The Man from Uruguay

Danny Bergara - A footballing journey

Written by Phil Brennan

Published by Rose-Martin Publications

The Man from Uruguay

First paperback edition printed 2013 in the United Kingdom

A catalogue record for this book is available from the British Library.
ISBN 978-0-9927853-0-7

Published by Rose-Martin Publications.

For more copies of this book, please email: bergarabook@outlook.com

Designed and Set by 75Media www.75media.co.uk. Printed in Great Britain

Acknowledgements

This book was made possible thanks to the help of all those listed below who very kindly made available photographs, scrapbooks, memorabilia or other information concerning the life of Alberto Daniel 'Danny' Bergara:

Danny, Jan, Pilar, Simon & Elena Bergara, Chris Beaumont, Alan Biggs, John Bishop, Stuart Brennan, Aiden Casey, David Conn, Chris Davies, Keith Edwards, Dave Espley, Kevin Francis, Mike Flynn, Ged Gibbons, Richard Harnwell, Phil Henson, Jon Keighren, Tony Kenworthy, Andy King, Dave Marchbank-Smith, Mick McCarthy, Peter Mead, David Pleat, Andy Preece, John Sainty, Ian Watts, Stuart White.

Vital information has been gleaned from various sources including:

El Pais, Marca, Deporte, The Stockport Express, The Stockport Messenger, The Stockport Times, The Manchester Evening News, The Daily Mirror, The Daily Express, The Daily Star, The Daily Mail, The Northern Echo, Getty Images, The Press Association, Football Confidential 2 - Scams, Scandals & Screw-ups, The Sheffield Star, The Sheffield Weekly Gazette, The Morning Telegraph, The Green 'un, The Daily Telegraph, The Independent, The Sun, Luton News, Evening Post, Post Echo, Herts. Advertiser, The Herald, Shoot Magazine, Goal Magazine, The Evening Gazette.

Also from publications & Internet sites for:

Racing Club Montevideo, RCD Mallorca, Seville FC, CD Tenerife, Luton Town FC, Sheffield United FC, Rochdale FC, Stockport County FC, Sheffield Wednesday FC, The FA.

Although every precaution has been taken in the preparation of this book, the publisher and author assume no responsibility for errors or omissions. Neither is any liability assumed for damages resulting from the use of this information contained herein.

My sincere thanks to Mary Jinks for her sponsorship, to Andy Calvert for his help in designing the front cover and subsequent help in finalising it, Laura Allen, who spent much time typing and 'proof reading' many of the original articles and Steve Bailey who provided the final proof read.

My thanks also to Jon Hudson of 75Media for his help with the illustrations throughout the book and the setting up and running of the websites www.facebook.com/TheManfromUruguay and www.DannyBergara.co.uk

Finally I would like to thank my long suffering wife Liz, and my children Amy, Ellie and Joe for their continued love, support, help and most of all understanding, for the hours spent working on this project.

Phil Brennan 2013

The Man from Uruguay

Introduction

I spoke with Danny Bergara a couple of years after he had left Stockport County regarding the opportunity to write about his incredible reign at Edgeley Park. As a longstanding County fan I thought it would be of interest to my fellow supporters to read about his take on the good and bad times he had had whilst at the club. I had done a bit of detective work and procured his home telephone number and, having plucked up the courage, rang his house. Having had no reply I left a message regarding my proposal on his answer-phone and waited for his return call.

As a bit of background information I should state that Danny had in the past called me Stuart rather than my real name. I never did find out whether he confused me with Stuart Brennan (no relation), who was a reporter for the Stockport Express, or whether he was just showing his wicked sense of humour.

A day later the phone rang at my house and my eldest daughter Amy, a season ticket holder at Edgeley Park, answered it. With a look of extreme surprise, and with her hand over the mouthpiece she said:

"Dad, its Danny Bergara for you" she handed the phone to me, completely star struck.

"Hello Stuart" said the unmistakable voice at the other end

"Hi Danny, it's Phil" I said

"Whatever" came his, by now, usual response

I explained my thoughts to the great man, and thankfully, he was more than happy to help me. We agreed to meet up in a few weeks time and discuss the idea further. Within a week or so, Danny again rang me, this time though it wasn't good news as far as I was concerned. He had been approached by a leading sports journalist from one of the national papers who wanted to co-write Danny's autobiography. Although a little disappointed, I had to agree that the idea of his complete life story being written, and by a leading journalist, was the better way to go.

Several years later, for whatever reason, the intended book hadn't been written and I decided to give Danny a call to see if I could resurrect my original idea. Having answered the phone with his usual "Hello Stuart", he went on to tell me how disappointed he had been that the book hadn't been written. Then, to my surprise, he asked me if I would be interested in taking on the task.

Having accepted his offer, I agreed to travel over to his house in a couple of weeks time to begin the task. I rang Danny to let him know that I had arranged a few days off work to enable me to spend time with him. His wife Jan answered the phone with the awful news that Danny had been taken ill. There was even worse news to follow on my next call with Jan, Danny had suffered a stroke and his condition was deteriorating.

Danny sadly passed away on July 25th 2007, one day after his 65th birthday.

Three days later Stockport County played a pre-season friendly against Cardiff City. County were by now managed by one of Danny's first signings, Jim Gannon. City were managed by Dave

Jones, the man who had replaced Danny at Edgeley Park twelve years earlier.

The match was dedicated to Danny. In an emotionally charged atmosphere, the ground's PA system belted out Frank Sinatra's 'My Way', Danny's favourite song. Both managers paid their tributes by laying down a bunch of flowers which spelt 'DANNY' in front of his beloved Cheadle End. Then followed a specially designated two minutes to allow County supporters to sing 'Danny Bergara's Blue & White Army'. A thoroughly entertaining game ended with County beating the Championship outfit 6-4.

In a real twist of fate both sides would reach Wembley for the end of season play-offs. County finally winning at the National Stadium as if in tribute to the little Uruguayan.

Several years later, a chance conversation with Angela White, the wife of former club Director Grahame, and an old friend of Jan, led to me meeting up with Jan to discuss the possibility of finally writing Danny's story. Thankfully Jan agreed that we should go ahead.

I have thoroughly enjoyed my meetings and conversations with Jan and her children, Simon and Ellen, and also Danny's sister Pilar and her husband Pocho, whilst researching the life of Danny Bergara. I truly hope that this biography does justice to a man who, without doubt, was a trailblazer for the legion of 'foreign' managers that followed him into the English game.

Foreword

In recent years English football supporters have seen the impact that Arsène Wenger, José Mourinho, Rafael Benítez, Carlo Ancelotti, Roberto di Matteo and Roberto Mancini have made at the top level in club football. Even the English national team has been managed by foreigners Sven-Göran Eriksson and Fabio Capello.

Long before foreign managers were commonplace in the English game, Uruguayan Danny Bergara had already blazed the trail for the rest to follow.

The name Danny Bergara is linked with several English football clubs, most famously Stockport County, although it is a little known fact that he was used as a scout and coach by Dave Mackay when his Derby County side played Real Madrid in the European Cup 2nd round way back in 1975. Danny also spent a two year period working for the England youth team as assistant to John Cartwright, the first foreign national to do so, almost twenty years before Eriksson took charge of the first team.

It is probably fair to say that without Danny Bergara's success, both as a coach and manager, the influx of foreign managers into the English game may never have happened. Danny himself, although always believing that his methods and ideas would work, mentioned on many an occasion that he thought he had probably arrived in the country too early.

What is certain however is that, back in 1962, two mothers on opposite sides of the world both made a decision, regarding the future of their child, which helped change the face of English football forever.

A farmer's son, born in Montevideo, Danny Bergara was one of seven children. His elder brother Mario represented Uruguay at the 1962 World Cup whilst Danny himself grew to be a skilful and prolific inside-forward and at the tender age of 14 joined local side Racing Club.

Having helped the club win the Second Division title he made his début in the Uruguayan First Division aged 16, and also represented his country at youth level. His form attracted the attention of clubs in Italy and Spain and in particular Real Mallorca, who he joined in 1962 aged 19.

Danny went on to have a successful 11 year spell in Spain finishing top scorer on many occasions, winning the Second Division title with both Real Mallorca and his next club Seville, who finished joint third on their return to the top flight, before ending his career in an injury plagued spell at Tenerife FC.

Having met and married his English girlfriend Jan whilst playing in Spain, the couple decided to move their young family to England. The original plan was to open a travel agency but fate was going to play a part in the future of Alberto Daniel 'Danny' Bergara.

In an effort to keep his fitness levels up, Danny had spoken to Paddy Sowden, a friend of Jan's cousin Graham, about training with nearby Luton Town. The gods of football were looking down on Danny as he was invited to train with the juniors and very quickly earned himself a position within the coaching staff at Kenilworth Road.

Prior to leaving for England Danny had spoken to Vic Buckingham, an English former manager at Seville, who had warned him that it would be a struggle for him to gain a position in English football due to the way that it was structured, but suddenly that opportunity was being made available, and he was certainly going to give it a try.

Uruguay

Alberto Daniel 'Danny' Bergara was born in July 1942 in Pocitos, a residential area of Montevideo, the capital of Uruguay. The Bergara family owned a ranch, 180km from Montevideo, in Garzon, with 500 head of cattle and 3,000 sheep, but moved to Rocha in 1947, allowing the children to attend better schools, returning to the family ranch during the holidays.

As a young boy on the ranch Alberto almost drowned in the sheep's disinfecting bath yet he loved the life his family had, particularly the opportunity to carry out his favourite pastimes such as fishing in the river in Garzon, shooting partridges, bareback horse riding and outdoor barbeques.

Every house in Uruguay seemed to have a built-in barbeque, as it was very much a meat producing and eating country. Alberto's favourite food was always steak.

His father Mario had died, aged just 36, in 1949, leaving his wife Maria Elena a widow with seven children. Alberto was just 7 whilst his youngest sister Pilar was still a baby.

The family moved back to Montevideo in 1953 when Alberto was 11 years old where the children attended secondary school and university respectively. The ranch was rented out before it was eventually sold to very good friends of the family.

The Bergaras were a very cultured and educated family, with accountants, solicitors, doctors, a defence minister and even a bishop amongst their numbers. Alberto's upbringing was based on true Christian values.

The Bergara children were schooled in Rocha, with the Marista brotherhood. The Marist brothers, a Catholic Religious Institute came from Germany, and the founder of the school, brother Gandolfo Hengeled, had been the headmaster who went on to become the chief inspector of all the Marista schools in South America.

Pilar Bergara remembers their schooldays:

This period prepared all the boys, especially Alberto, where they learnt discipline, to concentrate on their studies, friendship, team spirit/unity, perseverance, order and all the virtues needed from childhood, to demonstrate when the child becomes a man. All this teaching served Alberto when he played football, worked in the bank, then as a manager, and above all, as a good person.

As adolescents/teenagers we all attended Colegio Pio (liceo) secondary school in Montevideo, run by the Salesiamo priests in Villa Colon where our mother and the remaining brothers and sister still live near each other. I live 30km from Montevideo in Medanos de Solymar in the department of Canelones.

Circa 1955/6 in Colegio Pio, Alberto would help the youngest pupils with their studies and the most undisciplined, giving them private classes, drilling into them the discipline, the love of studying and respect. In effect, putting into practice what he had learnt from the Maristas.

A very talented individual, he wrote plays, acted in Colegio Pio's theatre, without having studied the piano, played amazingly well by ear, and played football for the school team. He and his brothers formed their own football team called Media Luna (half moon), playing against other local teams.

They played on land adjacent to our house next to the house of some very dear neighbours and friends who still live there today. Pedro Bustos had 4 daughters so he regarded Alberto as a son and loved him very much.

He mentored him in his youth and used to say to all of us "This lad, Alberto, is going to be a cracking footballer and people are going to have to pay to watch him play!".

In Rocha, 1950, on the first day back to school, in clean, smart uniforms, Alberto and his companions were involved in a commotion in the main avenue of the town centre of Rocha. A group of boys from the Marista school were running, shouting, raising their arms, following something, which happened to be a pig, that had fallen off a cart which was taking some pigs to market. The frightened pig was running all over the place being followed by a growing group of people. Who was leading the crowd? Alberto, of course, went in front with his classmates, trying to get the pig into the police station.

Bergara's footballing potential as a skilful and prolific inside-forward had been noticed at a very early age and he joined the youth team at Racing Club of Montevideo aged 14.

On the day of his debut, the gate man wouldn't let him into the player's entrance because he had short trousers on and he didn't believe he was playing. In that era, at least in Uruguay, long trousers were not worn until a boy reached 15 years of age, which then signified/symbolised the beginning of the stage of maturity for boys.

Bergara's rise from youth team to first team came rapidly, making his debut against Rampla Juniors, he went on to help Racing Club

Young Danny

Holy Communion (right)

Maria Elena Bergara and her seven children

Los Juveniles

In action for Racing

Uruguay Youth

In action for Uruguay Youth v Chile Youth

Action from Racing v Defensor (Danny has written names and scores on photo)

Action from Racing v Defensor

Racing - 2nd Division Champions 1958
Nacho Bergara (back row, 1st left)
Danny Bergara (front row, 2nd right)

Danny and brother Mario
(Racing v Nacional)

Racing Portrait

Celebration dinner one week before Danny and
Nacho leave for Spain

win the Second Division title in 1958, and thereby a return to the top flight. He made his début in the Uruguayan First Division the following season aged 16, going on to make around 50 appearances in the Uruguayan First Division, in which there were only 18 games per season. His first goal for the club coming against Defensor in the Artigas Cup.

With his family's work ethic in mind, Bergara worked in the Banco Transatlantico whilst continuing his football 'education' and also during this period he won 3 caps for his country at youth international level, twice against Argentina and once against Chile.

Even as a young player Bergara often featured in the national press:

Our newspapers are adorned today by the small figure of a good future player for our club Racing. We are referring to Alberto Bergara, who has just celebrated his 15th birthday. His merits have gained a mention in the 'Racing' corner of the press.

What can we say about him? Well, quite a lot, despite his young years. He would distribute his hours of studying with practising football. He immediately captured the affection of all at the club. He was friendly and cordial, telling us of his anecdotes and dreams. He could do marvellous things with the ball for all to see. He played in the Racing reserves against Nacional and scored a goal. Against Penarol he was the best forward and his pass allowed his elder brother Mario to score. It's a pleasure to talk to the 'young boy', how many illusions in his words and how much purity in his smile. He just wants to 'arrive', to see the net move. We hope you triumph too, you deserve it and because, quite honestly, you play well 'young boy'

After having in our editorial office Mariolo and Ignacio, the two elder brothers, we now have Alberto Bergara - an extraordinary intelligence and facility to express himself. We have seen in this future star of our football, all but a man, even though he is only 17 years old. He joined Racing Club at 14 in 1956 and immediately played against Nacional FC, the first time against the shirt of one of the 'big teams', in the reserves and scored against the two 'big clubs' Nacional and Penarol.

Racing Club 4 Defensor 2

Alberto Bergara scored one goal and made two others, a lively, opportunist player who had a brilliant game.

Racing Club 1 Nacional 0

An extraordinary performance by the 19 year old Alberto Bergara. In this immense battle of 'sweat and effort' between Racing and Nacional, if all the players were a wall, there is no doubt as to who rose above it.

Alberto Bergara the 19 year old youngster, who helped everyone, who assisted everyone, who ran, fought and played with the strength of a Titan.

When the game finished he hugged his elder brother Mariolo, who had played for Nacional. They had been rivals, but in a sea of emotions the younger Bergara cried as he left the pitch, a triumphant winner. He had fought like a man and cried like a boy.

He continues to ascend the technical hierarchy of his brother Mario, now at Nacional and in the Uruguayan national team selection. Alberto Bergara continues to show brilliant work, an impressive and elegant player who works to help the rearguard and also as a link player to the forwards. One of the most skilful forwards - man of the match.

Bergara's form had not gone unnoticed by the many scouts that travelled to South America on behalf of European clubs and in 1961 Fiorentina of Italy wanted to sign him, but in that era the rules stated that a player had to have a parent or grandparent of Italian origin, so the move couldn't happen.

Having been told of the opportunity and the subsequent reason for the breakdown of the move, in a moment of youthful frustration he said to his mother *"You should have married an Italian"*, a comment that earned him a slap from his mother.

However, his continued excellent form had been brought to the attention of Spanish club Real Mallorca, whose coach Jose Luis Saso had seen Danny whilst over in Uruguay on one of his regular scouting missions. Saso then sent Jaime Porres, a representative of the club, over to speak to the Bergara family about a possible move to Europe for the young star.

Bergara's mother Maria Elena, believing that her son was too young at the age of 19 to travel such a distance, was somewhat reluctant for him to sign, although she came up with a compromise for the Spanish club. Maria Elena told Porres that she would agree to her son moving to Spain if Real Mallorca signed Bergara's brother Ignacio (Nacho), a defender who was two years older than Alberto, too.

After consulting with his employers Porres agreed to both Bergara boys joining Real Mallorca for 800,000 pesetas. Although Bergara often mentioned with a wry smile, his annoyance at having to share his 'signing on' fee with his sibling. Both players moved to Spain in August 1962.

RCD Mallorca

Danny and his brother Nacho settled into their new surroundings on the idyllic island of Mallorca along with another young Uruguayan footballer, Armando 'Tito' Castilla.

Meanwhile, in Hampstead, London, 19 year old Janet 'Jan' Turner, a secretary in a travel agents, was preparing to set off on her own Spanish adventure. The previous summer Jan had wanted to go and work in Mallorca but her parents persuaded her that she was too young, telling her to wait another year to see if she still wanted to go, bearing in mind that foreign travel was still in its infancy.

Jan's desire to travel hadn't waned and, following discussions with her parents, she prepared to leave for Mallorca in March 1963. Jan's good friend Lynn had hitchhiked to Spain the previous year but Jan's mother Ellen insisted and convinced the girls to take the ferry to France and an overnight train to Spain, before a ferry crossing to the island of Mallorca.

The two girls had become friends whilst at secretarial college and Lynn, who had spent the previous summer season working in a boutique in Mallorca, had told Jan that there would be a job there for her as the owner was looking for English speaking girls to work for him. After several months working in the boutique, Jan took up the offer to work for travel agents Sunflight & Globalair, which was a return to the industry she knew well.

Upon taking up her new role Jan moved into an apartment with her two new workmates Val and Moira. The apartment just happened to be next door to an apartment which was being shared by the three young Uruguayan footballers that had joined the local football clubs the previous summer. Val and Moira were dating Nacho and Tito respectively, and whilst Jan and Danny began seeing each other as friends to begin with, their relationship was to blossom over the next two summers.

Jan Bergara remembers those early days:

On the 9th of March 1963, when tourism was just taking off, with a bible (from my brother) in my pocket, I set off aged 20 from Dover by boat and then train and ferry to Mallorca with a college friend of mine.

Who would have imagined my destiny was about to unfold just two months later

I met Daniel at the end of May 1963. I do remember asking Daniel in 'broken Spanish' when first meeting him what he was studying or what was his profession aside from playing football. His answer was simple "I am a professional footballer" I hadn't realised that you could actually earn a living from playing football.

His English and my Spanish were in their infancy so my O Level, GCE French came in handy and we spoke in French for the most part to start with. He lived in the next block of apartments to where I shared with two other English girls, Moira and Valerie, who I worked with at Sunflight & Globalair, an English travel agency based in Palma.

Daniel lived with his elder brother Nacho and another young Uruguayan Tito Castilla. Dan and Nacho were signed on by Mallorca whilst Tito played for Constancia.

We bumped into each other outside the apartments as he was waiting to take his brother and Tito to the beach, at the end of the season. I said I was going to the 'peluqueria' (hairdressers) and he offered to take me. I said thank you but I had already booked a taxi. Apparently he said afterwards to his brother "Damn, why didn't I think to pay for the taxi and take her myself?". He was that annoyed with himself as his brother and Tito weren't ready to go to the beach anyway.

The three of them went on a tour of Spain, Italy and France soon after our meeting in June, whilst on their summer break. Dan was the one with the car, and the one who got things going. They visited Madrid, Barcelona and Rome, where they even saw the Pope, as well as Milan, Paris, Cannes and St Tropez.

Moira and Valerie were already going out with Nacho and Tito respectively and on the boys return from their tour, we were all invited around for 'tapas' and caviar and to see all the photos and postcards from the trip, Daniel being a keen photographer. It was all very exciting then as travel was still very much a novelty and just beginning to be accessible to everyone with the dawn of 'package holidays'.

We became inseparable from very early on in our courtship. We shared the same taste and love of music. Our courtship was made up of beautiful Uruguayan folklore, Spanish flamenco, Charles Aznevour and of course 'The Beatles' - Spanish, French and English music!!

I think he only put up with my love of classical music though!!

At the end of the 'summer holiday season' in October, I would return to London and travel back to Palma the following

March/April. We wrote to each other almost every day and spoke on the phone. In those days you had to book calls via Madrid, and couldn't always get through if the lines were busy.

Bergara needed time to adapt to the pace of the Spanish League, compared with Uruguay, and so struggled to break into the Mallorca side in the early part of the season, Nacho however had made his debut in the first game, a 5-0 hammering of Malaga. Danny finally made his debut coming on as a substitute in a home win against Athletic Bilbao in December. His first goal for the club coming against a Real Madrid side featuring Ferenc Puskas and fellow Uruguayan Jose Santamaria. The eventual champions winning handsomely 2-5.

Unfortunately, several heavy defeats saw Mallorca struggling at the wrong end of the table and, although they were to beat Barcelona in the last game of the campaign, they finished in the bottom four and were relegated as rivals Seville beat Valencia to stay up at their expense.

Mallorca were to feature at the top end of the Second Division for much of the following season. With Danny scoring regularly they lost just six games going into the final three fixtures and were set for a quick return to the Primera Division.

Defeat at Las Palmas was followed by a home win against Melilla placing the club third with just a visit to Granada remaining, where anything better than a defeat would see them return at the first attempt. Unfortunately with rivals Hercules managing a draw and Sporting Gijon winning, Mallorca's heavy 1-4 defeat meant that they missed out on promotion by a point.

Danny was happy both in his private life and on the football field, helping Mallorca to win the Second Division championship in 1965. Having lost five of their opening sixteen games, Mallorca were to lose just one of the last fourteen, at Hercules (0-1) and that in January. A superb run of six wins and four draws saw them clinch the title. Bergara, again amongst the goals, his form bringing him to the attention of the bigger clubs on the mainland.

In the summer of 1966 Danny and Jan were married at Christ Church, Hampstead in London and in true footballers wives style, the newlywed's honeymoon included a visit to Wembley Stadium to watch England against Uruguay in the opening game of the World Cup courtesy of the Uruguayan coaching staff. The two young newlyweds finished their honeymoon in the Lake District.

On his return to Mallorca Danny was again in great form and the club were struggling to fight off the attentions of Real Madrid, Barcelona, Atletico Madrid and Valencia.

Jan Bergara:

We got engaged on my 21st birthday, Dan was also 21, at least for another two months. At some time during the 1965/66 season Atletico Madrid put an offer in for Dan, he was the player of the year at Mallorca, and were told that 'Bergara is not for sale'. He signed a new 3 year contract at Mallorca, the maximum a foreign player could sign for at the time.

We married in June 66 in my church 'Christchurch' in Hampstead, London. His mother came over from Uruguay and Nacho, who was now playing on the mainland for Espanyol in Barcelona, flew over from Spain. We were invited to the opening game of the 1966 World Cup which saw our two nations pitted against each other as

England took on Uruguay at Wembley Stadium, we had also been invited to a training session in Harlow and met the playing squad afterwards.

The invitation had come from the Uruguayan delegation, and although it wasn't the best of games, a goalless draw was a happy result for the 'honeymooners'. We honeymooned in 'the district lakes' as Dan called them.

We returned to Mallorca a month after our wedding. Not long after talks began again regarding his transfer to a 'big' First Division club. Fans, season ticket holders and shareholders didn't see eye to eye with the president selling 'Bergara' and there were many protesting against it. The main message being that the team would be weakened without him. The local press published a statement "Fans would divorce from the club if it sold Bergara, to retain that support they must not sell him"

There was interest from Real Madrid, Barcelona, Atletico Madrid and Valencia. President Josep Barona asked for 5M Pts. Barcelona offered 3.5M Pts.

The agent Senor Guijarro was already holding talks with us both regarding where we would live, it appeared that within 24 hours it would be confirmed that Daniel was a Barcelona player.

President Barona told Daniel "The supporters will chop my balls off if I let you go now, for less than 5M Pts" to which Daniel replied "But senor Presidente if you don't let me go, you will chop off mine" He was disconsolate, the dream of playing for a 'big' club was gone .... for now!

I remember reading in the press: "This is only the beginning of this matter. The last word has not been said over Bergara, just wait and see, it will happen sooner or later"

One local reporter wrote an 'open letter' in the newspaper to the Club President regarding the situation:

My Dear President, you will receive many letters regarding Bergara (that cheeky young boy Saso brought over and converted into a star). I have to confess that if there is a fan that loves Bergara, then that is me. I have demonstrated my passion for his play in my column on many occasions. As and when he leaves Mallorca I will be disappointed, displeased and upset. I have just spoken to Bergara, as you have, I am sure we have both come to the same conclusion - we have to sell him.

For my readers I should write down what was discussed between Bergara and I, but I feel it only proper that I write this open letter to you.

Bergara needs to go where his calling takes him, where they have wet his appetite. No-one is to blame here - not you, not Bergara nor I. The blame is with those with the type of money that cause this upset. Despite our heavy heart, if Bergara stays in Mallorca he will never be able to forget what he has lost, he who is so professional, came so far leaving behind his family, friends and financial security. We have to understand he did not do this to become a Mallorcan for the rest of his life.

When you have been offered millions you have to accept, it pains us all but you have to do it - to the contrary (listen to what I say) you will lose the money but more importantly the player Bergara.

After what has happened, he could stop being the player we love, he could lose his appetite and our supporters could lose faith in him, thereby losing his status. Bergara is amongst the best, and should he not move, would wish to continue to give 100% for the Club, and remain in our hearts.

We would all want this to be so, but I believe it has gone too far for there to be any other outcome, therefore I believe the best course of action is for you to sell my favourite player on one condition.....Mallorca see the 5M Pts he is worth as this money will be for the long term benefit of the club.

We cannot afford the luxury of a player who is worth this type of money (beggars cannot be choosers) we have our cross to bear. Don't be fearful of the consequences. You will see that our supporters will come to terms with it.

Bergara finished the season at Mallorca going on to grab thirteen goals, his best goal scoring tally for the club, as they were relegated back to Segunda Division. He remained with the club for the following season, when disappointingly, Mallorca, who were 5th with just six games to play, managed only one more win to tail off, finishing ninth. This despite him reaching double figures again, notching ten goals.

In the summer of 1967 Atletico Madrid, Espanyol and Seville all showed interest in signing the by now 25 year old Bergara, with Seville winning the race for his signature. The deal, a record at the time, was 2.5M Pts plus a player and a game between the clubs with the gate money staying with Mallorca.

Danny with Uruguayan
legend Jose Santamaria

Bergara goal against Real Madrid

Another Bergara goal against Real Madrid

Danny in action against Real Madrid

Nacho and Danny with fellow Uruguayan Hector
Ramos (Mallorca v Elche)

Champions 1965

Mallorca portrait

Mallorca v Espanyol - Danny with brother Nacho
and Alfredo di Stefano

OS GOLES, TRES GOLES...

EN SEGUNDA DIVISION

VENCIO POR 3 - 0 AL PONTEVEDRA

BERGARA   ACHURI

2 Goles

Fueron los goleadores ayer

...ente del Mallorca, Sr. Barona, habla del traspaso
...na, de Bergara y de otros futuros traspasos.

...gara no se venderá por este precio (3.500.000)

...traspasado al
...a sido sin duda,
...la semana en el
...raspaso de Molí-
...posible de Berga-

★ A MI ME HA DOLIDO MAS QUE A NADIE EL DES-
PRENDERNOS DE MOLINA, PERO EL CLUB HA SALIDO
MUY BENEFICIADO.

★ QUEDAN EN LA PLANTILLA UNOS SEÑORES QUE

...orca, 3 - Español, 0

...OBRE
...TUACION
...NQUIAZUL
...ERECIDA
...OTA

BERGARA 2 GOLES

Mallorca, 2 - R. Madrid,

...eligroso
...VENCIO
...O AL
...2)

BERGARAS DEBUT IN MALLORCA FOOTBALL CLUB

Mi churro
A.D. Bergara-T

...A parte el Mallorca re...
...ficultades, Herrera—qu...
...xter luchando contra l...

Supporters had to finally accept that Mallorca couldn't keep their favourite son any longer. There were economical problems and debts to deal with for the club to survive and progress.

Bergara's standing with the supporters at Mallorca had actually been tested on one famous occasion, after he was fined and suspended for his reaction to a section of the crowd during a friendly against Badalona in which Mallorca were struggling. The local press carried the following report:

It was a poor game and Bergara was doing all he could to straighten out the game. A small section of the crowd were getting on his back and his teammates. He eventually scored a sensational goal as only Bergara can, after dribbling past half the Badalona team, but instead of his usual jubilant celebration, he gestured to that section of the fans in an offensive way. He was fined and suspended two weeks. He said in an interview held in his apartment: "I was forcing myself for the triumph and after scoring the goal I made the gesture impulsively without thought. I just wanted to say "now what hey?" It was never my intention to offend the public. There was no personal malice. You know whenever I score a goal I always direct myself to the stand or the dugout. My reaction even surprised myself and I can only say how sorry I am to Mallorca and the public, who I hold in great esteem. How I wish I hadn't scored that goal - I've never regretted so much scoring a goal!"

Later the local press reported the following:

The goal that forgave

Alberto Bergara, top goal scorer of RCD Mallorca, is today without question Real Mallorca's indispensable player. At the start of his next match after suspension, Bergara publicly apologised to the fans. That apology will remain with the fans, as will his beautiful winning goal on his comeback. Bergara - all is forgiven!

Afterwards at a club dinner, Bergara was used as an example - The President and directors agreed to return his fine and gave him an added bonus due to his reaction as a professional, to train hard through his suspension, playing well, scoring a goal and becoming a hero once again with the Mallorca FC fans!

Bergara had been top scorer for three consecutive seasons in Mallorca, he had scored 39 league goals and helped the club win the Second Division title during his time on the island, and after he left the club the press said: *"The best period without question of Mallorca FC was Bergara's time there and it's a great pity that afterwards, when he left, there was no continuation."*

A selection of press reports from Bergara's time in Mallorca:

Mallorca 5-2 Real Madrid

Bergara and Jose Santamaria, who both played for Racing Club of Montevideo, played against each other in this match where Mallorca had a resounding victory against the mighty Madrid. The little Bergara was the revelation of the afternoon and crowned his great exhibition with a goal, the kind that go down in history.

Down in the changing rooms Bergara jumped for joy, crying "No less than 5 goals against Real Madrid, marvellous isn't it?!" When asked about Santamaria he said "My compatriot is a great player. Today he was tough, but noble."

Santamaria for his part said "Mallorca played very well, better than us if that is possible. Bergara gave me an enormous amount of

*work, which you will have seen! I believe that he is one of the best
inside forwards to come to Spain. He will go far!"*

Mallorca 3-1 Athletic Bilbao

'Brilliant performance by Bergara - 20 Carat Gold'

*Jose Iribar, a great goalkeeper had plenty of good work, but even
better were the 3 goals by Bergara! The Uruguayan Bergara was
without doubt the triumph of the afternoon with three magnificent
goals - which place him on the table of goal scorers as one of the
best forwards in Spanish football.*

*Bergara won the match for his club. Once more it was the
inspiration of Bergara and his great goals for Mallorca, his goals
that are so characteristic of the little Uruguayan and why everyone
saw him as the only saviour of Mallorca. The only player, as always,
capable of taking the danger to Iribar's net.*

Mallorca 3-0 Espanyol

'Inspirational Bergara Man of the Match!'

*Bergara demonstrated - as he has demonstrated so many times
already - a spirited, elegant attacking performance with a beautiful
technique against Espanyol who were full of world stars (Di Stefano,
Carmelo, Kubala)!*

*Bergara delighted the fans. His brother Nacho, who played for
Espanyol, had said when they recently arrived from Uruguay "My
brother is phenomenal, you'll see!" After this match, he commented
"We are seeing just that! He scored a splendid goal."*

Mallorca 2-5 Real Madrid

'Bergara 2-5 Real Madrid!'

On 30 minutes a fantastic execution by Bergara, who evaded various opponents before running to the right and shooting, made the score 1-2. The international goalkeeper Betancourt had no chance to save...One of the best goals seen in the Lluis Sitjar Stadium this season!

On 44 minutes, 1-3. Then, a superb impeccable header by the man Bergara made it 2-3. 18 minutes into the second half, Danny Bergara had a great chance to make it 3-3 with a header just wide.

Bergara was named man of the match against the fabulous Real Madrid. He was the most effective of the attacking quintet of Mallorca FC, not only scoring two goals but with good movement all over the pitch which was worthy of more luck. He fought end to end throughout the game and is therefore named Man of the Match! Madrid had just come from a defeat against Barcelona, the cat played with the mouse and then gulped it down in 5 bites! 5-2 to Real Madrid.

Mallorca 4-2 Elche

Whether he plays home or away, whichever system, only Bergara is capable of scoring enormous goals like yesterday.

Mallorca 3-0 Pontevedra

Proclaimed champions of Division II! Bergara, a revelation of the league, a great forward. The little Uruguayan was the Giant of the whole match. There are people who can make the difficult look easy in the blink of an eye, and Mallorca possesses one of those people -

precisely the Uruguayan Bergara, who once again made the difficult easy, the boring exciting and the lost cause a winning one - a triumph. What we saw yesterday didn't surprise us at all of Bergara! He shone above his teammates and gave a master class, an outstanding performance.

Sevilla FC

Jan Bergara remembers the move from Mallorca to Seville:

I was pregnant with our first baby which was due at the end of July 1967 when Daniel was transferred to Seville. My mother had arranged to come over to be with me for the birth but Daniel had to report for pre-season training and an international tournament.

It was decided that I would fly back to London at the end of June, the latest date that I would be allowed to fly whilst pregnant. Daniel was given permission to take three days off at the end of July and he flew over hoping to be at the birth of our first child.

The first I knew of this was when I was having breakfast in bed and my dad said "You have a visitor" and Daniel's head appeared around the door. What a lovely surprise, I couldn't believe it.

Unfortunately baby was 10 days late so we had to wave Daniel goodbye at the train station as he left for Heathrow. It would be well over a month before I saw him again.

There were no direct flights to Seville so we had booked into a hotel near Malaga, my mother wanted me to rest before going down to Seville. I phoned Daniel, who had been playing against Real Madrid in the first game of the season that evening, to tell him we had arrived in Spain. I wanted Dan to have a good sleep and not to attempt the three and half hour drive from Seville during the night - that's what I wanted but I wasn't convinced he would do that.

The idea of spending some time relaxing with my mother and baby went with that phone call. Wild horses would not have prevented him from driving on the winding roads all the way to Malaga from

Seville. Having grabbed some sleep, on his arrival he paced up and down the beach and waited in the hotel reception until 7-00 am when he asked the concierge to call our room to make sure it was ok for him to come up.

I will never forget that wonderful moment when he saw his month old son, Simon Daniel, for the first time. We then all travelled to Seville where Daniel had bought a lovely apartment and although it was in a residential area, I think that seeing the flags all around the stadium in the distance and being able to hear the roar of supporters on match days, may have influenced his choice........well I know it did!

Games in Seville were often played at 10-00 at night because of the heat. Daniel used to get under the cold shower during the night and sprinkle water on the bed. They call Seville 'the frying pan of Spain' - inland and unbelievably hot in the summer.

On his arrival at the club he described himself as an attacking player, rather than striker: *"With the heavy defensive play, I play in every attacking position, my favourite being inside left and playing from midfield going forward."*

Having made his Seville debut in the home defeat by eventual champions Real Madrid, Bergara then made that mad dash up to see his new born son for the first time.

Simon's birth was one of few highlights in Bergara's first season as Seville were relegated to the Second Division for the first time in many years. There had been questions asked before a ball was kicked, as Seville had given the manager's job to Antonio Barrios. Although Barrios was one of their former managers, the problem

for many was that he had gained promotion at the end of the previous campaign with City rivals Real Betis.

The decision to name Barrios was not popular amongst the supporters and, as the team were heading for relegation, he was sacked with his side sitting bottom of the table.

Under Barrios, Seville had struggled with consistency, winning only two of the opening twelve games. Bergara scoring twice against Espanyol (3-0). The team's next win was the only real highlight of the campaign, Bergara grabbing a late winner at home against runners up Barcelona (2-1).

With 12 games to play Seville turned to another former manager, their former player Juan Arza, to see if he could perform a miracle. Arza had the nickname 'the golden boy' from his days as a player. He had scored a hat trick on his debut and helped Seville win their first ever Primera Division title in 1946.

Under Arza the side's form improved but they were to win only three further games, Bergara netting four times, including the winner against CE Sabadell, as they finished second bottom, the only consolation being that Betis finished below them. Bergara finishing the campaign as top scorer with 13 goals playing more games than any other outfield player.

The following season saw Seville clinch the Second Division title on a dramatic last day as they beat CD Mestalla (who needed to win to avoid relegation) at home to finish above title rivals Celta Vigo who also won on the last day, beating Real Valladolid.

The Board had backed Arza in an effort to make sure they made an immediate return to top flight football, allowing him to bring in several new players such as Berruezo, Chacón, Lebron and

Catalan. The move paid off handsomely as they were to lose just seven times in thirty eight games with Bergara again finishing top scorer with 14, Berruezo (10) and Lebron (9) the club's other top scorers. Bergara was also voted the best player in the League in his position of inside forward.

Unfortunately Arza's reward for winning promotion was to be replaced by Austrian coach Maximilian Merkel. The Board decided that they needed a different style of coaching if they were to continue their growth. Merkel repaid their faith by leading Seville to a joint third finish in the Primera Division and qualifying for the Inter City Fairs Cup at the first time of asking.

Merkel, who had played for both the Austrian and German national teams, was certainly a different type of coach to what the Spanish were used to. Born in Austria, where he played all his football, he had begun his coaching career in Holland, including a spell as national team manager, before moving back to SK Rapid Wien where he had played the majority of his football. In his two year spell back in Vienna he won his first title as his side won the Championship.

This was followed by more than ten years in Germany with Borussia Dortmund, TSV 1860 Munchen and FC Nurnberg, leading both Munchen and Nurnberg to Championships as well as reaching several Cup Finals with all three.

Having been a shock choice, Merkel, a methodical technician who concentrated on the physical side of his team, saw his Seville team exceed all expectations with the Sanchez Pizjuan Stadium almost a fortress. Having lost the first home game of the season to eventual champions Atletico Madrid, they didn't lose again, beating Barcelona, Real Madrid and Valencia amongst other visitors.

On the road their best result was an extraordinary victory at the Bernabeu (2-3) where only a late goal from Pirri had made the final score flatter the home side. The only black spot in the season came in The Spanish Cup as they lost to Murcia of the Segunda Division.

All in all a great season for his team, and Bergara, although not playing as many games as he would have liked due to a niggling groin injury which kept recurring, had certainly played his part with some vital goals including the winner at home against Real Madrid.

Bergara's groin injury had the medical staff at the club baffled. The injury was strange in that he could run and sprint with no pain but whenever he put effort into shooting or passing he would feel discomfort. Bergara was eventually sent to a specialist in Barcelona who discovered that there was a deep rooted infection which needed operating on to remove, meaning six weeks out of action.

Eager to regain his place Bergara then returned to first team action too early and suffered a relapse. Merkel who was renowned for his stance on having a completely fit team would continue with his squad 'rotation' meaning Bergara would spend much of his time on the bench. Bergara was not the only Seville player to suffer with injuries during the season due to the emphasis on the physical aspect of training that Merkel had imposed.

Just two days after the final game of the campaign he received some great news on the personal front.

Jan Bergara:

April 21st 1970 saw the birth of our daughter Elena Jane during 'the Feria of Seville' a famous and traditional two week festival after 'Saint week' and Easter.

'Saint week' was a very solemn time with only religious programmes on the radio and TV, followed by 'Feria' which was a time of celebrations, camping out in rows and rows of decorated and colourful marquees, singing and dancing into the early hours, flamenco, sevillanas, parading and horseback riding. In the days before mobile phones the gynaecologist had given me his direct line to call him on, should my labour begin during the festival, which it of course did.

I had called my mother who was to come over for the birth but there was a delay in Madrid where she had to change flights for Seville, so she arrived a few hours after Elena was born.

There were no midwives or ante-natal classes in Spain then, so when my waters broke, Daniel knowing nothing about labour, grabbed a large towel and told me not to worry about getting the car wet. He promptly rang my gynaecologist who was at the 'Feria'

"The bag's broken"

"What, the shopping bag?"

"No the water bag, and the placentas coming out"

"Oh, and where's the baby?"

46

In Dan's defence I feel that I should explain that in Spain the sac of fluid protecting the baby, is called the bag.

The much anticipated return to European football fell flat as the adventure was over almost before it began. A single goal home win against Turkish outfit Eskisehirspor wasn't enough as the Turks won the second leg by the two goals required (3-1).

The Primera League campaign began well for the team with three straight wins, away from home against Espanyol and Valencia as well as a big win over Real Madrid at the Sanchez Pizjuan (3-1). Unfortunately for Bergara he was finding it difficult to fit into Merkel's plans as he was used mostly as a substitute due to the manager's rotation system.

Frustratingly he was to score the winning goal in his first start of the season against Granada (1-0), twice in his second start against Athletic Bilbao (3-2) and again in his fourth start against Elche (2-1) before spending another spell out of the side.

Merkel, who had admitted that Bergara was one of the best strikers of the ball, with the best shot at goal at the club, was to suffer the wrath of both the Seville supporters and the press over his treatment of the Uruguayan:

After scoring the first and third goal in the 3-2 win against Athletic Bilbao, Merkel had told the press that Bergara had a place in the team playing like that. Bergara was asked by the press if Merkel had said anything to him after the game: "Not afterwards, but before. He said that today he expected a lot from me. I told him that I expected a lot from myself. As things went, we are all pleased"

Bergara goal from the penalty spot

Another Bergara goal for Sevilla

In action for Sevilla

Sevilla FC 1970/71

ESTADIO RAMÓN SÁNCHEZ - PIZJUÁN — Temp. 1970/71

Sevilla portrait

The Sevilla team that beat Real Madrid 1-0 in November 1969 thanks to a Bergara goal

Bergara with Spain's number one keeper Jose Iribar after 'That Goal'

On an official engagement

...dad y su fuerza arrolladora y los ...
...n de manifiesto que también CONTAMOS CON ELLOS

... BOTE EN BOTE

...ANCOS DE PISTA - TRIBUNA
...OLADIZO Y GRADA ALTA

FONDO

HOJA del LU

ASOCIACION DE LA PRENSA
SEVILLA   Editada por la Asociación de la Prensa, integrada en el Sindic...
Televisión y Publicidad. — Director: Juan José Gén...
DEPOSITO LEGAL: SE. 17 - 1958

10 NOVIEMBRE
DE 1969

Año XXX. Número 1.568.   Redacción y Administra...
Plaza de Falange Española número 9. — Teléfono 22...

...OTE EN BOTE

...ANCOS DE PI...
...OLADIZO Y G...

FON...

EL TRIUNFO Y LO...
GOLES DE BERGA...

El uruguayo —gesto característico— acen...
los seguidores con la expresiva exterioriza...
lo titularidad. Grist marcó dos goles y recuperó con tan sóli...
su titularidad. Grist, peca abierta y dos equipos...
fútbol, partido en el «sánchez...
El primer gol de Bergara sorprendió a todos...
te, acosado por Eloy, marcaría en propia pu...
timo. Bexara remataría su afortunadísima r...
el gol del triunfo. (Fotos Serran...

...hay entradas. Sobre...
...breves ventanillas ta...
...a terror...

The article finished with the following:

Bergara is today the most celebrated player by the Sevilla fans. If the fans had been consulted they would be overwhelmingly in favour of his inclusion in every game. With Bergara, Sevilla would already have the two points in the bag for certain and not have to rely on the 'opportunist' goal from Acosta. The good thing about this game was Sevilla had Bergara in their artillery. If it wasn't for Bergara, Sevilla would not have won this game. Merkel beat Ronnie Allen's Bilbao again - thank goodness Bergara played. If Acosta had counted on the collaboration of Bergara from the start of the season, Sevilla would be higher up the table. Bergara is a player who scores one or two goals when he plays....Merkel also knows this but has chosen to ignore it.

As if to prove a point Bergara had come to his side's rescue as a second half substitute in a hard fought win against Valencia, who had taken an early two goal lead. Merkel had thrown the Uruguayan into the action and once again he had come up with the goods:

The Public were Right

With their team two goals behind, the Seville supporters were chanting incessantly for the inclusion of Bergara in the team. At last Merkel put him on in the second half and his work rate was as brilliant as it was efficient. Having played his part in dragging his side level, he forced an own goal and then scored the all important fourth goal to put his side two in front. The fans were delirious. For it was demonstrated yet again that the public were right!! Woe betide Merkel - if Bergara doesn't play next Sunday

Bergara's last goal for Seville came in the home win over Malaga (1-0), the team losing four of the last seven games as they finished seventh in the table and the following season another change of manager saw Greek coach Dan Geordiadis take the helm. Bergara, now aged 29 and with no sign of first team action under the new regime moved to Tenerife in the Segunda Division in December 1971.

Before Bergara left Seville the club presented him with the club's badge, gold and studded with diamonds. That showed the great esteem in which he was held at the club with the President saying: *"I can assure you that Bergara is a luxury for Tenerife. That's not to say the club doesn't deserve to have players of quality but for the division that they actually found themselves in (2nd division). Bergara is an authentic player of the 1st division, you will soon see the proof for yourselves"*

A selection of press reports from Bergara's time in Seville:

<u>Marca</u>

If his goals are spectacular, his reaction after scoring is uncontrollable. On his reaction, he explained "To see the ball in the enemies net transformed into a goal has a significance like the kiss of a woman, electrifying, I go crazy!" Bergara remembers when playing in the youth team of Racing, he scored a goal and ran round the whole pitch. His elder brother Nacio, already playing in the 1st team, told him, 'Muchacho, kid, don't run round so much after every goal because afterwards you'll need time to recover!'. 'It's an irrepressible emotion he said!' With his admirable fitness, he fights bravely in all areas of the pitch and shoots at goal with infinite great danger, he settles the play of the team and owns the pitch!

Seville 2 Barcelona 1

The star of Seville F.C., Bergara who scored the winning goal, approachable, intelligent and quick in his responses to question. A likeable, excellent boy, noble on and off the pitch.

Seville 1 - Granada 0

Bergara's 90th minute goal, struck with the force of a torpedo, will be remembered by fans for a very long time, the most tenacious player in search of goals, whose free kick struck with such venom rattled the woodwork, the explosion of joy was enormous after the goal and the seat pads were thrown into the air in jubilation!

Seville 3 - Bilbao 2

Bergara scored 2 goals of impeccable quality. The most significant praise must go to Bergara, his first goal was a tremendous shot, only he can score goals like yesterday! The third goal, Bergara was involved in the execution, from start to finish, ending up scoring. Man of the match, great player, fantastic centre forward. Iribar stopped everything except the unstoppable.

Seville 1 - Real Madrid 0

Madrid resisted until the 80th minute. Betancourt had no chance with Bergara's goal that won the game for Seville, the first club to win against Real Madrid in this league and knock them off top spot, sensational triumph, breaking Real's winning run, in front of a crowd of 50,000.

Bergara still holding the match ball told press "It wasn't difficult for me to keep the ball in the game against Real Madrid. A throw-in was given in the dying seconds. I knew the referee was about to blow his whistle, he was looking at his watch. I controlled the ball with my chest, ref blew his whistle. I gave the ball a squeeze and kept it, I think I deserved to". **(Jan Bergara still has that ball, over forty years later)**

Jan remembers their time in Seville:

"We spent nearly five very happy years in Seville, a beautiful city and warm natured people. A wonderful family who lived next door were to become Elena's godparents, and we still keep in touch to this day. Their son Antonio, who was a young boy when Daniel played for Seville, told me when we spoke in many years later, that Daniel was his hero and he still remembers 'that goal' against Athletic Bilbao in November 1970.

Daniel scored the first and third goals in a 3-2 win which was still being talked about over 40 years later, "From an impossible angle, to score - Iribar didn't see it coming!!"

It seems that Antonio wasn't the only one remembering 'that goal'. An account of the goal appeared in an article in Seville FC monthly magazine as recently as the January 2012 edition, remembering past heroes.

The article was called 'A dream come true' by Spanish novelist Francisco Perez Gandul.

The volume of a human river of fans flowed down from the Gran Plaza, down Eduardo Dato to the Ramon Sanchez-Pizjuan Stadium. It was in this stadium where the dreams of the week, from time to time, came true.

If the history of this club was brimming with fabulous footballers who become idols from childhood onwards, the youngster will remember a footballer almost forgotten today but of extraordinary significance in his era.

He personified the 'hope' the actual 'we can' the 'everything is possible' when the minutes on the referee's watch had almost run out and you felt he would blow the whistle before time!

His name was Alberto Daniel Bergara and the crowds never needed so much his convincing and continued presence as when things were not going so well, which sometimes happened and the scoreboard spelled disaster.

That day when 'the dream came true' Iribar was between his posts and Bergara at the right corner post. The Uruguayan hit a clean shot towards the first post. Iribar palmed it out towards the corner hitting the chalk. Bergara again, with his team mates in the area anticipating his shot, sees the ball descending as if in slow motion.

The ball doesn't reach the ground. With the outside of his left foot Bergara hits a volley and the ball, before sat-nav was invented, takes the perfect orbit towards the inside square of the Bilbao's goalkeeper's second post with Iribar ending up flat out on the ground, a stone dead position. The Stadium erupts.

Final score: Seville 3 A Bilbao 2

Bergara scored 7 goals in 3 games against Athletic Bilbao - a record against Jose Angel Iribar Spain's international keeper

Jan Bergara:

In 2010 we visited Seville for Elena's 40th birthday as she was born there. We met the President of Seville FC Jose Maria Del Nido. His father had been the vice-president when Daniel played and his grandfather a director in his time.

The President and the historian of the club both remembered Daniel and his goals from 1967-1972. They said they were all spectacular goals and even described to us some of his free kicks.

The President, who was a boy when Daniel played told us "If the score was 0-0 with about 20 minutes to play - no problem, Bergara will score...and he usually did"

CD Tenerife

Jan Bergara:

The hardest move was from Seville to Tenerife in 1971 when Daniel was 29, after nearly five great years and leaving Elena's godparents and wonderful friends behind. But once in Tenerife, you again settle down and meet great new friends. A completely different accent again which you pick up quickly.

Daniel loved the climate in Tenerife as he could sleep more comfortably. In his retirement he wanted to spend six months there during our winter and six months spent between England and Uruguay where possible.

There had been interest in Bergara from several First and Second Division clubs but Bergara had decided on Tenerife and on his arrival he stated: *"I'll put my grain of sand to get Tenerife to where they belong. Tenerife possesses a refined technique, I like that. I like to play quality football"*

Tenerife had won promotion to the Second Division after two seasons in the Third Division but were struggling to win games at the next level. Shortly after signing, Bergara was joined at the club by fellow Uruguayan Héctor Núñez, who replaced former Spanish international Ignacio Eizaguirre, to become the head coach after leaving Third Division outfit Calvo Sotelo.

A young Tenerife side began to work well with the experienced Uruguayan pair, Núñez off the field, Bergara on it, starting with the first match together against Hercules, Bergara making two goals in a comfortable victory (3-0). Tenerife went on to record another nine home wins including victories against two of the

sides promoted CD Castellon (2-0) and Elche CF (1-0) as they finished in a respectable ninth place in the table.

Bergara's second season at Tenerife saw him receive the calf injury that was to end his playing career, but not before he picked up several man of the match awards for some scintillating performances as an attacking midfielder.

A selection of press reports from Bergara's games whilst in Tenerife:

Tenerife 2 - Osasuna 0

Bergara's first goal bent the goalkeeper's fingers backwards, Bergara, the true motor of the team, he would also be that even if he was lame and with his eyes bandaged up.

Tenerife 3 Orense 1

The visitors, already one goal behind, were undone by two quick goals from Bergara and Cantudo. The little Uruguayan, turned in the area, to score the second with a goal that was beautifully crafted.

Tenerife 3 - Cultural Leonesa 0

Bergara, the best on the field, gave an authentic lesson in football. That was football! Bergara the great conductor who fed the forwards. He only lost one ball in the entire match. Man of the match.

Tenerife 2 - Valladolid 1

Bergara again the great star - 2 great goals! He is the solution of the team. Scored a skilful goal in 3 minutes and after 10 minutes continued to be the director of the orchestra. After 19 minutes, Bergara scored a header. As always the best. This is a true centre-forward, what a player gentleman, if only we had eleven Bergara's - we would be playing the European Cup! Man of the match.

Tenerife 4 - Barcelona 0

Barcelona were surprised by Second Division side Tenerife, a sensational performance by Bergara, the real motor of the Tenerife team. That was an exhibition of Bergara and his boys, Bergara is the indispensable organizer, playmaker, a great player, irreplaceable. He made the first and fourth goal. man of the match, without question.

Tenerife 4 v San Andres 1

At the end of Bergara's first season, he is considered as an extremely profitable buy. With both directors and fans celebrating his performances. The quality of the South American's play, together with his technique and delivery make him a player of the highest standard. In the game against San Andres, the fans could see the proof of his great movement and excellent organisation in the middle of the park, from this player who occupies the inside left position!

His flair and ease at dribbling, his pass always practical and delivered, his drive, all demonstrate an athlete who always gives everything. The power in his shot from a direct free kick produced the goal. It was a goal of 'ovation', a goal that had the public out of their seats, genuinely astonished! An ovation for the individuals intelligence, in short, knowing how to and delivering the end product.

Bergara goal for Tenerife

Tenerife FC

Tenerife portrait

Another Bergara goal for Tenerife

BERGARA, DE NUEVO, L

TENERIFE, 2 - VAL

EL REVERSO DE LA

Por Sal

los espectadores una mediana calidad.

Se presentaba el Tenerife con muchos nervios. Parecía pesar en los jugadores el ánimo de las dos últimas derrotas. Por lo que de entrada, desde un principio, no salieron las cosas bien. Y posteriormente, conforme avanzaba el cronómetro, tampoco llegaban agüeros de mejorar. En esta circunstancia, fue el San Andrés el que diera claras muestras de peligro en un par de contrataques que a punto estuvieron de fructificar, en especial, en la falta que a los cinco minutos sacó Vidal y que Domingo salvó en la misma raya, tras no haber blocado primeramente el esférico.

Esta ocasión, parecía indicar que los sanandrenos no renunciarían al ataque. Todo lo contrario; hacía suponer que junto a una bien montada defensiva, estaría la rapidez y lo

quedar detrás los zagueros y Roberto.

El San Andrés, en tanto enfrascado defensivamente, ya había dejado de disgustar sus contragolpeadas en la sola intención de mantener a cero y, por ende, de la ineficacia de los locales, de despejar las esferas interiormente alidó de un ataque, en principio alidó de un te 4-3-3, alabé riormente había mета. De ahí frecuente ver jugadores por su área, achini sí son, los antes menero lo que se fútbol, ha los catalán guraron en escasos en cluir está aprovech a cero.

(Viene de la pág. TRECE)

piedad a los once hombres de la plantilla local. Todo lo ve negro. Todo son fallos. Todo es pesimismo. Se sientan los dos juntos porque ambos son socios. Y en el asiento de allá, don Jaime. Don Jaime es un hombre ponderado, respetuoso, enamorado de la técnica, enemigo de la "patada para delante". Don Matías, don Francisco y don Jaime se saludaron antes de comenzar el partido. A medida que éste transcurría, hacían en voz alta sus comentarios. Yo tuve la suerte de estar alli y poderlos recoger para ustedes.

DON MATIAS —(servicio): —Mire que yo, mire que yo, don Francisco, no soy hombre que le gusta hacer elogios, pero... ¿se la ha fijado usted en Bergara? Esta es la solución del equipo. Ha marcado un gol de maestro en el minuto tres y ahora, que ya estamos en el 10, sigue siendo el director de orquesta del Tenerife.

DON FRANCISCO —Sí, sí, hombre. Eso lo reconozco yo. Pero, junto a la buena labor de Bergara, dese cuenta en lo que

DIALOGO PARA TRES

Por Andrés CHAVES

22 minutos. Falta contra el Tenerife. Se saca. Rechaza el balón Manolo. Se ordena la repetición. El árbitro cuenta y recuenta los pasos. La tiran de nuevo Astrain chuta y... marca. Los tres personajes de mi crónica saltaron de sus asientos como un sólo hombre. He aquí sus frases:

DON MATIAS: —¡Este es el colmo de la injusticia!

DON FRANCISCO: —¡Ya

tro? ¿Nómbrele usted a todos, caray! De acuerdo en que Juanito, Laguna y Cabrera están flojos, pero no culpe usted a los demás incluso, Manolo, está haciendo su papel.

Termina el primer tiempo. El mal humor de los aficionados —no por el juego del equipo, sino porque el aficionado se daba cuenta de que el Tenerife estaba cohibido por la actua-

dicará a esa revista... ¿Cómo se llama? "Sansofé". A la que dice que es viejo y que está desentrenado. Técnicos hay muchos... ¿eh? Pero ahí es, Bergara, como siempre, el mejor. Este sí que es un centro delantero.

El entusiasmo era enorme. Don Francisco, que había hecho tragarse un cigarrillo al señor de delante, por el empujón mayúsculo

LA TARDE

ante triunfo del Tenerife sobre el Barcelona (4-0)

Marcaron los goles Juanito y Esteban (2), en el primer tiempo y Laguna, en la continuación

las doce en punto comenzaba a jugarse en el Estadio anunciado encuentro de fútbol patrocinado por el Gobernador Civil de la provincia, entre el Tenerife y el Barcelona, a favor de la campaña para la construcción de Guarderías infantiles.

La alineación inicial fue la siguiente:

Tenerife: Del Castillo; Oscar, Molina, Pepito; Mauro, Esteban; Juanito, Manolo, Bergara, Cabrera y Laguna.

Barcelona: Sadurní; Paredes, Romero, Fusté; Eladio, Zabalza; Alfonseda, Rifé, Bustillo, Martí Filosía y Dueñas.

Arbitro, el colegiado tinerfeño José Antonio Nazco.

El público ha respondido entusiastamente a los fines benéficos del encuentro, registrando el "Helio doro Rodríguez López" una magnífica entrada en la jornada de total éxito en la

pues en el orden deportivo se registra un magnífico partido, particularmente por parte del Tenerife, que, según nos informa el compañero Andrés Chaves, realiza una extraordinaria actuación, y gana en el primer tiempo por tres tantos a cero.

El primero fue a los 15 minutos, obra de Juanito a pase de Bergara. El segundo gol a los 21 minutos. Manolo sacó una falta se media vuelta, y finalmente en el minuto 41, otro gol de Esteban de tiro fortísimo desde fuera del área. Bergara está siendo la figura del partido. También Juanito tuvo unos comienzos inciales, pero en general, todos hacen un juego enlazado y eficaz.

El Barcelona comenzó ofreciendo una buena exhibición, y poco a poco el Tenerife fue imponiendo su juego efectivo que ha dado

al máximo para en la jornada del próximo domingo, también como la anterior de Liga, a las once y media de la mañana para confirmar su buen momento actual ante el Real Valladolid.

El Barcelona regresa esta sobre las cuatro de esta tarde a la Ciudad Condal. Buen viaje.

este resultado de 3-0 en el primer tiempo.

En la continuación balajó algo el rendimiento de nuestro equipo, pero continuó la buena actuación, pese a los muchos cambios que realizó Héctor Núñez, aprovechando la oportunidad para probar a varios jugadores. Así, a lo largo de esta segunda parte, Samblás sustituyó a Molina, Quico salió por Mauro, Herrera lo hizo por Manolo, Ramos por Juanito y García Prada por Cabrera.

En el Barcelona, sólo dos cambios: Marcial por Zabalza y Juan Carlos por Eladio.

El Tenerife, como decíamos, siguió actuando con eficacia y Bergara continuó siendo su gran figura de esta mañana, brillantemente culminada con un marcador en el minuto 40 de marcado por Laguna a pase de Ramos.

El público salió muy satisfecho.

LOS 10.000 METROS, PARA UN HOLANDES

SPPORO, 7.—El holandés Ard Schek conquistó la medalla de oro en la especialidad de los 10.000 metros, velocidad, de décimos Juegos Olímpicos de Invierno. Schek había conquistado

uguayo Berga

EL MEJOR JUGADOR TENERIFE

Sin lugar a dudas fue Bergara, no sólo el mejor del Tenerife, sino de los veintidós que saltaron al campo. Pleno de dominio del balón, de sentido de la penetración y derrochando facultades a raudales, Bergara hizo el domingo un formidable partido. El gol del triunfo fue servido por él magistralmente y el de él, que sus botas salieron los mejores pases, los mejores cambios de juego y una fuerza arrolladora, que le permitía estar en todas partes sin acusar cansancio. Con Bergara jugando de esta forma y la nueva fisonomía que se ha dado al equipo Héctor Núñez, hay que ir pensando con más optimismo. C.

¡un frutal en su despensa!

Tenerife 2 - Seville 0

Tenerife were superior to Sevilla, although Sevilla showed their great class. Bergara individually, had a truly sensational game and scored the first goal against his old club!

Unfortunately the calf injury which had required two operations ended his football career aged nearly 31, some believed prematurely. The following article appeared when the news broke that Bergara was leaving Tenerife:

Everyone knows what Bergara has given to Tenerife F.C. I don't need to explain the virtues of a sporting hero, nor have I needed to sing the praises of his sporting glories. The accomplishment of the Uruguayan forward is there for all to see, who've gone to the games or have read the newspapers, or heard on the radio, or watched on TV. His performances are in the archives of the press, on radio tapes and on video tapes from TV. A great footballer who showed so much that is rarely seen in these geographical football grounds. He gave his team so many victories. He was esteemed by all the Tenerife fans for his sporting honour and as a gentleman of high moral qualities, I still think it's a big mistake and find it hard to accept, that a player of such class is leaving Tenerife, when he still had so much to give. I have no alternative but to comply with his wishes to say publicly goodbye to his fans and friends.

Jan Bergara:

After we moved to England, we still kept in touch with all of our Spanish friends and Daniel's team mates, and would often visit them in the summer holidays.

With our young children we wanted to be with family and so put down roots in England. My parents and my elder brother and his family had moved to St Albans from London, so St Albans was going to be our first English home together.

Dan, having been raised in a democratic and very pro-British country in Uruguay, felt that he would be totally at home in England, a country that had ties with Uruguay going back to the formation of the British Uruguayan Society in 1945.

Luton Town FC

Having arrived in St Albans, England in June 1973 with the notion of opening a travel business, Bergara spoke to Paddy Sowden, an acquaintance of Jan's cousin Graham, about the possibility of training with Luton Town, where he was the Chief Scout, in an effort to keep fit.

Aware of Bergara's playing career, Sowden had been impressed by a series of scrapbooks that Jan had kept from his playing career in both Uruguay and Spain. Knowing how hard it would be to convince the club to allow the Uruguayan to train at the club, Sowden asked for permission to show the books to the manager Harry Haslam.

Having read the books, Haslam was keen to meet with Bergara and so invited him to Kenilworth Road for a chat. Although impressed with Bergara's experience and obvious ability, Haslam was aware that as a foreign national there was no immediate opportunity to use him as either a player or a coach, so he set about planning some way to find an opening. In the meantime Bergara was invited to join in with training at the club.

Haslam, well known as a 'wheeler and dealer', came up with a unique plan to ensure Bergara would be allowed to join him at Luton Town. He convinced one of the directors of the club to employ Bergara as a driver's assistant which meant that he would be in a position to gain a National Insurance number which would enable him to pay tax and insurance, thereby also being able to enrol on a coaching course. Once accepted on the FA list Bergara could also sign for the club as a player/coach.

Having offered Bergara a role as a full time coach with responsibility for looking after Luton Town's youth players, Haslam announced:

"He is a good coach and has sound ideas on continental coaching methods. Danny cannot play for our first team but he can play in our reserve side in the Football Combination and midweek league. He is very keen and we wanted a coach who was able to play with the youngsters and add a little experience to the midweek league side"

Jan Bergara remembers the introduction to Luton Town:

Daniel was invited to train at Luton Town to keep fit, whilst considering work in the travel business. The Chief Scout, Paddy Sowden, came to our house and took away a portfolio that I had been keeping during Daniel's football career in Spain. Sowden said he would be in touch.

As there were no foreign coaches or players in England at that time we thought it was a case of 'don't phone us we will phone you'. We were thrilled that the phone did actually ring........Luton's manager Harry Haslam offered Daniel an opportunity, he was made youth team coach.

He was teased by the players at his pronunciation of the 'Queens English', so he soon picked up 'footballer's English' from the players. He would have lunch at the club and when his order came he would say "Where's my rabbit, I ordered Welsh rabbit"

He came home one day and asked "What does 'sheet' mean?, the players are always saying 'sheet this' sheet that'. I'm afraid to say he mastered the art and joined in!! As it was common place, I suppose he wouldn't have survived without it, at least when he was at home he became very adept at switching a certain word to 'flippin this' and 'flippin that'.

Bergara was soon letting the people of England know who he was, with an early interview in the local press:

<u>England need some of that Latin skill</u>

If England had as much Uruguayan-type skill in their side as they have British teamwork, Sir Alf Ramsey would now be celebrating their entry into the World Cup finals this year. I played in the Uruguayan First and Second Divisions, and made my debut for Racing Club when I was 15 in 1957 and played for the national youth team. I've also played in Spain's First and Second Divisions, for my part. Uruguay can boast the most skilful players in the world.

But skill alone isn't enough to bring success at a national level. I can't remember seeing a team with as much teamwork as England. Unfortunately, they do lack skill. England work for each other. The Uruguayans place much emphasis on skill. One won't work without the other. Spanish teams try to mix the two. They have four or five star players in each league side, but they haven't quite managed to perfect it yet.

I reckon I must be one of the most travelled players in this country who no longer plays. After I played for Racing Club, I was transferred to Majorca in 1962. I left them in 1967 to join Seville. Then I was transferred again to Tenerife in 1972. I spent only two years there before I came to England with my wife last June. I'm now 31, and the opportunity to obtain a coaching position at Luton has given me a new start. Whether I will make the grade as a coach remains to be seen, but I'll always be grateful to Harry Haslam for giving me the chance to try.

Unfortunately, I can play only in the midweek league and Football Combination sides. I'm told I must wait for two years before I can qualify to play in the first team; but I'm getting a little old for that. But I do miss the atmosphere of competitive games. Seville attracted attendances of 45,000 for their home games, Majorca 25,000 and Tenerife 15,000. And the minimum admission charges were £1. It's a bit different from England.

The Spanish tend to panic if things aren't working out for their teams. Sacking managers and coaches is a regular thing for them and, just after I left Seville, they appointed Vic Buckingham to succeed Dan Giorgiadis who was sacked. I didn't get on with Dan. He didn't get on with me. He wouldn't put me in the team for reasons best known to himself, so I asked for a move. As soon as I left, out went Dan, and in came Buckingham. It was sometimes a difficult job to keep pace with which manager was boss of which club.

The training in Spain was also much different. All league games were played on Sundays, and it meant we often had to train six days a week. It didn't leave us much time to ourselves or families. But I still keep in touch with Spain on a Sunday evening when I listen to their national results on the radio. It brings back a few happy memories. I am now helping to coach Luton's youngsters. And there are some players there who should have a bright future in the game.

Having readily accepted his new role as youth coach, Bergara was quickly making friends both within the club and also amongst the opposing teams that his youth side came up against. His engaging coaching style impressed his new charges and, on the occasions that he was called upon to play, he often brought positive comments from the opposition.

One of his early games saw both he and 44 year old Sowden turn out for Luton Town at Hitchin Town. With the first team away at Carlisle United and the reserves playing a Combination League game against Fulham both men had to play alongside the likes of Alan Biley and Andy King. Biley giving the young Hatters an early lead in the game eventually ending 2-2.

Another game saw Bergara named as substitute for the Combination League visit of Plymouth Argyle. Unfortunately Kim Wassell suffered a dislocated shoulder early in the game meaning Bergara had to play the rest of the game.

Former Town junior Peter Mead who played right back in the game remembers Bergara:

I first met Danny when he joined Luton Town in the 1973/74 season. My first recollection was he signed as a player/coach. He must have been around 30 years of age and coming to the end of his career. I had just signed on as one of a group of about nine apprentices at the club which included youngsters such as Andy King, Lil Fuccillo, Alan Biley and David Carr all of whom went on to have really good careers in the game.

We played in the Midweek Reserve League which was made up of local clubs like Northampton Town, Cambridge United, Charlton Athletic, Millwall and Peterborough United. Danny started to play as a midfielder/forward in these games and straight away you could tell he could play and was technically very gifted, but what was evident was he was finding the physical side of English football very different to that of Uruguayan and Spanish football. So he was in and out of the side which gave him time to do some coaching.

At training we would be split up into three groups, 1st team squad, reserve team squad and finally the youth team squad. We would go off in our different groups to warm up and prepare for training sessions. Danny`s warm ups were full of flexibility exercises and always with the ball working in pairs which was completely different from the old regimental style warm ups which we were used to. After training we found out this caused quite a stir with the first team players who actually stopped and watched this small stocky foreigner take our warm up and could not believe that a warm up could be so enjoyable!

After this Danny quickly gained the respect of everyone at the club with his training methods and ability to show the technical skills required by demonstrating them himself during sessions. The following season he took over as youth team coach with David Pleat moving up to reserve team coach, so he accepted really that his playing days were coming to a end, but that didn't stop him being the best player in all of the small 5-a-side games we used to play in training!

The game against Plymouth Argyle reserves was played during the 1975/76 season on 3rd April 1976 over the Easter period. Danny by then was well established as the youth team coach and due to injuries and suspensions to players at the club we were left with no substitute for this Combination match, so Danny, who was registered still as a player at the club, was named by Dave Pleat (reserve team manager) as the sub, thinking Danny, who had not played a full game for nearly one and a half seasons, would hopefully not have to be called upon to make an appearance. How wrong could he have been with Kim Wassell picking up an injury only a couple of minutes into the match.

On came Danny, an ageing 33 year old, looking short, stocky and a bit overweight. Straight away the Plymouth players started taking the micky out of him and thinking they were in for an easy victory.

Danny then went on to produce an excellent display of technique, skill and passing ability and he completely dictated the midfield for the rest of the game. Not running all over the place, because he was quite unfit, but by keeping and looking after the ball, by twisting and turning in tight situations and moving the ball on quickly and not getting caught in possession. He made two of the goals with inch perfect passes and played with the passion and commitment of a 23 year old!

After the game all the Plymouth players wanted to know who he was and where he came from. It made me actually sit down and think, what an excellent player he must have been to be able to perform like that at his age, not really fit and hardly played any football for a long period of time, in what was a good quality reserve league, filled with experienced players. For the record we won 3-0 and the team that day was: Knight, Mead, Carr, Morgan, Jones, Malcolm, Simon, Smith, Ingram, Hill, Wassell. Sub - Bergara

The opposition had a couple of experienced players themselves that day, former Town player Neil Rioch and Mick Horswill, who had won the FA Cup with Sunderland only a few seasons earlier, but Bergara was the man who stood out. Future England star Ricky Hill gave Luton a half time lead before Bergara played in Wayne Morgan for the second. His delightful free kick then being headed home by Graham Jones to complete the scoring. The Plymouth keeper that day, Milija Aleksic, actually kept the score down with an outstanding display.

Aleksic was later to sign for Luton Town, going on to make 77 appearances for the Hatters before joining Tottenham Hotspur where he won FA Cup in 1981.

The 1973/74 season proved to be eventful for all concerned at Kenilworth Road as the first team finished runners-up in Division Two thereby gaining promotion to Division One for the first time in fourteen years. Promotion was clinched at The Hawthorns, as a Barry Butlin goal earned the Hatters the point required. Even a last day defeat at Kenilworth Road against Sunderland couldn't dampen the spirits at the club. Haslam had steered his side to the promised land.

Bergara continued his coaching education with the youth team over the next few seasons, his young charges featuring the likes of Alan Biley, Andy King, Ricky Hill and Lil Fuccillo, were to lose only one League game in his first two seasons, picking up League titles and Cups along the way.

Planning for the Future

Luton manager Harry Haslam this week outlined his future hopes for the club's youth policy. And his words couldn't have come at a better time because Luton won the Chiltern Premier League after beating Cambridge United 3-2 on Tuesday evening. Their last game of the season was against Harlow at Vauxhall this morning. And they were due to receive their championship trophy and pennant after the match. There may be people who think that a club of Luton's strength should automatically win the youth league. But it's never a foregone conclusion.

Youth team coach Danny Bergara explained some of the difficulties. "Because Luton have only a small professional staff compared with other clubs, we have been forced to include many schoolboys recently. Most other clubs in the league have been able to field a fairly regular side. But many of our youth players have continuously been called into the Football Combination team."

Until this morning Luton's youth team had not lost a match in the league, and dropped only two points. In their league games Luton scored a total of 87 goals with a season's total of 120. "It has been a difficult season" added Bergara. "I know people tend to think Luton should automatically win the competition, but we have not been able to field a settled team. In a way that has been a good thing, because we have been able to look at many prospective players in competitive matches. If we can find any apprentice professionals we feel will make the grade we will be satisfied".

Haslam has already admitted that the clubs future rests with home grown players. "It may be necessary, in the immediate future, to buy experience by signing a couple of players. But in the main we will have to rely on our own youngsters. There is no way Luton Town can go out and spend large sums on players" he said. "We will have to be self-supporting and produce our own players to exist within our own financial structure".

The manager continued: "You will find many clubs, including those in the First Division, will blend their future on their own youth players. The game is going through a bad period. There are only a few clubs who are making a profit and the majority are struggling to make ends meet. That's why a good youth policy is essential, and we believe our youngsters are going to come good and save us a small fortune".

Whilst at Luton Town Bergara wrote a regular feature in the first team's match day programme. The articles were an insight as to

how he and other coaching staff at the club worked and also offered supporters an insight to how they could help players. Here are a couple of samples of his informative articles:

Coaching – by Danny Bergara

In football, as in any other profession, all concerned expect to gain something. When it comes to the team performance on Saturday afternoon, although contributing from different angles, directors, managers, coaches and supporters, are all working towards the same end: the success of their team.

We coaches may not think in the same way about practical work at club level. However, we try to unite our ideas as much as possible to contribute as best we can to the necessities of the team. We can break down our work into three main areas: Fitness, Technical and Tactical aspects, and most important of all, Mental fitness. It is no good having the most skilful players in the world in top physical form if they are not enthusiastic in their approach to the game.

As coaches we have to be very careful how we instruct the players, especially those who are not quite making the grade. How is the best way to handle a player who is having problems? Do we tell him he is useless, and suggest he changes his career?

Or do we, as I believe we should, encourage him to believe in his own ability and thus build up his confidence? We must ask ourselves whether we are using the right approach. Perhaps we are imposing a way of playing that doesn't suit that particular type of player. There are so many questions we have to ask ourselves to try and ensure that we get the best from each player.

Supporters too, have their part to play in the overall success of the team (including you Oak Road lads). It is you who can give the team the special kind of encouragement and support they need, it is you who can lift their spirits when the game is in full action and things are going wrong and in this way help them to gain success.

Coaching – by Danny Bergara

In my last column I talked about the 3 main points over which we base ourselves to train the town players and they are: Technical and Tactical aspects, Physical fitness and Mental fitness. I also remarked on the tremendous help and vital influence of your support on the Saturday afternoon, contributing to the success of the team.

In other programmes we have asked you to help us in finding players with the qualities required to become in our case a Luton player. Today, I would like to give my views about what to look for when you are looking for quality players, for this purpose, I have to go back to the 3 main points mentioned above. Technical, Physical and Mental fitness, and if we based our training schedules on them, I believe we must base ourselves on them too, when we look for the ideal players.

The other vital points for would be players are: to want, to know, to be able.

To want: *this concerns the attitude of the player. It's the most important one of the three. Dedication to the game, willingness or desire to become great, are virtual in the performance of a player. Many times you see very good players having a poor game. Why? Family problems, girlfriends, nights out and so many more questions that you can think of, as well as ourselves.*

To know: *involves all the techniques in football which, if applied, will give us the skilful player. Can he pass, head control and shoot etc? What does a player do when he has not got the ball. A good*

75

player should be aware at all times, not only where the ball is, but more important, where team mates and opponents are. Also where spaces to attack or defend are. To spot this, depends on the ability of the observer. We ask the player to be aware of these facts, that is as far as we coaches must go.

__To be able:__ vital especially in English football is fitness. What can a dedicated player with all the skill in the world do if he cannot run or last the 90 minutes. To the young player this is the least important of the 3. We can get them fit. We cannot make a slow player into an Alan Pascoe but we will improve them. Flexibility, speed, power and balance are of great importance in the natural qualities of the player. We look for a good attitude and plenty of skill. We can improve them and make them fitter.

Remember:

If you know and you want but are not able

If you know and are able but you don't want

If you want and you are able but you do not know

You will only reach the lower levels of football.

Having worked with English Champions Derby County for their European Cup clash with Real Madrid in November (see next Chapter) Bergara's name was soon being mentioned in larger football circles.

In December 1975, amidst yet another financial crisis at Kenilworth Road, he was approached by Sheffield United manager Jimmy Sirrel with an offer of becoming the new youth team manager at Bramall Lane.

Roy McCrohan, Harry Haslam, David Pleat & Bergara

Harry Haslam and Bergara celebrate promotion to Division 1

Snow - a new phenomenon for Bergara

Danny and Jan Bergara at promotion dinner with Eric Morecambe

Danny and Jan Bergara with Paddy Sowden

this page we introduced you to Danny Bergara, team Coach and Dave Pleat who coaches Luton's ... eam and Dave have years of experience in th... ith Danny and Dave by taking note of what the...

an improve your game

can't pass . . .
. . . you can't play

this week I want to talk about passing. Let's get one thing straig... eginning – if you can't pass you can't play. Although this week... u the techniques of passing, and I want you to practice and keep o... t stress that passing is not just something you do with your fe... e important. Think before you pass. Also get out there and practi... of your mates, practice makes perfect. In the strip below is illustrat... es of good passing. Purpose the main point and the four things th... accuracy, weight, time and disguise. When you've got all five rig... ave improved your game tremendously. As a general rule it is alwa... orward, however there are times when a square pass or even a pa... needed, but more of that next edition.

DANNY BERGARA

Britain's ... think tha... outlook.

There ar... at Kenilwo... showing ... improvem... be forced... home gr... rather th... vast amo... fers.

I am pa... with the ... youngster... Luton. T... and are... hard fo... themselve...

Last ... diff Rev... they h... throug... for the...

Last ... but w... have ... Mid-w... season...

you... been ... into ... to ... mKing, ... Les ... fine... Bri...

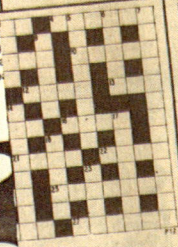

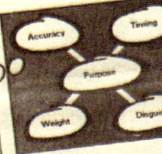

PASSING THE BALL...

Accuracy: Make sure you are positioned correctly. The non kicking foot along side ball and kick with the inside of the foot m... contact with the middle of the ball. Prac... accurate passing with BOTH feet.

Accuracy | Timing
Purpose
Weight | Disguise

... CLUES

... arrows (6), 4 Material for painters (6) ... Swan (3), 11 American coin (4), 12 ... 15 Importune for payment (3), 15 ... (4), 18 Declare to be true (4), 19 ... ortified (4), 21 To capacity (4), 24 ... ashire town (7), 26 Dilates (6), 27 ...

... DER CLUES

DOWN
... imals with ownership signs (6.5), 2 ... Bird's craw (4), 3 Cure of nom. (2 ... ienting clear, striking picture (6), 7 ... romatic substance (5), 14 'Footbia... rved form (7), 18 Colour, show ... (4), 23 Dismiss (4).

1 They impose the mark of the beast (6.5)

HERE they are — the men who carry Luton's pride into the First Division and, we all hope, to success in the premier competition in the world.

Pictured on the revitalised Kenilworth Road turf, they are, from left (back row): Jimmy Husband, Gordon Hindson, Andy King, Pasquale Fuccillo, Alex Malcolm,

Steve Buckley, Phil O'Co...
Matt Pollock, Danny ...
Second row: Ray King (...
(physiotherapist), B...
(captain): John Ryan, ...
Keith Barber, Graham H...
Steve Litt, Paul Price, D...
Roy McCrohan (chief co...

There is no doubt in my mind that many youngsters now with Luton will eventually make the first team and two examples of players who have been found in local soccer and who are ready to show their skills are Andy King and Lilly Fuccillo.

We have five apprentice professionals at Luton but it isn't just a case of playing regularly.

They have to clean the dressing rooms, issue the kit for the senior professionals in training sessions.

SCOTTISH CUP SEMI-FINAL
Celtic (0) 1 Dundee (0) 0

Reading win ...

Virginia wins

Seeded favourite Chris Evert, Martina Navratilova, Virginia Wade and Evonne Goolagong all scored victories in their Round-Robin matches in the 150,000 dollars ($87,000) in the Virginia Slims women's tennis tournament in Los Angeles last night.

half ... off th...

Birm... side ... prepa... with ... win t... to Li...

Am... Kend... Rober... Gordo... game ... Fran... night ... for th...

O REMEMBER

TOMORROW'S TOWN
— a winning team!

Danny pictured with Luton's 10 your apprentices. Tomorrow's Town

Fro...
star...

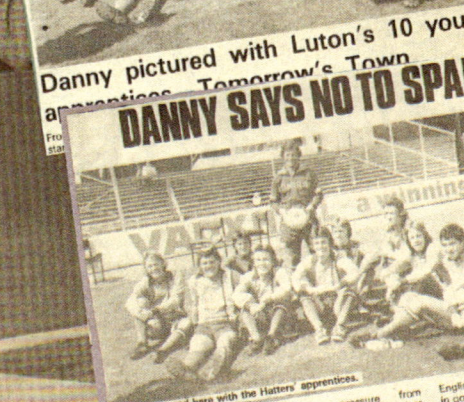

DANNY SAYS NO TO SPAI...

UST a few weeks ago ... ad four people on the ... aslam, Roy McCroha... ergara.

Today they have onl... leat, who earlier this ... f manager.

Roy McCrohan left ... ew life in American for... aslam, and youth team ... o join Sheffield Unite... t Kenilworth Road.

Make no mistakes, ... atonians as a Luton ... ood coach with me... uneaton as well as Le... uton.

It is perhaps unfortu... Englishe pieces, and one o... in good ... give confidence

OUVENIR

'D.

LOS...

DAN...

here with the Hatters' apprentices.
pressure from
just ...

...LE OF LUTON

...your Co-op now!

...er Mead,
...(coach);
...e Game
...homson
...aulkner,
...Garner,
...(coach),
...rd row:

Paul Futcher, Peter Anderson, Brian Chambers, Alan West, Harry Haslam (manager), Ron Futcher, Jimmy Ryan, Rod Fern, David Carr; Front row: Martin Chalmers, Alan Biley, Steve Russell, Laurence Coyne. Inset: Adrian Alston.

Picture: KEITH DOBNEY

...MATCH

...Bergara (Luton's Uruguayan coach) locked in ...rmined battle of tactics. What are they doing: ...tronic football called Videosport. This is a game ...an be played on your own T.V. set (details ...ain this new exciting sports game. Judging by ...s not having it all his own way.

BERGARA AND DAVE PLEAT

Last week I talked to you in my column about chipping ... position. This week I want to talk about chipping for dista... technique, when you can hit a ball straight, you can plac... achieving this your confidence will be tremendous. You'll ... and you'll have the advantage of placing the ball to a cho... an area of one yard more or less). Please practice and don't ... come right straight away. I have been going through this te... apprentices for three months and one lad still can't chip it pr...

CHIPPING THE BALL

When chipping a long ball stand at 40 degrees to the ball. Approach the ball and make the last stride with the non kicking foot, a long stride. The non kicking foot must be about half a yard to a yard from the ball but in line with it (the exact distance varies according to the height of the player). The non kicking foot MUST point to

TARGET

40°

...rs in training!

WHEN your job is to tune-up a squad of footballers into a keen, fighting ...capabl...

January 27, 1978

...oa News, November 4, 1976

...an and Co... ...n stars

...Division club staff ...o used to coach.

...ground staff today ...o smiles on their faces ...nasive boost to their ...arations for the new ...oday they were ...some ard graft. ...he pitch after the ...weather spell. ...day of spreading ...yesterday.

...night's downpour ...r them.

...LEATED' LUTON HARRY AND ...Y

...Football Club ...nt side, Harry ...eat and Danny

...at four left, D. ...ed the position

...ago to start a ...his week Harry ...ny Bergara left ...a hectic week

...nown to older ...exceptionally ...experience at ...coaching with

...has to pick up ...tasks will be ...r supporters

...portsNews 3

...ANNY TURNS ...OWN CHANCE TO GO HOME

...H of the success-
...oa Town team in
...Chiltern Premier
...Danny Bergara
...has turned down a lucra-
...tive top job in his native
...country of Uruguay.

Danny, who comes
from Montevideo, was
flown to South America
for talks with the na-
tional FA authorities.
They wanted him to be-
come manager of their
youth squad, to build a
team for the 1982 World
Cup.

"I was very tempted," said
Danny. "The salary they
offered was out of this
world. But I ...

bought a house at St Albans.
"It was looking around for
a job, and was prepared to
go out of football com-
pletely," he said.
"But I wanted to keep fit,
so I asked Luton Town if
I could use their training
facilities, and they agreed."

That request brought the
young South American to
the attention of Harry
Haslam and before long
Danny was taken on the
staff of Luton Town to
replace youth coach Ray
King.

● DANNY BERGA... still wearing the ... Town badge after ... ing down a top ... national job.

...made a big name for h...
...he turned down ...
...offers to join league ...
...in this country befor...
...offer from Uruguay cam...

..."I like it here at Lut...
...he said this week. "I get ...
...well with Mr. Haslam ...
...other coaches.

..."I expect one day I ...
...move because I ...

Bergara in action for Luton in January 1974

Bergara with Andy King

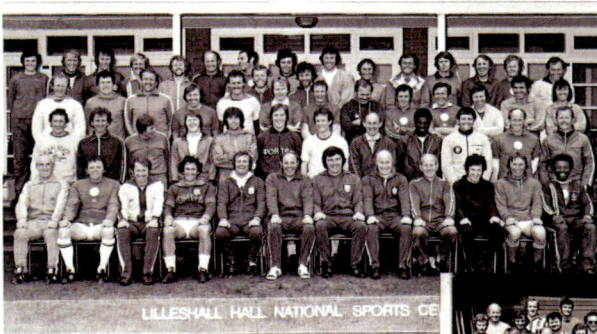

FA coaching courses at Lilleshall

David Pleat and Bergara at training

Bergara told the local paper: *It would be ridiculous to say that I and the other coaches have been able to ignore the current crisis, but the lads have stuck to their jobs and taken the manager's advice to maintain the attitude which is producing one of the best youth policies in the country. As far as I am concerned my future is still with Luton Town. Only last week I turned down an offer from Jimmy Sirrel to become Sheffield United's youth team coach. Harry Haslam and the club put their faith in me two years ago and now I am putting my faith in them. If the financial problems can be overcome, the future of the club lies with the young players being groomed for senior football, and from that aspect the prospects are looking very healthy indeed.*

The majority of the Football Combination side are now products of the clubs youth policy, and one player has now made it through to the first team - Andy King. Andy is a local boy who is still only 19 years old. he has begun to make his mark on the Second Division, and in his case the coaches can perhaps allow themselves a smile of satisfaction at one part of their job completed. There are several more players almost ready for first team action and in the current situation, when the club may be forced to sell leading players, we must keep working to make sure replacements are available. Once in the first team they begin to command a transfer fee. The market maybe depressed but club's must still pay good money for class players.

However my job is producing players not selling them, and I have been thrilled by the players' attitudes in the past couple of weeks. The Combination side won at Highbury on Saturday against a very strong Arsenal side and seven of the players have come through our ranks. Yet however much I want them to win, it is good to lose occasionally and prevent them from getting too cocky. It was interesting to see what happened after the defeat at Northampton. The lads came back with two 6-0 victories. That is the type of attitude that I like to see. Mental fitness is one of three aspects of a good footballer. Ally that to natural skill and fitness and the job becomes easier.

Having begun my football career in Uruguay and played in Spain, I believe that English football, a hard physical game, is offered much by the South American and continental attitudes. Conversely, the English game has its lessons for them, because they tend not to be as physical as necessary in today's top competitions.

At Luton, I am trying to give the players a combination of the best parts of each approach to the game, a combination which in its highest degree has produced such players as Pele and Di Stefano. I am concerned with producing two-footed players, patient players, who are not afraid to take people on. In the fifties it was control, look, pass, but the game has developed to a stage where it is now look, control and pass, so you can see why it is so necessary to allow young players to develop their natural skills, particularly while they are still at school. At that stage my advice is to give them the ball and let them play. We can teach them the intricacies of tactics when they come to us at 16 and 17 years old, and it makes it much easier, when we don't need to spend time on the basics.

With his charges hot favourites to win another League title, Bergara's coaching abilities had started to attract attention further afield. He was offered a position back at Seville as Head of Youth but the offer that almost saw him leave his new English home came from his home country.

Danny Turns Down Offer

Coach Danny Bergara, who has been working wonders with Luton's youth team, has turned down a lucrative offer to be youth team manager for Spanish First Division side Seville. "I would have earned twice as much as I am doing here," he told me. "But manager Harry Haslam advised me not to go. I trust Harry implicitly. He gave me my chance to get into English football. We had a long chat, and the boss said - don't go Danny"

Explained Mr Haslam: *"Danny has everything going for him in England at the moment. He got his full coaching badge this summer but he is still learning. Soon he will have a lot to offer the game, both here and on the continent, especially on the continent with his language advantages. But he is still learning the management side. We would not want him to go over there and find he was lost. I honestly don't think he has enough experience yet, and that is why I advised him to stick around for a bit".*

Danny, who came to England two years ago and applied to Luton for a job. Mr Haslam took him on, and now Danny is commanding respect of the FA as one of the fastest improving coaches in the game. "I haven't done badly in two years" he laughed. "But I have every confidence in Harry. I will do whatever he advises".

Danny says No to Spain

This past week our youth team coach, Danny Bergara made a most important decision both for himself and for Luton Town F.C. Danny had been approached by Seville F.C. of Spain to take over the full control of their reserve and youth sides with a salary that only top managers in this country could command and a two year contract. Despite pressure from Seville (their season is just about beginning) to make a quick decision, Danny had several long chats with the manager and finally decided to reject the offer. Naturally Danny feels there is a future at this club and at present he is learning, and learning quickly some of the ins and outs of management from the boss. The manager has put it on record that one day he feels Danny will have a big job abroad and at present his experience gained in English football will stand him in good stead.

It is not surprising that our youth team coach is in demand from Spain. You will recall the highly successful Englishmen like Jimmy Hagan, Vic Buckingham and Ronnie Allen who have proved that the lessons of British football coaching and training allied to the Spaniards' skill is a recipe for success. Remembering that Danny is fluent in several languages including Spanish and you will see that there is no problem of communication.

Bergara also flew to Uruguay and spent ten days with the Uruguayan FA after which he was offered the dual role as Director of Coaching to the Uruguayan FA and also a role as International Youth Coach. Upon his return to England it became apparent that there were issues within the Uruguayan FA and Bergara decided that his immediate future lay with Luton Town.

Danny Turns Down Chance to go Home

Coach of the successful Luton Town team in the Chiltern Premier League, Danny Bergara, has turned down a lucrative top job in his native country of Uruguay. Danny, who comes from Montevideo, was flown to South America for talks with the national FA authorities. They wanted him to become manager of their youth squad, to build a team for the 1982 World Cup. "I was very tempted" said Danny. "The salary they offered was out of this world. But I was not happy with some of the details of their organisation, and in the end I decided to stay with Luton".

Since he took over the Town's youth training, Danny has built a team which has lost only one game in two seasons in the Chiltern Premier League. So far this season they have dropped only one point, and are hot favourites to be champions for the second consecutive time. He came to Luton through pure luck. He started his football career in Uruguay, and was transferred to Majorca 14 years ago, when he was 20.

Bergara told the local press his side of the story:

<u>**Why I'm happy to stay with the Hatters**</u>

You may have read in the Post-Echo last night that I was almost made Director of Coaching to the Uruguayan FA. I was also offered the job of international youth coach in my home country. I went over there for ten days recently, and it looked as if I'd landed a fantastic job at a fabulous salary. And then things began to go sour. I got back to this country and heard that the board which had offered me the position had resigned. The thing blew hot and cold, and I realised that my future again lay at Luton. And, do you know, I wasn't all that sorry.

Two Second Division clubs - I prefer not to say which ones - also made enquiries about me, and I also nearly went to Seville in Spain where I enjoyed some success as a player. But to be honest, I am happy at Luton at the moment. Manager Harry Haslam and the board of directors have been fantastic to me. They have never stood in my way, and I have never forgotten that it was they who gave me my chance in English football. So I am staying - at least for the moment. Of course everyone wants to better himself, but I am convinced that Harry will advise me correctly when the right offer comes along.

We have a great youth team at Kenilworth Road, and last season they won the Chiltern Youth Premier League and the Cup. This season we are already in the semi-final of the East Anglian Cup, and the kids beat Hitchin 6-0 in the FA Youth Cup. I am working closely with assistant coach David Pleat, and our aim is to have a Second Division team made up entirely of players who have come up through the ranks. We are trying to get as many of the kids as possible through to the first team. We have already made it with players like Lilly Fuccillo, Andy King, Ricky Hill, Alan Biley. Goalkeeper Tony Knight is almost ready.

The only way a lot of clubs are going to survive is by producing their own players, and this is what we are working hard for at Kenilworth Road. I must say I am delighted at the way it is going. And this is one of the reasons I wasn't too disappointed when the Uruguayan job fell through.

Last summer I did a coaching course and emerged as an FA staff coach. This is another arrow in my bow. We teach people from all over the place who are interested in becoming soccer coaches. It's funny, some of them couldn't kick a ball properly. Others were top players. We take them on two week courses at either Bisham Abbey or at Lilleshall.

This has been a great help in my job as youth coach at Luton. You give people hints and you give them ideas. It's all a matter of making people think. We teach them the ABC of football; the basic principles. The only trouble about all this speculation about my future is that it's all been a bit unsettling for myself and my family. When you think about it one afternoon I thought I was an international manager, and then, all of a sudden, I was just Luton's youth team coach again. But, as I say, that doesn't bother me much. We all have great ambitions at Kenilworth Road. I am at Luton now, and that's it.

In the meantime there's a lot to be done here. Already a lot of our youngsters have a foot in the first team door. It is my job to make sure that if they have the ability they get in, that's why mine is such a satisfying job.

A typical press cutting from Bergara's days at Kenilworth Road

<u>Danny is a Real Bag of Tricks</u>

Luton Town have had success with players in the last couple of seasons, the Futcher twins, Steve Buckley, Andy King and latest discovery Pasquale Fuccillo ('Lil' to his mates). Occasionally the youngsters at Kenilworth Road have produced South American style skills. Not so surprising, however, as they have been coached by a South American! Uruguayan-born Danny Bergara has been with Luton for three years as youth team and reserve coach.

Bergara said: "I receive great enjoyment from coaching schoolboys. The boys are willing to learn and their enthusiasm is unlimited. I have now passed my coaching courses and have been appointed an FA staff coach", Danny tells me. "I don't know what the future holds, but at the moment I'm very happy coaching the youngsters at Luton. As a player I could do anything with the ball. Any trick Pele could do I could do as well. But there was a difference when it came to all-round ability. The kids like me to show them tricks with the ball. I don't see that as my job. I have to teach them the basics first. But natural players like Andy King and Pasquale 'Lil' Fuccillo can start to try some of the tricks now they have learned the basics".

Andy King: *"Danny is fantastic with a ball. He can almost make it talk. He shows you ways of beating a man you wouldn't dream of. But you have to gain the confidence first to try them".*

Having turned down several approaches to leave Kenilworth Road Danny Bergara eventually took the next step on his English adventure early in 1978 when Haslam accepted the vacant manager's role at Sheffield United. After a very successful spell at Kenilworth Road, he was once again to move on from a club where he had been very happy.

The local paper reported that there was more to Haslam and Bergara leaving than met the eye:

<u>Directors to blame claims Harry Haslam</u>

This week Harry Haslam and Danny Bergara have left Luton Town football club. A sad loss to all loyal supporters and the blame for their departure lies with the directors, claims Harry. This week in the Herald we can reveal exclusively what's been happening at Kenilworth Road. Harry Haslam left the club because the directors would not offer him a new contract that was acceptable. He claimed in an exclusive interview with Herald editor Keith Barwell that the directors had misled him and the new contract he had been offered was less in real terms than his existing contract, he was left with a decision to stay for peanuts, as he called it, or go. He went.

To understand the full story it is necessary to back-track to the beginning of the season. Harry told me that the subject of his new contract first came up on the tour before the season started. He wanted a new contract that offered him more security and he claimed that at that time extra money was not a consideration. 'The

*directors could have offered me a new contract there and then'
added Harry, but it was not to be.*

*The departure of both Haslam and Bergara could have far reaching
effects. Several members of the full time staff at the club are very
unhappy. One of them told me 'The board have gone their way,
they wanted to get rid of Harry who has stood between them and
their desire to sell several top players. The players respect Harry and
don't be surprised to see some of them go at the end of the season.'
Whether this happens remains to be seen.*

*My main concern is that what looked like a winning management
team has been disrupted. Harry Haslam was not a 'track suit'
manager. He was more of a General Manager, an ambassador for
the club. With David Pleat taking charge of the first team coaching
and Danny Bergara nursing along the kids. Although Haslam and
Bergara have gone, it is important to put the record straight.*

*One thing is for sure, directors must be open and honest with their
managers and supporters. Double dealings and personal battles for
power can only have an adverse effect on the club. David Pleat, the
new manager is a very capable guy, he won't be able to replace
Haslam as an ambassador for the club, that's not his style, but he
could be a manager of real style and power given the right support
from the board. It's such a pity however that the board couldn't see
their way clear to do the sensible and honourable thing, make
Haslam the general manager, give Pleat more power as team
manager, and keep the flood of youngsters coming into the first
team through the hands of talented Danny Bergara. If the board's
decisions turn out to be wrong, let them be warned, regular
supporters and shareholders will not stand idly by.*

Jan Bergara:

When Harry Haslam was offered the job of manager at Sheffield United he asked Daniel to be his assistant manager. David Pleat, who had been the reserve team coach at Luton Town and had now been offered the manager's job, also wanted Daniel to be his assistant.

As Harry had offered Daniel his chance in English football, when England was still very insular within football, he wanted to repay his loyalty to Harry and so joined him on a five year contract at Bramall Lane. Daniel was a pioneer who stuck at it with passion, self belief and he never gave up.

Derby County FC

In October of 1975, Bergara, whilst on the coaching staff at Luton Town, was approached by Derby County manager Dave Mackay with regard to his side's upcoming game against Real Madrid in the European Cup.

The Rams were England's sole representative in the tournament having won the First Division the previous season. The competition in those days was between the 32 teams in Europe that had won their respective Leagues. Having beaten Czechoslovakian champions Slovan Bratislava in the first round, thanks to two late Francis Lee goals in the second leg at the Baseball Ground, Derby were drawn against the might of Real Madrid for a place in the last eight.

Mackay had asked Luton Town if Bergara would be available to help him compile a dossier on the Spanish club. Bergara had only left Spain two years previously and the Scot wanted him to give him as much background information on the team and players as possible before the tie.

Bergara was allowed to give his help and advice and, having played against Real Madrid many times in his ten years in Spain, proved a good source of information to the Rams manager and his staff.

He provided a detailed breakdown on the probable team and individual players, in particular Madrid's most influential player, midfielder José Martínez Sánchez. Sanchez, nicknamed 'Pirri', was in fine form for the Spaniards as the Rams would find out to their cost over the two legs.

As the daily papers in England reported:

Wednesday's European Cup adventure against Real Madrid promises to be a world apart from First Division scuffling against Wolves. And goals will not be plucked as easily as they were in Saturday's 3-2 win. While English fans look forward to seeing Günter Netzer, Paul Breitner, giant centre-forward Santillana and perhaps the veteran Amancio at the Baseball Ground, Derby have been warned about the man who will really matter in this week's first leg. Madrid's prime objective will be to contain. For that they will rely on a player of less than Netzer and company's universal appeal. Jose Martinez Sánchez, better known under his nickname of Pirri flies to England today as the key man.

Mackay Studies Real File

An Irish-sounding Uruguayan, with strong Spanish connections, studying in England, this weekend added weight to Derby County's dossier on Real Madrid. Danny Bergara, Luton's youth team coach, who has played for Majorca and Seville, has supplied Derby with a detailed breakdown on Real's players, and the team the champions can expect to meet at the Baseball Ground on Wednesday.

Derby's managerial team, Dave MacKay and his assistant Des Anderson, have already digested Bergara's file. Today, Derby's inside information on their European Cup opponents will be completed when chief scout Bert Johnson presents his report on his spying mission to Spain on Saturday. The result the combined reports will have, I understand, is merely to underline Derby's fierce conviction that their most successful ploy lies in their attacking ability.

Anderson said: *"We know that three goals on Wednesday would be nice to take with us to Madrid in a fortnight but I believe that one or two could still be enough. We were not entirely happy that the tactics we used in Bratislava in the first round were right. Your heart is always in your mouth when you're trying to defend".*

Mackay adds significantly: *"I am not necessarily one of those who believe that this tie will be won at home".*

Derby's training today and tomorrow will be in a light vein as MacKay is aware of the dangers of the players leaving their energy on the training ground. The Derby manager explained last night: *"I thought we looked a tired team in the second half against Wolves. Fortunately, we got away with it because we had scored three goals in the first half. It would be easy for me to say that I told the lads to ease off in the second half... Easy, but not the truth".*

Striker Charlie George, who accepted his second half substitution without a whimper of complaint, said: *"This team hasn't played to its full potential once this season".*

Derby County 4 Real Madrid 1

In the first leg, played on 22nd October 1975 at Derby's Baseball Ground, the Rams' performance was easily their best of the season to date. Their possession and build up play appeared to surprise the Spaniards. Charlie George blasted home the first goal on 10 minutes before adding his second from the penalty spot 5 minutes later after Francis Lee had been brought down.

Danger man Pirri then scored a neat goal to reduce the arrears before defender David Nish lashed home from 25 yards to give Derby a two goal cushion going into the break. Pirri looked to have reduced the deficit again midway through the second half, his

93

Bergara with Derby staff and FA
Ambassador Bobby Charlton on
plane to Madrid

On Bernabeu pitch with Derby
players

With Derby Manager Dave Mackay
and his assistant Des Anderson

Charlie George puts Derby
ahead at The Baseball Ground

With Anderson and Charlton
training at The Bernabeu

Mackay studies Real file

MALCOLM FOLLEY checks Derby's plans

DERBY COUNTY FOOTBALL CLUB

Est. 1884

Derby County

by Danny Bergara

FIRST of all I would like to thank Harry and the club for allowing me to go on this

Dave asked me if I had something to say, I only reiterated his comments on concentration: that it must play a very important role during the game and if they normally give 100% concentration, I would ask them for 110%, especially in the first 15 minutes of each half and the last five. And so we went to the stadium to face the task.

From the first moment, Real Madrid came out like thunder, putting Derby under tremendous pressure and, as a result, they scored after three minutes when Martinez went through. In the rest of the first half Derby defended, trying to keep possession and only had two attempts at goal, only one of them presenting any danger.

Although 1-0 in the lead at half time, Real Madrid still had a tremendous task ahead of them to put the game in their favour, and I could not see them scoring another two goals. They were not allowing Derby to show much in the way of attack and I felt that they could have been much tighter in midfield, although Netzer, Del Bosque and Breitner were in command of the situation.

In the second half Madrid again came in strongly and within 15 minutes they were 3-0 up. Derby came back into the game and George, with a tremendous goal, put the game clearly on Derby's side, but Madrid, showing a lot of character and determination again pressurized Derby. As a result of this pressure and the inspiration of one player – Amancio – they were awarded a doubtful penalty. The game went into extra time and again Madrid started attacking as they had done for the first 90 minutes, resulting in a goal from their centre forward. Following this, Derby missed a good chance when Alan Hin...

DERBY COUNTY EUROPEAN CHAMPIONS CUP REAL MADRID

Bernabeu Stadium

Kick-off 21.00 hrs, Nov. 5 1975

Official Itinerary

MUNDO BALON

PROGRAMA OFICIAL DEL PARTIDO

Real Madrid C.F. – Derby County F.C.

Estadio Santiago Bernabeu   5 Noviembre 1975

Madrid players.

Mackay encouraged his players to attack and I do not

DANNY'S OFF TO SPAIN

NEXT week, Danny Bergara, our youth team coach, leaves for Madrid with the Derby County party for their return game with Real. Danny's knowledge of Spanish football and the Real players helped Assistant Manager, Des Anderson to compile a report which proved valuable.

Danny could not conceal his delight when Derby stormed to that three goal advantage at the Baseball Ground and after the game he was interviewed on the Spanish Radio network. In Spain Danny had played against Pirri, the skilful midfield player, many times and he made a studied report of this player, intimating that his breaks from midfield, strength in the tackle and competitiveness would prove the main danger to Derby. This proved to be the case.

After the game, Danny and our Assistant Coach, Dave Pleat, were entertained by the Derby management and they recorded their thanks to our Club for allowing Danny to help.

Next week Danny will get a deserved break from routine

EL ENTRENAMIENTO DEL DERBY COUNTY, EN FOTOS

(Reportaje gráfico de Antonio ALCOBA.)

GRUPO.—Finalizado el entrenamiento, pose de un reducido grupo de jugadores, acompañados de Bobby Charlton, Alberto Bergara y el preparador físico. Ellos son: Bourne, Gemmill, Lee, Moseley, Hinton y Todd.

LOLA LOLA

sweet strike being wrongly ruled out for offside, before George completed his hat trick from the spot after Netzer had brought down Kevin Hector in the box late in the game.

Bergara could not conceal his delight when Derby stormed to that three goal advantage at the Baseball Ground and after the game he was interviewed on the Spanish radio network. In Spain Danny had played against Pirri, the skilful midfield player, many times and he made a studied report of this player, intimating that his breaks from midfield, strength in the tackle and competiveness would prove the main danger to Derby. This proved to be the case.

The return leg took place two weeks later on 5th November when unfortunately the Rams had several problems with team selection, several players were suffering from knocks and more importantly striker Francis Lee was suspended.

Real Madrid, needing to overturn a three goal deficit, came out of the blocks on fire as they took a second-minute lead through Roberto Martínez, and though Derby managed to get to the break without conceding again, an incredible start to the second half saw Madrid score two more goals. Martínez notched again, in the 50th minute, and Santillana in the 54th to put the scores level overall but put the home side ahead on 'away' goals.

However, George made it 3-1 six minutes later, his superb strike from 30 yards being his fourth goal of the tie, forcing the home team to score at least one goal to level the contest. With just five minutes left to play Real were awarded a penalty after a foul by Nish, Pirri scoring from the spot to put the match into extra time. In extra time, Santillana scored a brilliant solo goal to clinch the tie for Real and break Derby's hearts.

Bergara's own report on the return leg at The Bernabeu

First of all I would like to thank Harry and the club for such an important game in which I was indirectly involved regarding assisting Dave MacKay with information on the Real Madrid players, most of whom I have played against. Secondly, I must also thank Dave MacKay and Des Anderson for inviting me to go.

The atmosphere before the game not just a few hours before the game, but since we arrived was tremendous and pointed to a great game. Many factors surrounded the game and most of them were against Derby. Even before we arrived, the papers were talking about the fight between Lee and Hunter in the Leeds v Derby game on the previous Saturday and were creating ill feeling for Derby. In their interviews, the Madrid players were saying that their morale was very high and were asking the fans, through the press, to cheer them all the way through and turn this tie in their favour.

Mackay had many problems with the formation of his side. Lee was suspended and three or four players doubtful right up until the morning of the game. In fact there was a doubt on McFarland right up until an hour and ten minutes before kickoff. Their three goal advantage could have meant some kind of relaxation and over confidence in some of the Derby players and all these factors could have affected the Derby players psychologically, not the least being the coverage of the Lee/Hunter affair by the Spanish press. I feel that this made the Derby players too aware of going into strong tackles on the good Real Madrid players.

Mackay encouraged his players to attack, and I do not think that either himself or Anderson left much to be said of the players, tying up every possible point that would help them to win the game. When Dave asked me if I had something to say, I only reiterated his comments on concentration: that it must play a very important role during the game and if they normally gave 100% concentration, I would ask them for 110%, especially in the first 15 minutes of each half and the last five. And so we went to the stadium to face the task.

From the first moment, Real Madrid came out like thunder, putting Derby under tremendous pressure and, as a result, they scored after three minutes when Martinez went through. In the rest of the first half, Derby defended, trying to keep possession and only had two attempts at goal, only one of them presenting any danger. Although 1-0 in the lead at half time, Real Madrid still had a tremendous task ahead of them to put the game in their favour, and I could not see them scoring another two goals. They were not allowing Derby to show much in the way of attack and I felt that they could have been much tighter in midfield, although Netzer, Del Bosque and Breitner were in command of the situation.

In the second half Madrid again came in strongly and within 15 minutes they were 3-0 up. Derby came back into the game and George, with a tremendous goal, put the game clearly on Derby's side, but Madrid, showing a lot of character and determination again pressured Derby. As a result of this pressure and the inspiration of one player; Amancio; they were awarded a doubtful penalty. The game went into extra time and again Madrid started attacking as they had done for the first 90 minutes, resulting in a goal from their centre forward. Following this, Derby missed a good chance when Alan Hinton crossed from the left and Roger Davies did not get to the ball six yards from goal. Although the result was obviously a disappointing one, it was a most enjoyable trip and thanks once again to all who made it possible for me to be a part of it

Sheffield United FC

Jan Bergara:

Another journey, this time up north. My twin brother assured me we would love it, and at least it was in England. One thing that you learn from very early on when you move around is that you can make friends anywhere in the world. Daniel had always loved travel and languages and had always made friends easily. We happily settled in Sheffield to this day, but Daniel's second home became his beloved Stockport County in 1989.

Daniel took up golf through our son Simon encouraging him to do so. He became a good golfer winning the vice-captain's trophy and also notching a 'hole in one'. His garden gradually took on the appearance of a beautiful football pitch with Wembley stripes. He had a huge sense of pride in all that he did.

One of my first visits to Bramall Lane was when River Plate of Argentina played Sheffield United in a pre-season friendly, I was on my way to the match with Alex Sabella's wife Viviana and former Argentina captain Antonio Rattin. The taxi couldn't get all the way to the ground so we decided to walk the last few hundred yards, as we were walking I had my bottom pinched. Rattin who was walking behind us saw what had happened and asked me to hold his watch.

Suddenly he hauled up the supporter who had pinched my bottom by the shirt and held him in the air. I kept saying "no pasa nada" (it's ok leave it) to him as I wanted us to get into the ground, but the look on the face of the supporter when confronted by the 6' 4" former footballer Rattin was priceless!

The Blades had finished sixth in the First Division at the end of the season, missing out on a UEFA Cup spot by a single point. Unfortunately the completion of the new South Stand at Bramall Lane in 1975 coincided with a slump in fortunes on the field for Sheffield United.

The following campaign was a complete disaster as the Blades finished bottom of the table and were relegated to the Second Division.

Relegation proved to be a financial disaster and the drop in season ticket sales meant limited funds for strengthening the team. With the banks reluctant to give additional loans on top of the debt on the new South Stand, the club were forced to sell club legend Tony Currie to arch rivals Leeds United. The £250,000 from his sale, as well as season ticket money, was quickly swallowed up.

In an effort to halt the club's slide out of the First Division, United had brought in Jimmy Sirrel from Notts County but he proved unpopular with both the players and fans and could not halt the decline, overseeing relegation and then being sacked in September 1977 with the Blades near the foot of Division Two.

Sirrel was replaced on a temporary basis by long serving Cec Coldwell, and whilst the initial results picked up, the lack of funds for new players was matched by the lack of reserve players suitable for the step up to the first team.

After a poor run of results in January, the board acted to bring in Harry Haslam from Luton Town. Haslam was seen as a bit of a 'wheeler dealer' who had successfully managed the Hatters in similar circumstances for nine years.

Haslam, who's Luton Town team had completed a league double over the Blades with a three goal victory at Bramall Lane just a few days earlier, brought Bergara in as his assistant manager. He had also offered a role to David Pleat but Pleat had been offered and accepted the first team role vacated by Haslam at Kenilworth Road. Pleat had also offered Bergara the assistant manager role under him, Bergara however felt that his first loyalty was to Haslam who had offered him a start in English football, and so joined him in Sheffield.

Local report after appointment of Haslam and Bergara

It's been the week of a new deal for Sheffield United in the appointment of Harry Haslam as manager and Danny Bergara as his assistant. In a five year spell, Haslam has been involved in transfer deals adding up to £1,600,000. Whatever the future brings the new management, one thing is certain - United are in for a new style of control. A combination of down-to-earth Lancashire humour and volatile South American temperament and flair in the mixture Sheffield United have hired to start the club's long haul back towards the sunlight of the First Division.

In Harry Haslam, their new manager, United have signed up a man with a formidable record of finding, grooming and selling fine players. Malcolm MacDonald, Andy King, John Ryan, Ian Seymour, David Sadler, Tony Burns, Des Anderson, the Futchers... the list is impressive.

And in Danny Bergara they have acquired a coach who brings to Sheffield , for the first time, a knowledge and experience of the South American and Spanish scene. The partnership is fascinating: the challenge daunting: the rewards considerable: failure unthinkable.

Contract for Cec top job for Bergara

Sheffield United have offered a five year contract to chief coach Cec Coldwell... but newcomer Danny Bergara gets the title of assistant manager with overall responsibility for coaching at Bramall Lane.

United's new manager, Harry Haslam, announced this proposed new set-up when he arrived at the club today.

He said: "Cec will remain chief coach and I have negotiated a contract for him of about five years on very good terms". This is the first time Coldwell has had a contract but he asked for time to think it over, probably until it became clear exactly how coaching duties would be divided.

Said Haslam: "Cec has given me no reason to doubt that he can work with me but naturally he wants to talk it over with his wife. We have had a nice chat and I sincerely hope he will join our team". Coldwell was due to see Chairman Mr. John Hassall later today with an indication of his decision.

Bergara, 35-year-old from Uruguay with experience in both South American and Spanish soccer, comes to Sheffield with a glowing testimony from Haslam. "He brings an appreciation of technique and skill plus a tremendous ability to put things across to players. He is a wonderful asset to our English football".

United's new chief spoke of his legacy to Luton - and the problems of Sheffield. "It was an emotional night last night when we played the Italian under 21 side," he said. "But now I'm here and the problems may have some comparison with what we once had at Luton but I look at the ground, I look at the facilities, I remember the traditions and obviously things are not so bad as Luton's. There is a lot of work to be done but I want to create a club of enjoyment.

Sheffield United 1978

Bergara on plane back
from successful
pre-season tour

Bergara on the bench at Bramall Lane

ergara relaxing with Antonio Rattin, Alex
Sabella and Oscar Arce

Sheffield Soccer
Forum with Brian
Clough and Jack
Charlton

UGH CLOUGH

The Express panel at Sheffield: Brian Clough, Danny Bergara, Stuart Linnel, Jackie Charlton and Pe

'Wednesday job? I have got enough problems'

United

RIVER PLATE

GRAND CHALLENGE MATCH
Wednesday 30 August 1978 · Kick-o
Official Match Day Magazine 20p Vol

CONTRACT FOR CEC —
TOP JOB FOR BERGARA

The Prime Minister of Soccer

STARTING in The Star next week, a super soccer series on the local boy who made good to such a degree that he

great visionary because he first:
● Wanted floodlit football

By Tony Pritchett

SHEFFIELD UNITED have offered a five-year contract to chief coach Cec Coldwell . . . but newcomer Danny Bergara gets the title of assistant-manager with overall responsibility for coaching at Bramall Lane.

United's new manager, Harry Haslam, announced this proposed new set-up when he arrived at the club today.

He said: "Cec will remain chief

"It was an emotional night last night when we played

United's new team

N, Sheffield, Saturday, January 28, 1978

PPY HARRY – THE MANAGER WHOSE DEALS IN A FIVE-YEAR SPELL ADDED UP TO

THE BIGGEST GAMBLE
OF HIS SOCCER CAREE

k of a field

arry er. ara as a five m was fter to atever s the nt, one w style of

NETT

ATION of Lancashire d volatile an temper- is the mix- United have the club's ack towards the First

Haslam, their United have

The Star Football Special, 1980

THE SOUTH AMERICAN WAY

Smiling Harry Haslam (left) and one of his assistants Danny Bergara getting ready for the new season.

SHEFFIELD is a proud place these days. Its belching black factory chimneys once earned the unkindly reputation of "the floor of hell" but, after six and a half million pounds expense and 13 years of battle against the grime, it boasts that it is now the cleanest industrial city in Europe.

Business is booming. Thousands of people from all parts of the world pour into the Steel City each year for conferences and, at Sheffield United the directors intend keeping in step with the city's progress.

The club sits in a prime spot, a mere stroll from the city centre, and chairman John Hassall and his board have, in the past four months, made the appointments that should bring in the first class football entertainment.

They have sprinkled five year contracts around on new manager Harry Haslam and his assistants can build the team properly.

Now in his mid-50s, Haslam recognises the challenge at Sheffield could be the highlight of his career and he is putting everything into the job in his own inimitable way — which means with a grin as wide as the High Street and jokey ad-libs which make interviews and Press conferences so different from the "inquisition sessions" too often held up and down the country.

A full-back with Manchester United in 1938/39, after the War he played for Brighton and Orient before managing non-League clubs Eastbourne, Barry and Tunbridge Wells (nine years).

Chief-scout duties for Fulham and Luton came next. His eventual managership of Luton earned him acclaim from all quarters. His discovery of players and astuteness in the players' market reduced the club's debts by £500,000.

Looking back, he said: "The nicest thing was getting Luton to stay, but it was an achievement with a small staff."

With forgettable see-saw League performances last term behind them, the Sheffield United supporters will be wondering what is in store for them next season. They may have to see it through wire fences after a foolish ground invasion in the last minutes of the last game of the season.

The minority's action stopped Haslam sending the real supporters home with words of encouragement. He could have broadcast over the club's loudspeaker system for instance about building up tem the reserve's strength.

"I thought it advisable to get some young players in straight away rather than try and get them at the start of the new season," he told SHOOT.

"While we had enough matches to play the youngsters in I tried them in the second, third and fourth teams . . . we had to get some standard."

Some new faces, including £100,000 buy from Chelsea Steve Finnieston, can be expected in the first team next term but Haslam was quick to praise the current squad.

"They did a good job . . . they were on a hiding to nothing and sometimes, trying too hard, they slipped up. They need the Summer break to kindle everything.

"I'm contracted here," he went on, "to try and bring stability into the team's play . . . to generally recreate a few things . . . to breed a winning attitude and work from there. And I believe we have the lads on the staff and by adding some new talent to the squad we'll be able to come out and have a go!"

In the short time he has been in office Haslam has made some important back-room signings which illustrate his thinking and explains why those in his regular presence are so optimistic again.

George McCabe, the former F.A. Cup Final and World Cup referee, has been recruited along with Argentinian Oscar Arce to fertilise the youth set-up at the club.

Their credentials — McCabe as a most successful schoolboy talent spotter, Arce for Millwall's young team players will mean that before team players will to keep the position

By the age of three Uruguayan youth caps and played Racing Club of Monte team in the nation.

His eldest brother international caps a model

Bergara left Montevideo age of 29 (he joined FC in Spain's First learn to know Europe experience.

Married to Janet here and, after a couple of in a friendly game which Haslam said he don't you take up coaching have a go in this country started a four-year stay with Haslam.

It's about time the United emerged once football's shadows. The Bergara duo have the right qualifications to do the job.

Training United sty[le]

☐ THE URUGUAYAN SNOWMAN, United's new coaching supremo, South American [star Danny] Bergara copes with an English winter on his first full day at the club.

☐ WATCHING BRIEF . . . Sheffield United assistant manager Danny Bergara, rig[ht] United's Argentinian star Alex Sabella watch Saturday's match from the dug-out

It looks like start of a new United era

THEY went to cheer Finnieston, they broke off their adulation for the two-goal hero by rapturously welcoming the ...

Manager with the Morecambe touch . . .

SHEFFIELD UNITED'S Keith Walker had been taking some stick with comics on the phone asking if that was Sheffield 505151.

What with a bunch of fives headline in the Green 'Un, Hawaii Five-O and five-a-side cracks coming thick and fast, it was all a strain on the sense of humour.

"Just you wait until Harry Haslam gets here, he'll sort you out with the jokes."

Mind you, Harry had a head start in a week when five was the dominating number — he's 55. Now we know!

INTRIGUED

Certainly, the Walker forecast stood up in the light of Harry Haslam's first day

DANNY BERGARA AND A TOUCH OF LATIN COACHING A[...]

United do it the South American way

TONY PRITCHETT WITH UNITED

efficient and first imp sions must be that on cut transfer prices, he's bargain at £100,000.

I want the board to enjoy our football even when we lose... we have no bad players until I prove it to myself. And I have five years... I want to finish my football career with Sheffield United".

Mr. Hassall confirmed that his club had engaged Haslam for five years. He said: "We are all aware of what has to be done and we think the manager should be allowed to get on with it without fear of change. It will need patience and time but naturally our aim is the quickest possible return to the First Division". Saturday's team for the friendly at Swindon will be largely Cec Coldwell's choosing. But Mr. Haslam and his new assistant Bergara will be there to see the team for the first time.

Simple rule of Danny

After coping with the heavy Glasgow accent of Jimmy Sirrel, the Sheffield United players may have nothing more to fear in the way of language problems. However, new United assistant manager Danny Bergara from Uruguay, may cause a few snags initially. Says Danny: "I had no trouble at Luton after I got to know the players. But I have a simple rule. If players don't understand me, they should ask, otherwise it's their fault if we don't communicate. On the other hand, if they ask and I still don't get through, then it's my fault".

On his move to Sheffield United Bergara stated: *"I could have stayed behind and worked with David Pleat but I am a great believer in loyalty. Harry was the person who had faith in me when nobody had heard of me and it is part of my make-up to repay loyalty".*

Even back in 1978 Bergara was campaigning for a change in the way the English game was being run regarding junior football. He

was probably the first FA Coach to recognise that the game in England needed to change:

"I think that basically, League clubs receive the youngsters too late on in their development, and I find that many of them are lacking in the basics which are taken for granted in South America. I have also found that the negative aspects are encouraged in this country, the youngsters should be encouraged to learn attacking and positive techniques. It should be a gradual process, they should not learn to run before they can walk. Here many really young kids, the under 12's, are made to go out and play on a full size pitch. It is stupid, the players just get tired and cannot use the pitch fully. They should use pitches designed for their age group, a smaller and narrower pitch which encourages dribbling and makes the player aware of what is going on around him. Unfortunately many of the youngsters who first come to me know more about tactics than they do about playing football. The coaches who have taught them teach to treat the ball as something that should be cleared as soon as possible, instead of realising what alternatives are available. That is what I will try to achieve here at Sheffield United. I hope that my players will become better and more skilful players who will go on to the first team".

United finished in a comfortable mid-table position at the end of Haslam's first season, unfortunately that was to be his highest finish whilst at the club. With a reputation for finding talent, Haslam brought in a number of players, most notably Argentinean Alex Sabella.

Haslam had tried to sign the teenage sensation Diego Maradona from Argentinos Juniors but the club wouldn't accept the Blades offer of £400,000. Haslam switched his attention to Sabella who they signed for £160,000 in July 1978. Sabella made his full debut for United at Bramhall Lane in the opening day defeat against Leyton Orient (1-2).

Sabella played for United until 1980 when Haslam agreed a fee of £600,000 with Second Division Sunderland, Sabella however had ambitions to play in the First Division and refused to join the Wearside outfit. The Argentinean eventually joined Leeds United during the close season for £400,000.

One factor during Haslam's reign was that he had to balance the books, forcing him to sell several of the club's promising young players. The likes of Keith Edwards, Imre Varadi and Simon Stainrod were all allowed to leave Bramall Lane in an effort to raise funds.

Old stager Alan Woodward also left the club to play in America, and with his side struggling at the wrong end of the Second Division, Haslam brought in another veteran, Bruce Rioch, whose eight game loan spell from Derby County brought a mini-revival in the club's fortunes.

After the home win over relegation rivals Charlton Athletic at the end of March (2-1) the Blades fate was in their own hands. They were now level on points with the Addicks, but crucially had three games left whilst the Londoners only had one.

One point from those last three games saw United relegated to the Third Division. The new campaign would see them play their first ever season outside the top two divisions.

During the season the Daily Express had held a 'SOCCER FORUM' in the City with Bergara joining guests Brian Clough and Jack Charlton alongside Peter Thomas from the Daily Express and host Stewart Linnell of local station Radio Hallam.

During the evening Bergara had stated at the end of one his answers to a question from the floor, that he was honoured to be working in the country that had given football to the world.

Clough was quick to quip *"And so you should be"*

Bergara's response brought a great cheer from the room and an almost apologetic nod of the head from Clough *"I am, but my country are no mugs either. We have won two World Cups, two Olympic Titles and been champions of South America eleven times".*

Ted Dickinson, the editor of the Daily Express, sent Bergara the following letter after the event:

"Dear Danny, It was a night to remember and I shall remember it as the night Danny Bergara put Brian Clough down. In spite of all the difficulties you handled it superbly and I don't believe Harry Haslam could've done it any better. Kind regards to Jan and again many thanks"

The new season started promisingly enough with eleven wins before the end of October, but their early form dipped and the team spent the majority of the season in mid-table, never threatening the promotion places. Worse still City rivals Sheffield Wednesday earned themselves promotion as well as thrashing the Blades at Hillsborough (4-0).

It was during this period that Bergara was invited by the Welsh FA to apply for the vacant manager's role following the resignation of Mike Smith. The Uruguayan actually made the short list and but for the inclusion of former Wales captain Mike England, who was eventually named as Smith's successor, it was widely accepted in the province that the job could well have gone to Bergara.

When asked about the Welsh job at the time Bergara told the press: *"It's a great honour to make the shortlist for a job of this size. It doesn't mean I am unhappy at Sheffield United. On the contrary, my family is very settled. But to be in the running for an International job is very pleasing"*

There was a significant change at Bramall Lane in the lead up to the new campaign as Haslam agreed a deal to bring former England international, and World Cup winner, Martin Peters to the club. Peters was to join the Blades as player/coach with a view to eventually becoming manager, Haslam was to move upstairs when the time came.

Bergara was to be moved to a 'head of youth' position with complete responsibility for the recruitment, training and coaching of all the club's young players.

Haslam stated: *"Sheffield United regard this as a key appointment, and Danny is uniquely qualified to undertake it He has enjoyed outstanding success with the young players and has willingly accepted new responsibilities. He is the best man in the club to do the job and the club looks forward with confidence to an improved youth policy under his guidance".*

Not long after Bergara had taken charge of the United youth set-up he was invited to help on a special three day course for the England international youth squad at Lilleshall. The invitation was an important breakthrough for the Uruguayan as it was almost certainly the first ever time that the English FA had called upon a foreign coach to assist them.

Haslam was quoted at the time: *"I am delighted for the club and for Danny, but I am not surprised. He is an immensely gifted coach, particularly with young players and he could go a very long way in the game"*

Bergara having turned down a role with the Uruguayan FA as Youth Team Manager whilst with Luton Town, said on his appointment to the England youth set-up: *"John Cartwright (England Youth Manager) told me he wants to use my experience and ability in the future and I want to go as far as I can. I will go to Lilleshall and we will take it from there"*

Bergara had a chance to catch up with a lifelong friend, Juan Martin Mujica, when Brian Clough's European Champions Nottingham Forest were due to play Uruguayan club Nacional of Montevideo in the 'World Club Championship' in Tokyo. Mujica was now the coach of Bergara's boyhood club.

The newly named Toyota Cup was starting out its new life as a 'one-off' match between the champions of Europe and the champions of South America. The Cup had always been played for on a home and away basis up until now, but with new sponsors on board and with FIFA keen to grow the popularity of football in Asia the trophy now had a new format and a new regular venue.

Mujica, the most successful coach in South America, contacted Bergara with a view to gaining information on his team's Toyota Cup opponents. Bergara, only too happy to help, arranged to accompany Mujica to Forest's home games against Ipswich Town in the League and Valencia in the European Super Cup.

As well as helping his compatriot with a dossier on Forest, Bergara was charged with gaining information from Mujica on the South American football scene as part of his England Youth duties. By now a regular in the national youth coaching set-up, Bergara was

able to provide England manager Ron Greenwood with his completed dossier.

The 1980/81 season saw another good start, with Haslam's team top of the table after eight games, only for the manager to suffer with ill health which eventually forced him to stand down in mid-January.

Martin Peters succeeded Haslam as had been agreed as part of the deal to bring the former international to Bramall Lane, but under Peters the Blades went into free fall, winning only three of the last sixteen games and were relegated to the bottom tier of English football.

On the last day of the season, in a winner takes all showdown against Walsall, United could have stayed up at their visitors expense but Don Givens missed a late penalty which, had it been successful, would have put the Saddlers down instead. Peters resigned after the game.

Having dropped to the lowest level in their history, United appointed Ian Porterfield as their new manager. The Scot who left neighbours Rotherham United to take charge was given funds by new United Chairman Reg Brealey and given the remit of returning the club back to the Third Division at the first time of asking. Porterfield's side lost only four times as they clinched the Fourth Division championship in his first season.

Unfortunately Bergara, who had continued to work within Martin Peters' management team after Haslam's early retirement, was one of the early casualties as Porterfield began to bring in his own men.

England Youth

Bergara became the first ever foreign coach to be involved in an official FA coaching party when he was invited to join the England youth set-up early in 1981 whilst at Sheffield United. Bergara had been moved to Head of Youth following Martin Peters move to manager after Harry Haslam had resigned due to health issues. Bergara had been involved with many FA coaching courses since his first visit to Lilleshall during his Luton Town days. He had often been asked to present coaching sessions during courses and had obviously impressed the on-looking FA officials.

The England Head of Youth, John Cartwright, had come across Bergara on many occasions when his Crystal Palace youth team played Bergara's Luton Town youngsters and liked the way the Uruguayan worked: *"I invited Danny along because he can help me to achieve a compromise in our game, I want to carry the better aspects of our game with those of the Latin countries. Danny can show my players certain techniques from another part of the world, such as accurate and powerful finishing from distance. He has introduced another tack, another dimension, and I have enormous respect for his work".*

When asked about his call up Bergara said: *"I am as chuffed as if I was going to coach my own country. It's a tremendous honour for me, the club and the City. I am delighted for the opportunity to work at this level. John is working along similar lines to me, he is trying to combine the qualities of English and South American football, and he has the perfect stage to demonstrate the kind of football which uses the best of both worlds. I can show the very talented England players things which no English coach can, and they will become a good all-round team if our hopes are fulfilled".*

When asked if there is anything working in England had taught him, Bergara replied: *"Yes indeed, wherever you go in the world of football you never stop learning. The main thing I have admired here is how the football is organised and controlled. The way John has organised the national team at Lilleshall is fantastic. English coaches are perhaps the best in the world at organising training and get-togethers. I have learned this from other great coaches such as Terry Venables, they have certainly opened my eyes, and we have helped one and other".*

Bergara's views are certainly forthright, and he believes our short-comings at international level owe a great deal to our shortcomings at teaching the game: *"England have a few natural players, who are basically skilful, such as Keegan and Mariner. But when they are injured England are in trouble. It all stems from when the player is developing, the coaches shouldn't have to waste time teaching elementary skills. In Germany for example, they produce all-round players at 16 years of age and we always beat them at youth level. However when we play them at international level, they nearly always beat us. That is because their football education continues all the time".*

Bergara's first involvement in a competitive match with the national youth squad came at Fellows Park, home of Walsall FC in a European Youth Championship qualifying game against Northern Ireland Youth, won by a single Paul Walsh goal.

The return in Belfast a month later saw Terry Connor score twice and Ian Handysides once to see the young Lions beat the young Irish both home and away. Bergara was then invited to join the Youth squad for the finals in West Germany.

Although Bergara proudly wore his England colours, the young England squad, featuring the likes of Paul Walsh, Ian Snodin, Paul Allen, Terry Connor, Paul Parker and Mike Phelan, failed to get out of the group stage, losing to both Spain and Scotland before winning their last game against Austria.

Results:

25/5/1981 (Leimbach Stadion, Siegen) Spain 2 England 1 (Connor)

27/5/1981 (Tivoli Stadion, Aachen) Scotland 1 England 0

29/5/1981 (Sportpark Nord Stadion, Bonn) England 7 (Walsh 3, Allen, Barnes, Brooks, Connor) Austria 0

Following the appointment of Ian Porterfield as the new manager of Sheffield United, Bergara left his role as Head of Youth at Bramall Lane but he was soon on his travels again. With the local Sheffield newspaper reporting:

The topsy turvy world of Bergara

The upside down world of Danny Bergara saw him report to travel to Australia with the cream of England's young footballers for a world championship clash on the very day the club who sacked him had a match with Fourth Division Scunthorpe!

Just 24 hours after Uruguayan-born Bergara was paid up by Sheffield United, he reported to England's training head-quarters to prepare for the World Youth Cup on the other side of the world. It was a rueful weekend for Danny, the man who was brought from Luton by Harry Haslam four years ago to add that touch of South American swagger to the Second Division of the Football League. But the chemistry did not work and now Bergara finds himself not

115

wanted by his club but still highly regarded by England as one of the best youth coaches in the business. England picked Bergara and continue to use him despite his South American background; he gets to wear the badge of England while so many English coaches are rejected.

Bergara is sad about leaving United. He said: "The club has a wonderful Chairman, some fine young players coming through, and great support. I accept the statement that they wished to finish with me to get in a new face and new methods; I cannot accept that it was done on grounds of economy."

This clearly indicates that Bergara was paid up the full unexpired term of his contract at Bramall Lane. In addition - or perhaps as part of the settlement - he keeps the new Audi club car recently put on the road for him. Bergara was put in charge of Bramall Lane's young players in a re-shuffle of duties under former boss Harry Haslam. Danny is now convinced that the club has its best youth base for years and points to Geoff Dey's inclusion in the England party in Australia as proof. Dey is the only boy from a Fourth Division club in the squad.

Before leaving for Australia, Bergara expressed strong views on youth coaching in England: *"We go about it all wrong, the tendency is to pick the biggest strongest lads because they will win cups and medals. Too much emphasis is put on winning at too early an age in England. The result is the smaller players are thrown out in favour of bigger stronger players, and never get the chance to realise their potential. People running youth sides are busy chasing silver trophies instead of using their time to encourage players to play well - it is win at all costs. Of course I want to win everything but my motto is 'win, but win through skill'.*

Youth Squad in Australia

Junior World Cup Squad

Cannes 1982

England Youth Squad 1982

 FOOTBALL WEEKLY NEWS, November 5 – 11, 1980

The Latin tutor

DANNY BERGARA the Uruguayan helping England's future stars talks to Paul Lamb

FOR many years we, in this country, have cast envious eyes across the water and admired the football skills and artistry of the Latin American countries.

John Cartwright, the man in charge of the cream of England's youngsters, is endeavouring to combine the best aspects of our own style of play with that of the South Americans to produce a brand of football that will become the envy of the world.

And to acquaint his players with techniques and mastery of the foreign game, Cartwright has invited Sheffield United's Uruguayan youth coach, Danny Bergara, to join him on his coaching sessions.

"I invited Danny along because he can help me to achieve a compromise in our game. I want to carry the better aspects of our natural game with those of the Latin countries," said Cartwright.

"Danny can show my players certain techniques and skills from another part of the world, such as accurate and powerful finishing from distance. He has introduced another tack, another dimension and I have enormous respect for his work."

Cartwright and Bergara first encountered one another when they were in charge of the respective youth teams of Crystal Palace and Luton. Bergara recalls their meetings well.

Fortune

"Our youth teams had some great games against each other. We continued to be very successful at our clubs, John helped to produce many good players and I like to think I did the same at Luton."

Bergara first came to England seven years ago with his English-born wife after a serious calf injury forced him to give up playing. As a youngster he played for the Uruguayan youth team and then travelled to Spain to play for Majorca, Seville and Tenerife, then decided to seek his fortune in England.

On the advice of one of his wife's relatives, he telephoned the then Luton manager Harry Haslam asking for a job and became chief scout. After helping the youth side he became assistant coach under Haslam, and was one of the first men to stand by Haslam when he moved to Sheffield.

"I could have stayed behind and worked with David Pleat, but I am a great believer in loyalty. Harry was the person who had faith in me when nobody had heard of me, and it is part of my make-up to repay loyalty."

Bergara is now busily engaged in shaping the Sheffield United youth team into a good all-round team, but what problems has he found.

"I think that basically the League clubs receive the youngsters too late on in their development, and I find that many of them are lacking in the basics which are taken for granted in South America.

Encouraged

"I have also found that the negative aspects are encouraged in this country, the youngsters should be encouraged to learn attacking and positive techniques. It should be a gradual process, they should not learn to run before they can walk."

Continued Bergara: "Here many really young kids, the under-12s, are made to go out and play on a full-size pitch. It is stupid, the players just get tired and cannot use the pitch fully. They should use pitches designed for their age group, a smaller and narrower pitch which encourages dribbling and makes the player aware of what's going on around him."

Bergara has also had these type of hurdles to overcome at Bramall Lane: "Unfortunately many of the youngsters who first come along to me know more about tactics than they do about playing football.

"The coaches who have taught them teach them to treat the ball as something that should be cleared as soon as possible, instead of realising what alternatives are available.

Delighted

"That is what I am trying to achieve here at Sheffield United, I hope that my players will become better and more skilful players who will go on to the first team."

Bergara was delighted when his friend and former adversary, John Cartwright, invited him along to assist in the Lilleshall development training sessions.

"John is working along similar lines to me, he is trying to combine the qualities of English and South American football. And he has the perfect stage to demonstrate the kind of football which uses the best of both worlds.

"I can show the very talented England players things which an English coach could, and they will become a good all-round team if our hopes are fulfilled."

I wondered if there was anything this country has taught him: "Yes indeed, wherever you go in the world of football, you never stop learning. The main thing I have admired here is how the football is organised and controlled.

"The way John has organised the national team at Lilleshall is fantastic. English coaches are perhaps the best in the world at organising training and get-togethers. I have learned this from other good coaches such as Terry Venables, they have certainly opened my eyes and we have helped one another."

Shortcomings

Bergara's views are certainly forthright, and he believes that our shortcomings at full-international level owe a great deal to our shortcomings at teaching the game.

"England have a few natural players, who are basically skilful such as Keegan or Mariner. But when they are injured England are in trouble. It all stems from when the player is developing, the coaches shouldn't have to waste time teaching elementary skills," says Bergara.

"In Germany for example, they produce all-round players at the age of 16, and we always beat them at youth level. However, when we play against them at international level, they nearly always beat us because their football education continues all the time."

Of course the acid test of the policies of Messrs Cartwright and Bergara will come next year in Australia, when England contest the FIFA World Youth Cup, the youth equivalent to the World Cup. Although England have already added the UEFA Youth Tournament to their list of honours, a singularly marvellous achievement.

The fruits of Bergara's labour will not be realised until the youngsters under his care make it through to League football. But whatever happens, it is encouraging to see that real steps are being taken to ensure a future brand of football which will not only win trophies, but excite as well.

Danny Bergara

Bergara for Australia

SHEFFIELD United's youth coach Danny Bergara may be in line for a trip to Australia with the England youth team in October.

England qualified for the European Youth Championship in West Germany in May with a 3-0 win over Northern Ireland in Belfast yesterday — and were then named as one of the 16 nations for the World Youth Championship in Australia.

Bergara has assisted England youth supremo John Cartwright regularly and was on duty in Belfast, giving rise to speculation that he will be asked to travel to Australia with the national side again next autumn.

England promote Bergara

By Tony Pritchett

SHEFFFIELD UNITED youth coach Danny Bergara is to move up in the England set-up.

Bergara has been invited to help with the match-day duties when England Youth meet Northern Ireland at Walsall on February 11.

England's youth boss John Carwright said: "We have used Danny with our training sessions at Lilleshall and he has become very useful and very valuable. To ask him to work with us on Cup day is a natural progression. He has done a fine job with the youngsters."

Bergara is the first foreign coach — he is Uruguayan — to work with an England team.

Bergara joins World Cup party

FORMER Sheffield United youth coach Danny Bergara travels South today to join the England youth squad which competes in the mini-World Cup tournament in Australia next month.

For the former Uruguayan international it is a reassuring sign that his coaching talents are genuinely appreciated at international level, in a year which has seen him move from assistant manager at Bramall Lane to youth coach, before parting company with the club after Ian Porterfield took over as manager this summer.

England youth team manager John Cartwright considers Bergara to be very much part of the England youth set-up and said: "We will be travelling with a squad of 18 players.

"This has been weakened by the withdrawal of several players because of first team duty and in a situation like this the back up staff can come into their own".

Bergara has travelled extensively since he left Uruguay, but when he arrives with the squad, which includes a former protege at the Lane, midfielder Geoff Day, it will be his first visit to Australia.

Last night he said: "This is a great honour for me and I intend to do my very best to justify it. We will be playing Argentina, which will be a great personal challenge for me, but even if we meet Uruguay my loyalties lie very firmly with the England squad.

"After what has happened to the full England team, we want to make up for it in some way with the youngsters."

Bergara has strong views on coaching systems and the way that football is organised in England. He believes there should be a greater emphasis on encouraging individual skills.

"Too much emphasis is put on winning at too early an age in England. The result is that smaller kids are thrown out in favour of bigger, stronger players and never get the chance to realise their potential.

"People running youth sides are all chasing silver trophies instead of using the time to encourage players to play well — it's win at any cost. My motto is win, but win through skill."

Bergara is also concerned that clubs do not take enough time with their younger players. "In the main it is the best coaches coaching the first team, but if the best coaches were with the youths they wouldn't need to be coached by the time they reach the first team.

"You wouldn't go to a doctor who wasn't qualified, but too many players are coached by people who can't see what's wrong.

"Instead of worrying about who should manage the England team, more concern should be shown over how the game as a whole is organised."

JIM FERGUSON

DANNY BERGARA 'Great honour'

Bergara to join England coaching squad

By Tony Pritchett

SHEFFIELD UNITED'S youth coach Danny Bergara is to join the England coaching squad.

Bergara, born in Uruguay, and put incharge of the teenagers at Bramall Lane in a shuffle of duties when Martin Peters was appointed, has been invited to help a special course for the FA Youth International team at Lilleshall next week.

I understand this is not a one-off invitation and that Bergara will work with the England players in future after his three day stint which begins on Monday.

Danny Bergara

The invitation is an important breakthrough for Bergara as it is almost certainly the first time that the FA have called up the foreign coach for assistance.

United manager Harry Haslam said: "I am delighted for the club and for Danny — but I'm not surprised. He is an immensely gifted coach particularly with young players and could go a very long way."

WHITWORTH

"It depressed me — all those broken spearheads made me think of Wednesday without McCulloch and Curran!"

Bergara, aged 38, turned down the job of Uruguay youth team manager and director of coaching when he was with Luton four years ago because of differences between the Uruguayan set-up's board of directors and the government.

He said of his England appointment: "I'm as chuffed as if I was going to my own country. It's tremendous to have been asked to go and help.

"John Cartwright (the England youth team manager) told me that he wants to use my experience and ability in future and I want to go as far as I can.

"I'm going to Lilleshall and we'll take it from there."

Bergara set for international duty

Danny Bergara, Sheffield United's former assistant manager now in charge of the youth team, yesterday made a further step towards fulfilling his international coaching ambitions, writes **Jon Culley**.

Bergara, recently helping with England's youth team training at Lilleshall, has been invited to assist with match-day duties when England meet Northern Ireland at Walsall a week today in a qualifier for the UEFA European Youth Championship.

Last night Bergara, whose long-term ambitions lie, I believe, in international soccer, said: "I am delighted that England have thought of me in their coaching plans and I hope I can continue to help.

"I am also delighted that the Sheffield United board, Harry Haslam and now Martin Peters, have allowed me to serve a country to which I owe a lot.

"It is an honour for me, and I hope for the club, to have someone on the staff who is helping an international team."

Bergara, whose reputation as a coach was underlined when he was pipped by Mike England for the management of the Wales international team last year, has a good record with United's youngsters this season.

The Northern Intermediate League team has lost only six times in 26 matches this season and were unlucky to lose to holders Aston Villa after a replay in the FA Youth Cup.

Bergara's boys meet Sheffield Wednesday at Hillsborough on February 25 in a Northern Intermediate League Cup quarter final.

Decisions

The Uruguayan, who is possibly the first South American to assist with an England team, is obviously proud of his achievements this season.

"I want to say a million thanks to the people who have turned up at the Ball Inn Ground on Saturday mornings in all kinds of weather to watch the lads," he said.

"I will continue to do my very best for those people. It is out of a duty to make sure we do not let them down and provide them with future Sheffield United first-team players."

Meanwhile, the man whose arrival at Bramall Lane as player-coach to the first team coincided with Bergara's appointment as youth coach, has made one of his first big decisions as manager.

In a cost-cutting exercise, Martin Peters yesterday made five players available for free transfer.

Peters, who says United have too many professionals on the staff, has allowed goalkeeper Keith Solomon, defenders Andy Kesley and Paul Casey, midfield player Mick Jones and striker Mark Smith, to seek new clubs.

There may be more players made available later in the season, he said.

Ante stars as Wednesday win

Sheffield Wed Res	2
Nottm F Res	0

Yugoslav Ante Mirocevic had an outstanding match, inspiring Sheffield Wednesday who outplayed and deservedly defeated a strong Nottingham Forest team.

Though exerting continual pressure from the start, Wednesday did not take the lead until the 47th minute, when Paul Shirtliff scored. Brian Sigat (88 min) completed the scoring.

Bergara gets England coaching call

By Tony Pritchett

SHEFFIELD United's youth coach Danny Bergara is to join the England coaching squad.

Bergara, born in Uruguay, and put incharge of the teenagers at Bramall Lane in a shuffle of duties when Martin Peters was appointed, has been invited to help a special course for the FA Youth International team at Lilleshall next week.

I understand this is not a one-off invitation and that Bergara will work with the England players in future after his three day stint which begins on Monday.

Bergara, aged 38, turned down the job of Uruguay youth team manager and director of coaching when he was with Luton four years ago because of differences between the Uruguayan set-up's board of directors and the government.

He said of his England appointment: "I'm as chuffed as if I was going to my own country. It's tremendous to have been asked to go and help.

Danny gets call again

DANNY BERGARA, Sheffield United's youth coach, has again been called up by England.

Danny, the first foreign coach to be invited into the England set-up last month, goes as assistant coach to youth manager John Cartwright at a three-day session beginning on October 13.

Bergara for England

Sheffield United youth coach Danny Bergara travels south today to work on his first international duty since being appointed assistant coach to the England Youth squad.

Bergara, whose appointment was confirmed on Friday evening, has been invited to help on a three-day course at Lilleshall, starting today.

Last night the former Uruguayan youth international said: "It's a tremendous honour for me, the club and the city. I am delighted at the opportunity to work at this level."

Bergara will help with assessing trialists and arranging coaching for England under-18 players.

"At so many clubs the job of youth coach is given to some old pro at the end of his playing days. Long term, the job with young players is probably the most important in a club after the manager, but usually it goes to lowest paid, least qualified member of staff. You wouldn't go to see a doctor who wasn't qualified, yet too many young players with receptive minds are coached by people who simply cannot see what's wrong. How can you put something right in a player unless you spot what he is doing wrong? There is so much talk about the job of team manager of England. This is important but what we should be doing is concentrating more on who is handling the raw material".

The young England side were weakened by several withdrawals through players being kept by their clubs due to first team commitments. The team performed well enough in the group stages to qualify for the knock out stages, Dey justifying his selection with a goal in the opening victory against Cameroon, before a goal in each game from Michael Small earned draws against Argentina and hosts Australia to see England finish top of the group. A hat trick from Neil Webb and a goal from John Cooke saw the team beat Egypt Youth in the quarter final but the surprise team of the tournament, Qatar Youth, won the semi-final with Small scoring the consolation goal for the young Lions. Romania Youth then won the 3rd place play-off match to see England finish fourth.

Results:

3/10/1981 (Sydney Football Stadium) England 2 (Finnegan, Dey) Cameroon 0

5/10/1981 (Sydney Football Stadium) England 1 (Small) Argentina 1

8/10/1981 (Sydney Football Stadium) Australia 1 England 1 (Small)

11/10/1981 (Sydney Football Stadium) England 4 (Webb 3, Cooke) Egypt 2

14/10/1981 (Sydney Football Stadium) England 1 (Small) Qatar 2

17/10/1981 (Adelaide) England 0 Romania 1

Bergara was assistant coach to manager John Cartwright again as a strong England team featuring the likes of Paul Elliott, Paul Parker, Stuart Robson, Trevor Steven and Mark Walters were eliminated from the next European Youth Championships by Scotland early in 1982.

Results:

23/2/1982 (Ibrox Stadium) Scotland 1 England 0

23/3/1982 (Highfield Road) England 2 (Pearson, Walters) Scotland 2

Bergara remained part of the England Youth set up for the Tournoi Juniors Under 18 Tournament in Cannes. The young Lions performed well in beating both Portugal and the Netherlands Youth teams, a defeat in the last group game against Czechoslovakia youth didn't prevent them from topping the table to earn a final place against the hosts. Unfortunately France were to win a close Final to lift the trophy to leave England as runners-up.

Results:

7/4/1982 (Stade Pierre de Coubertin) England 3 (Bell 2, Kerslake) Portugal 0

9/4/1982 (Stade Pierre de Coubertin) England 1 (Little) Netherlands 0

11/4/1982 (Stade Pierre de Coubertin) England 0 Czechoslovakia 1

12/4/1982 (Stade Pierre de Coubertin) France 1 England 0

Bergara's blossoming England career was unfortunately ended with the retirement of national manager Ron Greenwood, new man Bobby Robson preferring to appoint his own men.

Many years later the Uruguayan, still hurt by being cast aside by the FA said: *"I hadn't done anything wrong, in fact I was being congratulated for my methods during the two years I had coached the England youth team under John Cartwright. It seems that Bobby Robson did not want foreigners in his camp. I couldn't understand it, my strength was developing technique and skill, and I could have offered England a lot more than they wanted from me".*

Sheffield FC

Prior to the start of the 1983/84 season Bergara had been helping out with the coaching at his local club Sheffield FC, famously known as the world's oldest football club having been founded in 1857. The club were in turmoil after previous manager Paddy Buckley had moved to Retford Town, taking nine of his established first team players with him. Following his coaching work at the club during the summer, Sheffield FC Chairman Keith Healey had approached Bergara and offered him the role of manager.

The local paper ran the story:

Danny thinks it over

Former Sheffield United assistant manager Danny Bergara is poised to take over as manager of Sheffield FC, the world's oldest soccer club. Club Chairman Keith Healey is very hopeful that Bergara, who is currently involved in the making of instructional video soccer films, will accept the voluntary position. Bergara said last night: "I would very much like to give a hand at Sheffield FC in some capacity, whether it is an advisory capacity, or as manager. I have some business affairs to sort out next week but I hope that I can give Keith Healey, and the oldest football club in the world, the answer they want"

Having accepted the voluntary role, Bergara set about building a squad for the forthcoming Northern Counties Eastern League campaign. The attitude of his players really impressed him as he told the local press: *"These lads deserve all the respect anyone can give them, they go to work in the morning, come straight home and* *then out again to attend training. To do that you have got to have the attitude of real pros. Some professionals, when they are asked to go back training in the afternoons, will say they are tired. These lads do a day's work and then train as well, that's real enthusiasm. I'm looking forward to a good season"*

He pledged to carry on as manager, with the aim of winning the league's Division One title, even though it had been announced that Sheffield FC couldn't be promoted to the Premier division because of the lack of facilities at their Abbeydale ground.

Bergara started his new campaign in the east Sheffield sunshine, and having had just six weeks to build a side, he saw them produce a display of clinical finishing to beat a hard running Denaby United side 4-1 on the opening day.

Dream Start for Bergara

Featuring only two of the previous campaigns players, Sheffield got off to a dream start when Smith opened the scoring in the fifth minute, Smith then won a penalty after being brought down, Shepherd making no mistake from the spot kick. Despite the half-time lead Sheffield had spent long periods fighting a rearguard action. Held together by the organisation and aerial power of Hugh Dowd, the former Wednesday and Doncaster Rovers player. Not surprisingly Kennedy reduced the arrears within minutes of the restart, on hand to head home a smartly taken goal. However the irrepressible Smith added a third for Sheffield before skipper Hughes, who had been hobbling through injury, was on hand to round the Denaby goalkeeper to make it four. Sheffield picking up the points thanks to an all-round fine team effort.

With Christmas approaching, in a remarkable upheaval, Bergara had taken his side to an unbeaten run into second place, with a game in hand on leaders Borrowash Vics, winning six and drawing one of their opening seven fixtures. Unfortunately for the football club, they were about to lose their inspirational manager, who had been offered the opportunity of a lifetime: *"The offer of the chance to coach the national team in Brunei was just too much temptation, but I leave the team fighting for top spot in Division One. I have had a tremendous six months with the club and I would like to thank the board, the players and the supporters for all their backing"*

Sheffield FC Chairman Keith Healey said: *"We can't thank Danny enough for what he has done. His dedication and hard work with the players has been an example to the four men who will be carrying on the team management. We wish him well because it is a fantastic opportunity for him and one he richly deserves. Sheffield FC are a lot better club for having had Danny's involvement".*

Brunei

Having been without a permanent position since leaving Sheffield United, it was a Bramall Lane connection that saw Bergara back in work in January 1984.

Jan Bergara remembers the introduction to Bergara's appointment in Brunei:

Daniel said to me "Do you want the good news or the bad news first?"

I said "Give me the good news first"

"I've been offered a job" which was great news as he was without a full time job at the time.

"Where?" he was hesitant but I could see excitement in his face

"Is it down south?"

"No"

"Europe?"

"No"

"Middle East?"

"No, a little bit further.....the Far East"

Oh wow, I thought. He looked so happy to be back in football, how could I spoil it?

Oil rich Brunei, looking for a coach to lift their standards, hired Bergara on the recommendation of Sheffield United Chairman Reg Brealey. The businessman had previously set up the visit of the Blades two years earlier, as Sheffield United had officially opened the Brunei National Stadium.

Brealey had put the Uruguayan's name forward for the chance to become the national coach for the Brunei national team, a role that would include setting up coaching sessions and courses for the Brunei FA as Director of Coaching.

The biggest problem for the Bergara family was that 17 year old Simon was by now making a name for himself as a player, earning himself an apprenticeship at Southampton FC and 14 year old Elena was at a very important stage of her education preparing for her 'O' Levels. It was agreed that Bergara would have to undertake his latest adventure on his own and the family would endeavour to visit him in Brunei at every opportunity.

Jan Bergara:

We joined him in the summer holidays. Regular phone calls and letters, our early life all over again, during the next year. Mr Brealey, whenever he travelled to Brunei, where he had business interests, would update me on his return and bring me the latest videos that Daniel had filmed, including one of him filming out of a helicopter whilst saying "Don't be scared Jan". (his feet dangling out of the helicopter)

He loved his time out in Brunei, apart from the hot, humid weather. A unique experience as we had to adapt to a completely different culture. Very polite, friendly people but certain rules had to be respected. No nightclubs and permission needed from the religious department for any entertainment in the hotels. Women's shoulders had to be covered. Elena had a finger pointed at her as her sundress exposed her shoulders and she was only a young girl. Taxi boats to and from the water village which had its own school and hospital.

Daniel stayed at the Sheraton Utama Hotel but as a special privilege ended up staying in the 'officer's mess' of the Brunei armed forces camp, as Daniel involved them in training the national team. He loved the whole experience especially meeting the Sultan of Brunei at his birthday celebrations and the success in reaching the final of the Borneo Cup. To think I had spent time in Malaya as a child when my father was in the Royal Marines 42 Commando and I was again travelling to Singapore on the way to Brunei over 30

A proud Uruguayan in the National Stadium

On Brunei TV

Brunei Squad 1984

Training with Squad

ergera
ooking in

KICK-OFF, Friday

Founded 1857
THE OLDEST FOOTBALL CLUB IN THE WORLD
Winners of the Amateur Cup 1903-4
F. A. Vase Finalists 1976-77
Founder Members of the Football Association

Sheffield Football Club

COLOURS:
Red Shirts
Black Shorts

GROUND:
Abbeydale Park
Tel: 362040

Official Programme
Season 1983/4

Danny Boy's go
astern promise

...ter six months   "I found a nation ...
...h their players   gentle, religious people wi...

..LA BORNEO 198
..34

...field United   Dann

..NG IN

22

..hb – 23hb
..PTEMBER
..84

years later, to spend the summer holidays with Daniel, this time with our children. We both could count in Malay now too.

Bergara would encounter several instances of a change in culture, not least during an early training session he noticed the players suddenly stopped training and went down on their hands and knees. When asking his charges what they were doing, he received the reply: "Pray, coach, pray" **- Bergara was quick to respond** "If you're training with me, it's play not pray"

After almost a year of working with over three hundred players in the overpowering conditions of heat and humidity Bergara achieved remarkable improvement in the players. He coached the national team and also the army team.

His main achievement coming when he plotted a 2-1 triumph for Brunei over Indonesia. Bergara said at the time: *"Indonesia have 60 years start on Brunei, that result was something like Luxembourg or Finland beating West Germany. I have found a nation of gentle, religious people with a magnificent natural talent for the game, but no ideas on training, coaching, organisation, diet or any of the areas we take for granted in Europe or South America"*

In early May Brunei had played in the Yusuf Cup in Indonesia against teams of semi-professionals. Bergara had taken a very young team, and picked up a trophy after his team's display. Having won three of their five games, losing two by a single goal, Brunei were awarded the trophy for being the most attractive team to watch in the tournament.

Three of the players that had improved so much under Bergara, defender Rosanan Samak and strikers Zainnudin Kassim and

Majidi Ghani were all taken on trial by Ian Porterfield on Bergara's recommendation.

After spending so much time away Bergara took his family to Uruguay for Christmas. Simon receiving permission to travel by Southampton FC on the understanding that he kept up with his training. It was arranged for him to train with Nacional FC, his uncle Mario's old club.

Gibraltar

On the family's return to England in the New Year, Brealey again came to Bergara's aid when he recommended and sponsored the Uruguayan coach to present a two week football course on behalf of the FA of Gibraltar.

With the help of several teachers, albeit with limited coaching ability, Bergara provided sessions for under 12's, under 14's, under 16's and under 18's. Although frustrated by the lack of good facilities and basic needs such as balls, bibs, cones at certain venues, Bergara was pleased with the reaction to his methods by all of the players involved.

Following his visit to the Rock, Bergara provided a full in depth revue of his findings, including a 10 page advisory document, much of which formed the coaching curriculum still being used many years later.

Middlesbrough FC

After another spell out of the game Bergara was given the opportunity to work with one of his former players, Bruce Rioch, at Second Division Middlesbrough. Rioch and Bergara had become acquainted back when the Uruguayan had spent time with Derby County during their European tie with Real Madrid and again when the Scot had spent a brief period at Sheffield United on loan from Derby County several years earlier.

With Boro fighting the threat of administration and also relegation to the Third Division, Rioch and Bergara, who were both working at the club as coaches, were put in charge by Chairman Alf Duffield after the Club had been without a manager for over six weeks following the sacking of Willie Maddren. Duffield promoted the two following a home defeat to promotion chasing Sheffield United, following which the Boro team had received a standing ovation from their supporters. Duffield told the local press: *"That is the best display I have seen from a Middlesbrough team this season, they were brilliant even in defeat. I was going to review Rioch's position at the end of the season, but that performance has made me change my mind. Rioch and Danny Bergara have given the players tremendous confidence and I know they will do a first class job for the club"*

Rioch said: *"I am delighted and Danny is elated too. We have both been out of League football but were desperate for the chance to put our talents to the test again. We are hungry, we are committed, we want to do a good job and we feel we can do that, but with the help of a lot of people at the club"*

BERGARA IN WAIT

UNITED'S old friend Danny Bergara lies in wait for the team when it goes to Middlesbrough on Tuesday night.

Danny, out of the English game for so long after losing his job with United five years ago, was teamed up with Bruce Rioch at the Lane many times in recent seasons, will be able to acquaint the Boro players with much invaluable information.

And, of course, Danny will be extra keen to see his new team beat his old; that is always the way of things in the game.

United would be most unwise to underestimate the Bergara factor. I have always regarded Danny as one of the shrewdest assessors of a team I have ever met and Rioch is certain to have paid high regard to his advice about this fixture.

Do not forget, either, that Middlesbrough are very much a hoodoo team to United. They won in Sheffield with almost the last kick of the game earlier this season and did the double last season. Theya re facing their annual struggle against relegation and may well prove difficult to play against next Tuesday.

...field winner wi...

O RIVALS
SCREW

TERRY CURRAN'S 87th minute w... night has left Boro with a mountain... avoid the big drop.

Curran's late goal gave Huddersfield a 2-1 w... them three places up the Second Division table a...

As a result, third from bot... tom Boro are now two points behind the next club, Brad- ford City who have four games in hand.

The news of Curran's winner was an even bigger blow for Boro than team coach Bruce Rioch today because he watched the match but let ten minutes from time with the score 1-1.

Rioch remained philo- sophical today. He said: "While other teams' results are obviously relative to what we do ourselves, what we can't let ourselves won't be spending time looking at League tables. There's no point going pessimistic, we just have to go out to try to win every game.

...players, I will make them brilliant.
"All I ask of the players is first of all the will to play, secondly all the skill and thirdly a high standard of fitness.
"I also expect a good attitude not only on the field, but on the field. If I can be asking the players for 101 per cent, but 99 per cent will not be good enough.

One of four of five brothers who became internationals. Bergara left Uruguay to join Real Mallorca in Spain when he was only 19.

By ERI...

N BERGARA
QUITS BORO

By ERIC PAYLOR

DANNY BERGARA, Boro's chief coach since early March, is leaving Ayresome Park to become Second Division Sheffield United.

The Uruguayan-born coach will sign a contract at Bra... mall Lane on Sunday.

Bergara becomes the second "backroom boy" to leave Boro within a week following the departure of physiotherapist Steve Birnell to Sunderland on Monday.

Boro, whose winding-up order is heard in the High Court on Monday, are left with only two management officials in team manager Bruce Rioch and youth team and reserve coach Colin Todd.

Bergara turned down a simila... offer from ex- Tottenham boss David Pleat to rejoin United, having spent three and a half years at Bramall Lane in the late 1970s.

He said today: "I would like to thank everybody at Middlesbrough for giving me the chance to come back into League football. I'll always have a soft spot for the club.

"At the end of the day it was a difficult decision to make after such a short time but with Middlesbrough battling to stay alive they weren't able to guarantee me anything in the future.

"One of the saddest parts will be leaving behind the lads in the centre of excellence and I hope that I have contributed something to them that will prove bene- ficial.

"I'm sorry to break up my partnership with Bruce Rioch, but football is a merry-go-around and I've now got a new challenge."

Bergara will take up an appointment as technical coach under new Sheffield United boss Billy McEwan.

Memorable one of Boro's summer transfer, Sheffield United defender Tony Ken... worthy is expected to join Mansfield Town.

Midland Bank Limited, who have authorised a similar overdraft for a similar figure. I understand that most of the other creditors are satis- fied with their credits now.

A Midland Bank spokes- man said today: "The bank is still involved in discus- sions and awaits acceptable proposals.

"We are not aware that the consortium has come to an agreement with the other creditors.

"At the same time I must make it clear that the Mid- land Bank did not start the precipitous action and we have always confirmed our willingness to support."

Boro also owe more than £100,000 to the Inland Revenue and VAT but I believe that the consortium intends to pay the amount in full should all the other creditors be satisfied.

Yesterday's meeting in Middlesbrough between pro- visional liquidator Tony Richmond and Boro director Steve Gibson ended with neither side prepared to comment until after Mon- day's hearing.

But I believe the club will be saved if the consortium can overcome one final stumbling block by agreeing a settlement figure with one of the major creditors.

Boro have two major creditors, former chairman Alf Duffield, who is owed around £800,000, and the

MOVES TO
HOT SEAT

BERGARA BOUNCES BACK AT BORO

By Tony Pritchett

DANNY Bergara, former assistant manager and chief coach at Sheffield United, is set to bounce back into English football next week.

...John says he's fit to play in the First Division and that's good enough for me.

Danny Bergara

In understand Danny, who worked at Bramall Lane under Harry Haslam has been offered a coaching appointment with Middlesbrough and the team United should have been playing this afternoon.

Postponement of this match means that Bergara is likely to be involved in Boro's preparations when United's visit is re...

At Middlesbrough...

Bergara will link up with Bruce Rioch, who played on loan with United in March and April of 1979.

Bergara also assisted Derby, when Rioch was playing, on their visit to Real Madrid in the quarter- finals of the European Cup.

He said today: "I am delighted to be back. It is a magnificent break for me.

ALL those in favour ... Boro's board of directors cast their votes in favour of the £1m share capital is... extraordinary general meeting. Left to right, vice chairman Jack Hatfield, secretary David Thorne, chairman Dick Corden, Steve Gibson, George Kitching, Keith Varley.

Evenin...
MONDA...

I'M TO BLAME
SAYS DUFFIEL...

Another giveaway

ALF DUFFIELD today looked back on his firs... of office and admitted: "I take full responsibi... the position the club finds itself in."

The Boro chairman blames himself for the club's success since he took over the reins last February.

But at the same time Duffield made it clear that lesso... been learned from the mistakes of the past and a... already turning.

Unfortunately, even with the new management team in place, Boro succumbed to the inevitable relegation winning only two more games as they finished second bottom and with the club in danger of being wound-up in court Bergara decided to take up the offer of a return to Bramall Lane under new Sheffield United manager Billy McEwan.

Now Bergara quits Boro

Danny Bergara, Boro's chief coach since early March, is leaving Ayresome Park to join Second Division Sheffield United. The Uruguay-born coach will sign a contract at Bramall Lane on Sunday. Bergara becomes the second 'back room boy' to leave Boro within a week following the departure of physiotherapist Steve Smelt to Sunderland on Monday.

Boro, whose winding-up order is heard in the High Court on Monday, are left with only two management officials in manager Bruce Rioch and youth team and reserve coach Colin Todd. Bergara turned down a similar offer from new Tottenham boss David Pleat to rejoin United, having spent three and a half years at Bramall Lane in the late 1970s.

He said today: "I would like to thank everybody at Middlesbrough for giving me the chance to come back into league football. I'll always have a soft spot for the club. At the end of the day it was a difficult decision to leave after such a short time but with Middlesbrough battling to stay alive they weren't able to guarantee me anything in the future. One of the saddest parts will be leaving behind the lads in the Centre of Excellence and I hope that I have contributed something to them that will prove beneficial. I'm sorry to break up my partnership with Bruce Rioch, but football is a merry-go-around and I've now got a new challenge."

Bergara will take up an appointment as technical coach under new Sheffield United boss Billy McEwan. Meanwhile one of Boro's summer targets, Sheffield United defender Tony Kenworthy, is expected to join Mansfield Town. Yesterday's meeting in Middlesbrough between provisional liquidator Tony Richmond and Boro director Steve Gibson ended with neither side prepared to comment until after Monday's hearing. But I believe the club will be saved if the consortium can overcome one final stumbling block by agreeing a settlement figure with one of the major creditors. Boro have two major creditors, former chairman Alf Duffield, who is owed around £600,000, and the Midland Bank Limited, who have authorised a bank overdraft for a similar figure. I understand that most of the other creditors are satisfied with their offers.

A Midland Bank spokesman said today: "The bank is still involved in discussions and awaits acceptable proposals. We are not aware that the consortium has come to an agreement with the other creditors. At the same time I must make it clear that the Midland Bank did not start the precipitous action and we have always confirmed our willingness to support." Boro also owe more than £100,000 to the Inland Revenue and VAT, but I believe that the consortium intends to pay this amount in full should all the other creditors be satisfied.

Sheffield United FC

With a new ambitious board in place United had recruited Ian Porterfield as manager in June 1981. He had an immediate impact, winning the Division Four championship in his first season and taking the club back into the second tier two years later on a meagre budget.

Despite this, many Blades fans were unhappy with the style of football and Porterfield was sacked in 1986 following supporter protests, youth team manager Billy McEwan was promoted to be Porterfield's replacement in March 1986, and although he restored fans' favourite Keith Edwards to the starting eleven the Blades fell away in their push for promotion, finishing seventh in the final table.

One of McEwan's first signings in the summer, before his first full season in charge, saw the return of Bergara. The Uruguayan coach had been given a glowing reference from Chairman Reg Brealey and, after five years away from the club, he returned as reserve team manager.

Bergara again turned down an opportunity to work alongside his old friend David Pleat, who had offered him a role at Tottenham Hotspur, to rejoin the Blades.

McEwan told the local press: *"I have always had a great respect for Danny's work on the technical and skill side of the game. He will be a great asset to us and an important part of our team".*

Bergara said: *"I am glad to be back at a club I should never have left"*

Also joining McEwan's new backroom team were former Sheffield Wednesday players Phil Henson as youth team manager and Ian Bailey as the new club physiotherapist.

The Scots first full season in charge saw the Blades finish in ninth place in the Second Division. Bergara's reserve side had looked impressive, and with the first team lacking a spark at times, the local paper was quick to point out the influence Bergara was having on the club's youngsters:

Outlook bright in the rain

Danny Bergara, back with Sheffield United after almost five years, has been put in charge of the Central League team and tomorrow's United looked in good hands indeed, at rainy Bramall Lane on Wednesday night. United fans disenchanted with the seniors 0-0 draw on Saturday would've been thrilled by the performance and quality of the reserves as they crushed Aston Villa's reserves. If the result had been 6-1 it would've been more representative of United's dominance. Most clubs are desperate for young strikers, but in Clive Mendonca and Tony Daws, United have two likely lads who led the Villa players a real dance. At the back Jeff Eckhart, Kenny Geelan and Brian Smith must've interested watching managers, who included Brian Horton of Hull, Ian Greaves of Huddersfield and John Duncan of Chesterfield. It was United's third straight win over First Division opposition following victories over Leicester City and Newcastle United. In all it was their fourth win in a row.

The following season, and with the Blades sat second bottom of the Second Division, Bergara, who's reserve team were sitting unbeaten at the top of the Central League, had been promoted to

work alongside McEwan with the struggling first team. His appointment coinciding with a remarkable set of results:

Bergara gets first team job

Danny Bergara was today appointed first team coach by Sheffield United manager Billy McEwan. Said McEwan "This is a step up for Danny. He has done a terrific job with the reserves, and now he will be with the senior side. I have done it all by myself for over a year, but we need to pool all our resources and Danny has an important contribution to make". The Central League side, under Bergara, is unbeaten this season and sit top of the First Division of the Central League. They have already beaten the reserve sides of Liverpool and Nottingham Forest.

The fortunes of the first team took an almost miraculous turn for the better, picking up two wins and a draw from their next three games

Billy and Danny for revival act

It has been a good week for Billy McEwan and his players after a dreadful performance at Bury had thrown up all sorts of murmurs and moans about Sheffield United going back to the Third Division. There may be troubles ahead... but at least the club is now tackling the task by pooling all its available resources. That is how I see the promotion of Danny Bergara as first team coach. Maybe it is coincidence that the club has taken four points from two away games when previously it had none from three, but whatever the reason, the revival, if revival it is, has come just in time to stifle the talk about an anti-relegation season. McEwan and Bergara are so different. The manager is Scottish, a believer in old established virtues of fitness, dedication and responsibility and his code of discipline makes no allowance for slackness. Bergara is South American, full of fun and flair with a passionate belief that he has a gift for coaching and can get the best out of any player he commands. Ultimate responsibility is with Billy, but together they might just make it work and end all those unpleasant whispers about a possible change at Bramall Lane, which forced managing director Derek Dooley into an official denial on the morning of the Barnsley match. McEwan has been in football long enough to know that the threat of change has been on the board's minds, concerned as they are at the dismal results so far. And so Billy moved Danny up to first team involvement, and the South American, who is popular with the players, is in his element.

Bergara's influence was quickly seen with youngsters Tony Daws, Chris Wilder and Clive Mendonca all seeing first team action. Another player to benefit from the Uruguayan coach's methods was the popular winger Peter Beagrie who had followed Bergara from Middlesbrough in the summer.

Beagrie saying of his mentor: *"I really enjoy working with Danny. The great thing is that he has tremendous skill himself, and can demonstrate what it is he wants you to do"*

Bold revival by 'timid' Blades

How much of the credit is due to new first team coach Danny Bergara?. That is the question Sheffield United supporters have been asking following the dramatic improvement at Bramall Lane. Since the Uruguayan became involved with the senior side United have taken seven points from three matches. But the answer within the complicated chemistry of football, is not as simple as the facts might imply. Certainly United players have replaced timidity with freedom of expression since the extrovert Bergara's promotion and manager Billy McEwan jokingly admits of his cheery sidekick: "He's saved me from a heart attack"

Barnsley 1 Sheffield United 2

Last week I saw a Second Division team, previously languishing at the foot of the table, give such a sparkling display of first-time football as to give the watching local journalists the surprise of their lives. When I asked why a team, playing such good football as this, should be anywhere near the bottom of the league, they admitted that they were at a complete loss to explain it.

They did mention, though, that Sheffield United had appointed a new coach and that this was his second game. It also turned out to be United's second win. Now I'm not suggesting that two swallows make a summer, or indeed, that two victories make a championship side, but I do say watch them. The point I find interesting is that Sheffield United go out and find themselves a man from Uruguay, one Danny Bergara, who performs a remarkable transformation on an ordinary side in such a short time. So why are most of our First Division teams persevering with their coaches who are doing nothing to improve the quality of their teams, or the enjoyment of their supporters? One thing is certain. Watch Sheffield United's inevitable climb up the league table.

Hull grounded at last

Hull suffered their first league defeat of the season at the hands of a Sheffield United team who have improved dramatically since the appointment of their new first team coach, Danny Bergara, a week ago. Mr. Bergara evidently believes that the best place to keep the ball is on the ground, at least while pitches are firm and grassy, and United responded with some attractive one-touch football.

Tony Philliskirk, Martin Pike, Kenny Geelan, John Burridge, Paul Tomlinso...
... Arnott, Brian Smith, Lee Walshaw, Phil Henso...
... physio, Peter Beagr...

Gutsy sho... from Unite...

CONGRATULATIONS to United on ... gutsy performance at Bournemouth last ... day.

For the first 20 minutes ... they looked like leaderless, head less chickens, then ... they got it all together. ... Stancliffe was outstand- ... ing, and it was fitting that ... he should score the ... winning goal.

Segers was brilliant: the ... first complete goalkeeper ... that we have had since Alan ... Hodgkinson. We have to do ... all we can to keep him.

In fact everyone played ... well. The only sad point is ... that Richard Cadette is just ... not up to it. He is too small ... to ever win a ball in the air. ... He is slow off the mark, and ... his close control leaves a lot ... to be desired.

He is a charming ... man but it would be ... all round to wire him ... off. Billy McEwan's exp... mistake, and give ... Mendness-Philliskirk ... bination an extended ... but that error is ... history.

And finally a world ... advice for the Portsmouth ... visit. Attack them with f... up front, as at Bourn... month, and we can be ... them. Defend and we're fo... a replay, and we will lose.

Fred Shenield, Winchester ... Terrace, Southampton.

Thanks all round

LL FOCUS

w faces for a new season

Crosspool: Jamiesons Chemists, 29, Sandygate Road.
Pollen count: 62, forecast: high.

SHEFFIELD UNITED F.C.
1889

McEWAN POISED TO CLINCH FIRST LANE SIGNINGS

By Tony Pritchett

BILLY McEWAN, Sheffield United's new team manager, is on the brink of his first signings for the club today.

But he began the build-up to the new season by hiring the club's former coach, Danny Bergara, who will return when the players report back on Monday.

Bergara's first move when he accepted Bramall Lane's terms was to tele-phone David Pleat, new boss of Spurs, who had also offered him a role at ...

United may also appoint a physio soon to complete their set-up fol-lowing the dismissals of Ian Porterfield, John McSeveney and Jim Dixon. Phil Henson has already been selected to manage the youth team.

Bergara, dismissed from United in the early days of Ian Porterfield in 1981, has been working all over the world in the last five ... He has been ...

Said Bergara today: "I am glad to be back at a club I should never have left."

Bergara has been work-ing recently with Bruce Rioch at Middlesbrough, but has accepted another contract with United, a club he first joined as Harry Haslam's assistant in January, 1977.

With the coaching appointment made, McEwan continued his determination to bring ... of new players ...

Your all-action Green 'Un

TOMORROW in your all-action Green 'Un . . .
★ SOCCER: How will United fill the Lewington gap — and focus on Owls new boy Brannigan.
★ GOLF: Lyle in mood for repeat win in The Open

Cup winners: 1899, 1902, 1915, 1925
RECORD TRANSFER FEE RECEIVED: £400,000 from Leeds for Alex Sabella.
RECORD TRANSFER FEE PAID: £160,000 to River Plate for Alex Sabella and to Leicester for Alan Y...

BACK ROW (left to right): Tony Philliskirk, Don Fenton, Geelan, John Burridge, Paul Stancliffe, Paul Tomlinson, McNaught, Peter Withe.

MIDDLE ROW: Kevin Arnott, Brian Smith, Henson (coach), ...

Geordie caps Latin magic

United's Latin look inspired a classic goal from the star pupil. New Latin American coach Danny Bergara has made a sensational impact with wins against two top sides. But the real hero was 19-year-old Geordie Clive Mendonca, the free scoring star from the juniors, who scored his first senior goal 15 minutes after coming on a substitute.

Despite the improvement in results and performances, Bergara was soon back working with the Central League side, with McEwan once again taking control. Unfortunately the first team's results and performances suffered and as they began to drop into the bottom half of the table, McEwan tendered his resignation on New Year's Day 1988 after an embarrassing home defeat to Oldham Athletic (0-5).

Bergara was asked by the board to take charge as 'caretaker manager' for the FA Cup match against Maidstone United at Bramall Lane which the Blades won (1-0) thanks to a goal from Mark Dempsey. Bergara's second game in charge also ended with a win, as the Blades picked up their first away win in over three months. His charges defeating Bournemouth at Dean Court in the League (2-1) thanks to goals from Tony Philliskirk and Paul Stancliffe. There was talk amongst the club's supporters that should the Blades beat Plymouth Argyle on the following Saturday, the Uruguayan would beat all contenders to take the manager's role himself. Unfortunately the winter weather saw the home game against the Pilgrims postponed, and with it the chance of a third straight win for Bergara had gone.

Danny's boys rescue mission

Danny Bergara launched Sheffield United's rescue mission today as he took charge of his first coaching session in the build-up to the visit of Maidstone United in the FA Cup on Saturday. Said Bergara "We have not done ourselves or poor Billy McEwan any favours lately. If our people go out on to that field just because they get paid for it, we might as well not bother. I shall do my utmost for the club, but the boys have got to want to play desperately for Sheffield United. The club is bigger than any of us, and we must give the supporters the victory they deserve on Saturday. We are not a bad side. We proved that at Barnsley, Villa and Manchester City. Now we have an opportunity, in the Cup, to get back in the groove". Managing director Derek Dooley spoke to the players before today's training session when he told them that he wanted to see the dressing room bubbling with life.

Caretaker dusts off the cobwebs

The big names make the big headlines in the nation's sporting press as Sheffield United look for a new manager. But meanwhile, the caretaker is taking care....Coach Danny Bergara gave his directors valuable breathing space - and did his own chances no harm either - by coaxing an uplifting performance, not to mention a priceless 2-1 win at Bournemouth. Bergara swapped Leaning for Segers in goal, stood by the rest of the side which had scraped through in the Cup against Maidstone and then watch them produce a vastly improved show.

United built their win around a step-up in quality from almost every player in the side, but notably from the midfield area which has often been their biggest problem.

The local paper also received a letter from an 'exiled' United fan, praising Bergara for his team's performance in the win at Dean Court:

Gutsy show from United

Congratulations to United on a real gutsy performance at Bournemouth last Saturday. For the first 20 minutes they looked like leaderless, headless chickens, then they got it all together. Stancliffe was outstanding and it was fitting that he scored the winning goal. Segers was brilliant, the first complete goalkeeper that we've had since Alan Hodgkinson. We have to do all we can to keep him, in fact everyone played well. (Fred Shemeld, Southampton)

Danny's key role in United quest

Caretaker Danny Bergara could be the key man in Sheffield United's search for a new manager. Not that Danny himself is likely to be handed a job which could now attract Watford's departed boss Dave Bassett. But I expect the Uruguayan coach to retain a key role whoever is appointed. Normally, men in Bergara's position - a legacy of an old regime - are the first to go when a new man arrives, bringing staff of his own choosing. But the key qualifications facing the leading candidates may not be whether they can work with Bergara but whether he can work with them.

I believe the board will insist on retaining the former England under-21 coach when the senior appointment is made and that the new man will be sufficiently of his acquaintance to establish a working relationship.

Days after the weather had denied Bergara the chance of a third game in charge, the Blades appointed a new manager, Dave

Bassett. Bergara remained as part of the management staff, however Bassett did bring in his old friend Geoff Taylor to work alongside him with Bergara concentrating his efforts on the reserve side.

As well as his 100% record as Sheffield United first team manager, by the end of the season Bergara had taken the club's reserve side to a fifth place finish in the Central League, the highest Sheffield United's reserve side had finished in eighteen years but following the first team's relegation to the Third Division, Bassett had decided to bring in his own backroom staff and Bergara was once again to leave Bramall Lane.

Deposed Bergara seeks to put the record straight

Sheffield United's deposed coach Danny Bergara spoke out this week in defence of his record and his methods. The flamboyant Uruguayan also put the record straight on his role during new manager David Bassett's determined but vain fight to keep United out of the Third Division.

Since then Bergara has become the first victim of Bassett's backroom shake-up, closely followed by youth team coach Phil Henson and physio Ian Bailey. All three have questioned the wisdom of the decision to part with their services to allow the manager to bring in his own staff, as is customary in football.

Bergara is disappointed that there was no apparent recognition of his efforts early last season when, with United second from bottom, he was promoted from reserve to first team coach under former manager Billy McEwan. "Within three weeks we climbed to tenth or eleventh in the table" he recalls. "But from then on Billy took command of coaching again and I was mainly training the juniors and the reserves. I was then made caretaker when Billy left and helped the lads out of a losing run by winning both my games in charge. Then Dave Bassett was appointed and after a week, brought in Geoff Taylor, unofficially, to help him with coaching the first team. It soon became obvious that they didn't like my style of football. I am naturally very upset that supporters are of the opinion that I have been first team coach since Dave arrived. This has not been the case. I am only sorry I was not given the opportunity to take full control of the team before Dave Bassett was appointed. One day I shall prove to a club that my methods, based on a mixture of South American skills and the British grit and organisation is a winning formula"

The next chapter in his adventure would finally see Danny Bergara step out from the shadows to become a manager in his own right as he took the short journey across the Pennines to Rochdale.

Rochdale FC

In the summer of 1988 Bergara became manager of perennial Fourth Division strugglers Rochdale, and in doing so became the first ever South American coach to take a first team manager's role with an English Football Club.

Dale manager Eddie Gray had resigned to take over at Second Division Hull City, and once again Sheffield United Chairman Reg Brealey was firmly in Bergara's camp, recommending to Jim Marsh, his counterpart at Spotland, that he give the Uruguayan a chance.

On rumours that Rochdale would soon be playing a South American style of football upon his appointment Bergara stated: *"I have lived in England almost as long as I lived in Uruguay, Rochdale cannot play the South American way as they have no South American players. What they can do is play without fear. When you are scared, you win nothing. This is my first chance as a manager, but I have not come to Rochdale to learn the job. I'm ready to apply all the experience I've gathered as a player/coach, assistant manager and caretaker manager. I don't know how it will work out but I am not going to worry that's for sure. I think that after 15 years hard work the chance has come - and you've got to take it. I am not taking a step back but a big step forward. I aim to reach the top if I can. I'll be aiming for a mixture of South American skill and British grit. I was brought up in the same way as Pele and Maradona - and that can't be wrong. I want my team to enjoy the game and play without fear"*

Of his new charges he said: *"It will be a hard task but it can be made easier if we all set out to enjoy what we are doing. If people* *pay to watch a team then the team has got to show how good it is. I paid a couple of scouting missions here last season. They tried to play good football, perhaps too much at times, if you can say that. I think there is a good nucleus of players, and I am looking forward to the new challenge. My aim is to improve things and get us as high in the Football League as I can. Rome wasn't built in a day, but we are not building Rome - just trying to get a bit of success for the club"*

He then stated that the ideal mixture for the team would be youth and experience, with the key, finding experienced players who would like to come to Rochdale and fight to get the club out of Division Four: *"I spoke to Ruud Gullit last week, but he didn't want to come"* he said with a twinkle in his eye.

Bergara had an early opportunity to outline his thoughts when he was introduced to Dale supporters at a 'fans forum' - a notorious 'lion's den' as many previous managers had found to their costs.

The Uruguayan certainly impressed the supporters with his forthright views and sense of humour, leaving many to believe that he could finally be the man to lead their team to some long awaited success.

One of the first questions asked was - 'What do you think about joining Dale', to which Bergara replied *"I was appointed on Tuesday and it was the greatest day of my life - I was a manager at last after 15 years of hard work. I was born in Uruguay which is a very small country but one which has won a lot at football. Rochdale is a small club compared with Manchester United and Liverpool. I am not saying we can become a Manchester United but I will try and get the people of Rochdale a football team they can be proud of. Here the supporters have had little to talk about for* years. I want to get them talking again. I am not saying success will come quickly. To all fans I say bear with us, have plenty of belief in us, but don't expect miracles. It is not a dream but a possibility to get this club to be respected everywhere. I hope to get the players in the right frame of mind, and they will have to work hard and earn their sweat. If we have a big heart and a bit of a brain we could become a successful club. After all who would have said that Wimbledon would go from Division Four to Division One"

When asked what his style of play would be, and if the team would be full of young players, he replied: *"We do need older heads to bring the young players on. Young players can do a very good job, but if you are 1-0 up with 10 minutes left to play, and the opposition start having a go at you, saying things to you, it is then that younger players start to get tense and worried. This is when experienced players prove invaluable. What we will have to do is make the younger players more manly. As for the style of play, when the other team has got the ball we have to chase them and get it back. After all you can't play without the ball. The best way is to play in their half, and when we have the ball, put it in the net - it is as simple as that"*

One Dale fan ventured that Dale had played most of the previous season in their own half, Bergara's reply was swift and to the point: *"You will not see that this season"*

Bergara would become well known over the next few years for his famous football quotes, one of his early quotes regarding his team preparation at Rochdale was: *"Preparing the side is just like the matador dressing up to go in the ring. The adrenalin is flowing and he feels ready. The only problem is, he has to face the bull. We will have to face the bull next season, and I don't intend to go jumping behind any barriers"*

Jan Bergara remembers Dan's early days at Rochdale:

There were leaks all over the changing rooms, buckets everywhere. We were both there once mopping up, when he first took over. He soon sorted that out and the main door that looked like it would collapse. He got the players involved in the cleaning and painting. He had pride and discipline in all he did, wherever he went clean kitchens just as important, not just discipline on the pitch. He even had a Mars bar, that he was saving in his desk drawer, eaten by mice!

Bergara's new role soon caught the attention of the national media, with the following report featuring in Shoot magazine:

The northern industrial town of Rochdale is not exactly the kind of place you would expect to find a South American diamond prospector, but for Uruguayan Danny Bergara, it's an exciting new field of operation.

Globetrotter Danny has checked in at Spotland via Montevideo, Seville and Brunei. But the Football League's first foreign manager believes the job of raising the profile of this archetypal Fourth Division club could be his most rewarding yet. Bergara became Rochdale's 18th manager since the war when he took over from Eddie Gray earlier this month. He's also been a coach with Luton, Sheffield United, Middlesbrough and the England youth team.

But the 46 year old protégé of the late Harry Haslam believes: "Whether you are manager of Rochdale or the Brunei national team, football is the same game." After more years than they care to remember scratching around the foot of the Fourth Division, the prospect of automatic relegation to the Vauxhall Conference has cast an ominous new shadow over the future of Rochdale. Bergara asks for patience, but knows time is not on his side. *"The people connected with this club must believe in what we are doing, but should not expect miracles overnight. Rochdale have finished in the bottom six for the past six or seven seasons, so our aim this time is to finish higher than that."*

And while the Tottenham and Manchester Uniteds of this world lash out millions on summer signings, Bergara must repair his team from the ranks of the free transfers. "There were only 12 players when I arrived here, but I've managed to add another four."

But even more important than the team's League position is the development of the young talent at the club. And Bergara, who helped Haslam bring Alex Sabella and Ossie Ardiles to England, believes that instead of looking to sign star players from abroad, our clubs should be importing foreign coaches. "I'd like to see brilliant, skilful players with coaching ability coming from abroad to show what skill is all about.

If you could have the natural talents of Uruguay and the organisation and guidance of England, I know it would be a winning formula. A young footballer is like a diamond, give him to a good jeweller and he'll be worth a million pounds. But a bad jeweller can crush him in two minutes. I do not want to be critical of English football because it has given me a marvellous living for the past 15 years and I will always be grateful for that. But England, who invented the game and gave it to the world, have only won one World Cup and nothing else. I see eight year old boys on a full sized pitch with a full sized goal. All they have to do to score is blast the ball over the goalkeeper's head. In Uruguay, you play in five a side goals until the age of 12.

You have to use your brain to score. You learn to bend the ball and you learn how to take the keeper on. I loved my time as assistant to John Cartwright with the England Youth team. I was very proud of the team we built, but the FA did not ask me to stay on."

Bergara's problem now is finding the time to develop a successful youth system at Rochdale. "I won't bring in 20 kids if I can't give them the best attention. I'd rather leave diamonds alone than ruin them. The previous managers of Rochdale have done very well just to keep the club in the League. We have a lot of hard work ahead , but if my boys don't enjoy it they might as well not be here."

After 15 years in England, does Bergara have any plans to finally accept British citizenship? *"Who knows. I was born in Uruguay and I'm a naturalised Spaniard. I've never been convicted except for a parking offence so maybe one day I will become an Englishman."*

Bergara used his Sheffield connections to good use as he brought in several players that he already knew from his days at Sheffield United and also at Sheffield FC, the world's oldest Football Club, where he had often coached during his time out of the professional game.

Defender Simon Copeland and midfielder David Frain both came in from United whilst strikers Chris Beaumont and Mark Smith, both previously at Sheffield FC, also joined Dale. Dave Sutton added experience to Bergara's defence when joining from Bolton Wanderers.

Despite earning just one point from the first three games, Bergara's Rochdale set about the season in good form, going on to win the next five games to sit proudly in third place in the table, A Rodger Wylde goal for Stockport County in a draw at Spotland

bringing the winning run to an end. Nevertheless Bergara had certainly made an impression on the people of Rochdale and also other managers in the Division.

With his side due to play Rochdale, who were still in and around the play-off places at the start of December, Peterborough United manager Mick Jones had the following to say: *"I watched Rochdale against York City in the League and Huddersfield United in the FA Cup and went home in disbelief at the transformation in Dale this season. I had seen more football in five minutes against Huddersfield Town, who are a division above, than in the whole of the televised match between Newcastle United and Manchester United last Sunday.*

"I was put through my own coaching badges some years ago by Danny Bergara and have been a disciple of his ever since. I know that any team managed by Danny will come out attacking, and I rate Dale as currently the best team in Division Four".

Following Rochdale's decent start to the season, Bergara was soon featured in another national magazine article:

What's a Uruguayan doing in Rochdale??

"It is a small place with not too many big ambitions and hopes, but with a great deal of pride and the team are now in with a chance of doing much better than they have for many years. There is a great deal of work to do here and success is based on many factors. I don't think you can talk in terms of good seasons and bad seasons. At one time there may be a lot of cash in the bank which is not spent so wisely and so what could have been a good season turns out to be a bad one and the club is in trouble. Having said that, I have managed to get new players who have cost us nothing. So we

LEAGUE

CRANES ALL·IN·ONE GARDEN CENTRE

ROCHDALE A.F.C.

ROC

...dale Observer Wednesday 29 March 1989

SCENE

Buenas noches . . .

BERGARA's flirtation with Football Club ended on when he resigned to manager of Stockport writes LES BARLOW.

breaker manager with son as his right-hand

t plan to advertise the veral applications have red.

culated since the mid-st Stockport were keen a replacement for the d. But the actual move Monday morning, only took the field against potland.

udden that some of the

Dale players didn't know he had gone until they arrived for the game against Carlisle.

Apparently, Stockport County chairman Brendan Elwood is an old friend of Bergara's and following his capture he was quoted as saying: "I have followed Danny's career with interest over the years and he has done a fantastic job at every club he has been with. I think we need a man of his experience as a replacement for Asa Hartford."

Dale director David Walkden said: "We wish Danny all the best in his new job. We have no one in mind for the job at Spotland and will give people chance to apply by ringing in. Dave Sutton will be given chance to apply."

There were rumours a few weeks ago that Bergara was on the brink of getting

already lined up a replacement.

Mr Walkden said: "There are always stories floating about when a team has a poor run, as we had done.

"I was told by a fan that Ronnie Moore had been virtually appointed as manager. It was news to me, and I am on the board of directors."

Moore is currently player-assistant manager with Tranmere Rovers.

More speculation came on Monday when former Bradford City manager and ex-Dale player Terry Dolan appeared at Spotland. Dolan is now working as a scout for Preston North End.

No doubt many more names will come out of the hat before an appointment is made. It remains to be seen which named floats to the top of the pool.

mer following the departure of Eddie Gray to Hull City. He became the first Latin-American manager in the Football League.

He often referred to Dale as "my little club" and one of his favourite quotes was: "The house is small but the heart is big, and if you have a big heart you can succeed."

Ironically, he penned in his programme notes for the game against Carlisle: "Win, lose, or draw, we must all keep together to the very end for everyone's benefit and above all that of Rochdale AFC."

Bergara did not take charge port team which drew against United at Edgeley Park on M But he did watch the game fr

He returned to Spotland

DAILY MIRROR, Friday, August 12, 1988

Danny's the boy to light up Rochdale

THE NEW PRIDE OF OUR ALLE

DANNY Begora always wanted to manage an English club.

ard says gara

gara yester-d into the eat at Roch-season's 89th in the League nk outsiders at n the title, and I feel great."

, 45-year-old , has his trc job with Roch-hose re-and of £12,000 is a far out of his pre-Sheffield United.

Dale Berga South

ALBERTO Daniel Bergara began his reign as Dale manager yesterday and aims to have two new players at his disposal by lunch-time today.

Danny, as he is known, made no promises of what the future holds for the club, but he aims to put a team on the field that gives value for money.

And that team could include three or four

First . . .

DANNY Bergara is believed to be the first

So w from t "string Berga chester spend f at least problem

"It wil but it ca if we all what we "If peo a team th got to sh is."

Bergar seen the his dispos He said couple of sions he The tear good footl

ROCHDALE A.F.C.

Diamond hunter Danny

"Rochdale have finished in the bottom six for the past six or seven seasons, so our aim this time is to finish higher than that." And while the Tottenhams and Manchester Uniteds of this world concentrate on superstar players, their repair bills from ...

"I do not want to be critical of English football because it has given me a marvellous living for the past 15 years and I will always be grateful for that. But England, who invented the game and gave it to the world, have only went one World Cup and nothing else.

"Last night one-side are a full sized pitch with a full sized goal. All they have to do to score is blast the ball over the goalkeeper's head.

"In Uruguay, we play in five-a-side goals until the age of 12. You have to use your brain to score. You learn to band the ball and you learn how to take the 'keeper on.

"I loved my time as assistant to John Cartwright with the England Youth team. I was very proud of the team we built, but the FA did not want me to stay on.

Successful

Bergara's problem now is finding the time to develop a successful youth system at Rochdale.

"I won't bring in 20 kids if I can't give them the best attention. I'd rather have a few diamonds alone than ruin them.

"The previous managers at Rochdale have done very well just to keep the club in the League. We have a lot of hard work ahead, but if my boys don't enjoy it they might as well not be here."

And after 15 years in England, does Bergara have any plans to finally accept British citizenship?

"Who knows. I was born in Uruguay and now I'm a naturalised Spaniard. I've never become anxious to maybe one day become an Englishman.

"Hasta La Vista" says Danny

by Les Barlow

DANNY Bergara settled into his new job as manager of Stockport County this week, but took time out to thank all who had helped him in his reign as Dale manager.

Danny said: "Rochdale gave me a chance to break into Football League management and I shall always be grateful to them for that.

"After nine hard working months at Spotland I would like to think I accomplished something.

"I managed to gather together a good young squad of players at no expense and at the same time brought in money for the club with the sale of some players.

"I tried to establish a new youth policy at the club, and I would like to think we were well on the way in terms of a youth policy."

Bergara said it was not easy leaving ...

... you have praised me, but it has been a joy to work with you as it has with all at Spotland.

But he did say our headline in Wednesday's Observer was a little wrong. The heading was Buenas Noches (good night) as Danny always used to wish those still left at Spotland on matchdays before he went home.

Danny said it should have been Hasta La Vista (until we meet again).

Fixtures

LAST NIGHT
Cambridge United v Wrexham
Colchester United v Rochdale
Torquay United v Crewe

TODAY
Burnley v Hereford United
Carlisle United v Hartlepool United
Darlington v Tranmere Rovers
Exeter City v Peterborough United
Leyton Orient v Grimsby Town
Lincoln City v Stockport County
Rotherham United v York City
Scarborough v Halifax Town
Scunthorpe United v Doncaster Rovers

TUESDAY
Burnley v Crewe
Cambridge United v York City
Lincoln City v Doncaster Rovers

---

new manager will do it the American way

Les Barlow

Man with national background

DANNY BERGARA was born in Uruguay but has lived in England for 15 years.

He played for the Uruguayan international youth team before moving to Spain, at the age of 20. He played in the Spanish First and Second Divisions for 11 years before coming to England in 1973.

He had a spell as England Youth coach under Ron Greenwood in 1980-81. England reached the European Youth Championship finals in West Germany. They lost against Spain, and Scotland, but scored a stunning 7-0 win over Austria in Basle.

Bergara spent five years as coach at Luton Town when David Pleat was manager, and later worked as assistant to Harry Haslam, who was manager of Sheffield United.

Bergara represented Sheffield United as coach to the Brunel Football Association and took charge of the Spanish national team for a time.

He was short-listed for the Welsh manager's job when Mike England was appointed.

Last season he was back with Sheffield United and took charge of their Central League side which finished fifth in the table — their highest position for 18 years.

He was United's caretaker manager for a short time last season before Dave Bassett was appointed.

Bergara succeeds Eddie Gray, who resigned last month to become manager of Hull City. Gray had been in charge at Spotland since December 1986.

Others who have tried at Spotland is ... Gray took over from Vic Halom, who was sacked.

mixture for a team would be youth and experience.

"Carl Harris has experience, and Geoff Lomax is ripening. The key is to find experienced players who would like to come here and fight to get us to the top of Division Four."

Tongue in cheek, he added: "I spoke to Rudi Gullit last week, but he didn't want to come."

He continued: "We cannot afford big signing-on fees, so it may be we have to stick to signing youngish players.

"Having said that, I will always have my eyes open for the occasional bargain. It is up to me to convince them there is still life at Spotland.

"I am well known in the game, and I know a lot of people in the game. If I see a player is on offer I will get in touch with people I know before making any signing.

"I have been with clubs in higher places than Dale, but they are always looking for promising young players in the lower Divisions, so I have seen a lot of Division Three and Four ...

games and know what the score is.

"I may make some mistakes, but I don't mind criticism as long as it's constructive."

Dale director David Walkden said Bergara will continue to live in Sheffield, but will live locally during the week.

He said: "He likes to work seven days a week, 24 hours a day because football is his life."

Members of Dale Supporters Club will be able to meet Bergara at their annual general meeting in the Ratcliffe Arms, Spotland, tomorrow night.

BERGARA NEW MA... AT ROCH...

By Tony Pritchett

DANNY Bergara will become the first foreign-born manager of an English League club when he is named as the new boss of Fourth Division Rochdale tomorrow.

Uruguayan-born and released by Sheffield United last week after Eddie Gray left to move to Hull. Announcement of the club ...

Since he left Bramall Lane Bergara had been strongly linked with ... Leicester City ...

Danny Bergara

now have five new players, Neil Evans on loan from Oldham and the 12 players who were here when I arrived. We have the nucleus of a good team. However, 18 players is not a healthy situation to be in, especially if we are hit with a spate of injuries. Many of the smaller clubs are in the same position as Rochdale. With little money to spare they are unable to give players lengthy contracts so it is a matter of renewing every year and recruiting new blood."

I wonder if he has ideas on changes he would like to make.

"There's not a great deal of scope for changes when you only have 12 players. In many cases changes don't necessarily mean that success will be achieved. In our case, it's a matter of the boys going out there and performing. They can do it, and have proved they can do it, as can be seen by the results of the past few months. I just hope they can sustain that kind of form. Also, finances are a problem. I, personally, have no input into the financial side of the club. Which I feel is as it should be. My job is to manage the team and let people who are more used to handling finance get on with it. So finances are down to the board. Obviously we consult when I'm after a new player or I need money for something, but in the end it's my job to get results out on the field. I don't see the point of crying and worrying over money when you haven't got any."

Obviously, with so little cash in the bank, and finances stretched to the limit, it must be very difficult for them to operate a youth policy.

"We have no youth policy as such, other than the YTS. One day we would like to build something decent, but at the moment that is impossible. I believe that if clubs such as Rochdale are going to have any chance at all, then it's got to be through the young players coming through. There are two ways of ensuring that we get the

158

youngsters here. The first one is through sponsorship, in that we get local businesses to sponsor the cost of a youngster as happened in the past, or go to the larger teams in the area, such as Manchester United, Manchester City, Liverpool and Everton and take the youngsters who they don't really want. This is not to say that they're no good - it's just that they don't fit into the scheme of things in the larger clubs.

In many cases, because we are a smaller club and are, therefore, able to spend more time with individuals, we can often bring the best out of them. Often it works to their advantage and many of them go on to better things. They are products of Rochdale and other teams like them, who, because of the chance we gave them, have realised their potential and when the opportunity has arisen, they have taken it. At present we have some good lads coming through, lads such as Jason Smart, Zach Hughes (who at 17 was one of the youngest people to ever play in the league), Stuart Mellish, Mycock, Armitage and Keith Welsh, who I'm sure will turn out to be outstanding players. When a club begins to do well, people begin to take more interest in it and they spend more money on it, which, in its turn, generates more interest, so in many respects, a club generates its own success.

On our present form we have a good chance of attracting more support as the season progresses. What people will not do is put money and effort into a team that is struggling and not producing the goods. If we continue to play all season as we have done in the first quarter, then we should have a chance of entering the Third Division next season. But being realistic, I don't think we have enough depth as yet. I would be happy to settle for the type of play we have achieved so far. I suspect we shall end up about mid-table.

If we can consolidate on that, then we can perhaps start looking for better things next season."

One of a manager's main tasks is motivating his players. How does Danny Bergara motivate players?

"To me motivation is to make them understand that they play for this team, for Rochdale. They must keep themselves fit, play to a pattern and die for the cause. There is no other way to motivate players for me. I expect everything from them when they play for this team. Whatever you do in this life you have to work hard. It's as simple as that."

So far things are looking good for Danny Bergara and Rochdale and the new manager is full of praise for the people of the town who have supported and continue to support the club. When he arrived he said: "Bear with us, believe in us, but don't expect miracles."

Dale went out of both the League Cup and the FA Cup at the first hurdle, but in keeping with Bergara's attacking rules, they ran their opponents close in both ties.

Fourth Division rivals Burnley won a two legged League Cup tie with the odd goal in nine. The first leg at Spotland finishing 3-3, before the Clarets earned a second round tie against eventual finalists Luton Town. Dale drew away at Leeds Road against Third Division Huddersfield Town (1-1) before losing the replay at Spotland after once again showing their attacking prowess (3-4).

Bergara was less than complimentary about his team giving goals away in League and Cup games: *"We keep on throwing goals away with silly mistakes, mainly brought on by inexperience. The goals against have meant we couldn't progress in two cup competitions, and hold only seventh place instead of being top of the table. We* *will keep on working and working until matters are put right - and they will come right, mark my words.*

"I thought the lads played some good football against Huddersfield and matched them in most ways. We are out of the cup and must now concentrate on reaching a good league position. The lads have now been together for four months and I feel that they are already a team. How many managers can say that?. At some places they spend a lot of money, bring in players, and still say after two years that they haven't got it right"

Bergara's side were playing attacking and enjoyable football, this season ticket holder was pleased to put his thoughts down on paper:

*To the Manager. Just a line to say how much I have enjoyed the football so far played home and away. In all the years I've been coming goals have been few and far between, now things have really taken off with 2's, 3's and 4's most every week, which is a great credit to yourself and the players. I wish you all the success you have built on and that promotion hopefully is not very far away. Good wishes to yourself, players and staff and the best of luck in the coming 12 months yours sincerely **A K Green (season ticket holder)***

Unfortunately after their good early season form, the thin squad at Spotland began to tell its own tale as Rochdale picked up only six points from nine games played in January and February, suffering heavy defeats against Exeter City and Stockport County. There were even rumblings amongst the supporters that Bergara would be sacked if results didn't improve.

Successive wins against Tranmere Rovers, Darlington and Scarborough Athletic soon calmed fears that the Uruguayan

would lose his job. The win against Scarborough had seen Dale just seven points off a play-off spot, but just over a week after that win against the 'seadogs', the news that most Dale fans didn't want to hear was out - Danny Bergara had resigned, and worse still he was joining North West rivals Stockport County.

The Rochdale Observer reported the news as:

<u>**Buenas Noches...**</u>

Danny Bergara's flirtation with Rochdale Football Club ended on Monday night when he resigned to become manager of Stockport County. Team captain Dave Sutton has been appointed as Dale's 'caretaker manager' with coach Jimmy Robson as his right hand man.

The club does not plan to advertise the vacant position. Several applications have already been received. Rumours had circulated since the middle of last week that Stockport were keen to sign Bergara as a replacement for the sacked Asa Hartford. But the actual move did not come until Monday morning, only hours before Dale took to the field against Carlisle United at Spotland. The move was so sudden that some of the Dale players didn't know he had gone until they arrived for the game against Carlisle.

Apparently, Stockport County Chairman Brendan Elwood is an old friend of Bergara's and following his capture was quoted as saying "I have followed Danny's career with interest over the years and he has done a fantastic job at every club he has been with. I think we need a man of his experience as a replacement for Asa Hartford"

Dale director David Walkden said: "We wish Danny all the best in his new job. We have no-one in mind for the job at Spotland and will give people the chance to apply by ringing in. Dave Sutton will be given the chance to apply"

Bergara, who had been working at Spotland without the security of a full time contract, contacted the Rochdale Observer to pass on his thanks via their reporter Les Barlow:

Danny Bergara settled into his new job as manager of Stockport County this week but took time out to thank all who had helped him in his reign as Dale manager.

"Rochdale gave me a chance to break into Football League management and I shall always be grateful to them for that. After nine hard working months at Spotland I would like to think I achieved something. I managed to gather together a good young squad of players at no expense and at the same time brought in money for the club with the sale of some players. I tried to establish a new youth policy at the club and would like to think we were well on the way in terms of a youth policy. It was not easy leaving Spotland where I have made so many friends. I did not want to leave, but certain circumstances and a very good offer from Stockport County prompted me to move. I would like to thank the Directors at Spotland, the fans and the players of whom I felt very proud as they gave me some great moments that money couldn't buy"

Stockport County FC

Without doubt the most successful spell of Danny Bergara's managerial career came at Stockport County. It is a huge measure of his achievements in the Edgeley Park hot seat that at the time of writing, almost 20 years after his departure, he is still the second longest serving manager in the club's history.

Jan Bergara:

Next came the six year love affair with Stockport County. Although it was rough going the first month or so and a very unprofessional dismissal after six great years, which should never have ended that way, what has since shone through to us is the never failing love and devotion to Danny from the County supporters, which meant so much to him and his family, as it still does to us today. He also loved Stockport County and his 'Blue & White Army'!

Chairman Brendan Elwood had first come across Bergara when he was out of work and coaching Sheffield FC. Elwood saw him at work and spotted his winning way with players, something that had struck a chord with him, and having followed the Uruguayan's career since, he knew that he was the man to take his club further.

However Bergara's introduction to the Edgeley Park faithful was, to say the least uninspiring, and comments regarding his appointment being a poor choice were plentiful towards the end of the season. He had joined County when they were mid-table having gathered 46 points. In his nine games in charge the Hatters had not won, drawing five and losing four. Rochdale on the other

hand had moved above County having been six places behind when he swapped clubs.

After the final game of the season, when County had finished just two points outside of the bottom two, the Stockport Express featured several letters from disgruntled County supporters including these scathing reviews of those first few weeks of his reign at Edgeley Park:

According to Danny Bergara in this paper on 25th May, Stockport County fans will be supporting a winning team sooner rather than later. If his first nine weeks in charge are anything to go by the team will be competing in the Vauxhall Conference, as for winning, that's another matter. As for Mr Bergara's boast 'that he didn't spend a penny at Rochdale, and they finished above us. What does he want, a pat on the back for what he didn't do at Rochdale, or a kick up the backside for what he has done at Stockport?. Perhaps he doesn't realise that when he took over at Edgeley Park, County were 12th in the table and had taken four points off Rochdale who were in 21st position, it looks like the best thing Mr Bergara did for Rochdale was to leave when he did.

As for the promise of a brighter future, the same promise was made on March 11th when he said 'You can rest assured that I and the lads will do our utmost to see this club through the season and prepare it for a much brighter future' and on Easter Monday he went on to say 'Win, lose or draw, we must all keep together to the very end for everyone's benefit and above all that of ROCHDALE FC'. Yes he made the same promise at Rochdale before he walked out on the Lancashire club.

Mentioning Lancashire reminds me, according to Chairman Brendon Elwood, in his programme notes for the Carlisle game,

166

Stockport was one of four Lancashire clubs, the others being Rochdale, Bury and Blackpool, that changed managers that week. Just read his programme notes from the last home game, he states 'we must establish our place on the map (if he looks in Cheshire - we are already on) and not let the same thing happen in Stockport as has happened in Southport, Newport, Workington etc etc...' If we are going to be successful, why mention failure, or is the writing on the wall??

He also states that the changes Danny Bergara has made are already bearing fruit (8 points from a possible 30 at the time - 8 points from 36 after Rotherham and York).

I question Mr Elwood's credibility if, as he says, he wants a sports complex, Owlerton Stadium is up for sale in Sheffield, as he comes from there I am sure he knows that is in Yorkshire and I know I speak for many genuine County fans when I say 'give County back to Stockport Mr Elwood'. Go back to Sheffield and take Mr Bergara with you. County will manage without you, people who care for the club will see to it. A very concerned County fan (name and address supplied)

Having watched County now for about 20 years through thick and thin, I think I will now call it a day. At the beginning of this season County fans for the first time in many years had hope, they had a solid base for success, a firm board of directors every one a local man and in the Chairman Dave Hunt, a man with ideas and who worked hard for the club.

On the football side we had Asa Hartford and Len Cantello, two men who had proven ability in the football world, maybe not as manager and assistant but as good professionals. Mr Hartford had built a good footballing side. Given a bit longer, I and many other County fans, thought he would have brought success to the club.

I think I would be right in saying when Mr Hunt, Asa and Len were kicked in the teeth by Mr Elwood and company that County had a chance, however slight, of making the play-offs, but as they went through the door, so did that slight chance.

Now we have Danny Bergara, a man who it is said had a good track record. Did this same man leave Rochdale in danger of relegation and maybe doing another Newport, and he now wants to bring the same Rochdale side to help County out of the Fourth Division? Forget it Danny, we want to go up not down.

Mr Elwood should also forget his pie in the sky development plans and take Mr Stevenson, Bergara and co back to Sheffield with him and leave it to local people who care about Stockport County Football Club and the supporters who love the club. **(A W Jones, Mile End, Stockport)**

What was the point?? Since the dismissal of Asa Hartford two months ago, statistics tell the story. County have not won a game, nor have they looked like winning, they have dropped from 10th to 20th and if results had gone against them, they could have easily finished next to bottom. The football played has not been entertaining and goodness knows where Mr Bergara's team selections have come from.

Thorpe in midfield, Cooke as centre forward, no Bob Colville, no Tony Hancock, no Brian Butler. Since Bergara came here from Rochdale they have climbed the table and we have gone the other way. So much for a 'tried and trusted' manager to put some pep into the club. Mr Elwood and the board made a big mistake the day they let Asa Hartford go and this has since been proved. I will not be returning to Edgeley Park next season, I do not like the way the club is being run - with Asa Hartford as manager, County stood a chance of going places, with Danny Bergara that chance is nil. **(J Withington, Reddish)**

There was however at least one County supporter who believed that Bergara just might be the man to take the club forward, his letter appearing after Bergara had been in charge for just two games, both away from home:

Let me open by stating I am a Stockport County supporter not a Brendan Elwood supporter. For those of us who follow County home and away throughout the season, there can be no doubt that the team has started to show an improvement over the past two weeks. Very creditable away draws at both Lincoln and Scunthorpe have, I feel been the result of the team being settled for the first time. Mr Bergara has decided on his best line-up and stuck to it, the result has been marked, if not remarkable. I am now convinced that the new manager is going to be a good man for the club, and it gives me great hope of his ability to continue the current improvement into next season.

Finally I would draw supporters attention to last season's league tables and note the team which drew 20 games over the season. That team was Crewe, who are now looking good at the top of the division with an excellent chance of automatic promotion. As this season's draw specialists, County could well follow Crewe's example of firstly learning how to avoid defeat, then developing into a team that can turn those draws into victories. **(Tod White, Heywood)**

The club then announced the departure of one bright young star and the arrival of a new player/coach. Local starlet, 22 year old

Tony Hancock, discovered playing for Stockport Georgians, had left County to sign for Burnley for £50,000. Manager Bergara defended his sale, saying: *"I didn't want him to go but Tony thought he would be better off with a bigger club, not only financially but also in terms of his career. I know a lot of supporters are going to be angry, but I don't want any players who are unsettled and who want to be somewhere else"*

Joining Bergara's backroom staff was experienced defender Paul Jones, with over 600 league games under his belt, centre half Jones had made his name with Bolton Wanderers where he spent fourteen years. Jones had recently spent time coaching in South Africa before playing under Bergara at Rochdale.

In the same paper Bergara took the opportunity to defend his position, saying: *"I know a lot of people think I got this job because I am an intimate friend of the Chairman. That's rubbish, I've worked hard at this game, and he's followed my progress. I repeat what I have already said to those genuine supporters and that is, give us a chance, wait and see. I will stop at nothing to show those who doubt me!!"*

In the build up to his first full season in charge Bergara and his Chairman would continue to raise concerns from supporters, with the weekly local paper following their every move:

Dan Plans Big Swoop

Danny Bergara has lined up an incredible ten new signings as the supporters' flack flies over the departures of Tony Hancock and Bob Colville. And chairman Brendan Elwood has hinted that among the names are some First and Second Division players.

He has angrily denied, amid rumours, that he has any plans for Edgeley Park other than turning County into a successful club. Fans favourite Bob Colville followed Tony Hancock out of the door within two days in a swap deal for York City's promising youngster Alan Dean. York also stand to make either 15 percent or £20,000 from any future transfer deal concerning Stockport lad Dean.

Another name being bandied about is Rochdale's tall right back, Malcolm Brown, a player who has First Division experience with Newcastle United. Bergara took him to Spotland from Huddersfield and now could bring him to Edgeley Park, depending on the outcome of talks with other players in the next few weeks.

But, apart from a goalkeeper, most of the signings he intends to make will be midfielders or forwards. One player who is believed to have caught Bergara's attention is Frank Worthington's nephew Gary, star player with relegated Darlington. In the meantime, there have been no offers for any of the players listed at Edgeley Park.

Bergara has refuted criticism about the players he has put on the transfer list: "People keep saying how can we let him go, and him go, but it's a matter of opinion. There must be some reason we finish fifth from the bottom for the last two seasons. I feel some new blood is needed," he said.

Colville was the latest casualty of Bergara's fresh approach. "I offered Bob terms of a three month contract - people think I offered him very little, but I haven't seen much of Bob. I can't say I'm sorry to see Bob go, but the fans should wait and see who I bring in," he said.

Chairman Brendan Elwood also hit back at his critics. "I understand public apprehension about late season results and the sale of Tony

Hancock. But they do not know what is in the pipeline. In the near future they will see players signed for Stockport from First Division clubs, players who would not normally come to the club. And we will be spending a lot more than the Tony Hancock money."

Elwood vowed he would leave the club if he has not achieved success within four years. "I make that declaration to stop all the gossips. I am fed up with all the backbiting about property speculation - if I wanted to make money I can think of a lot better investments!"

Future Lies With Youth

Youth is the key to Stockport County's future. That is the message from manager Danny Bergara in a week which has now seen a new name on the Edgeley Park team sheet, and some old ones disappearing from the club. In a week which Bergara has executed his vow to clear out players he sees as having no future with County, 17 year old Gary Dooner was the first product of the new youth set up to fight his way into the first team.

Amid the end of season gloom, that at least is a glimmer of hope and testimony to good work being carried out with the youths by Trevor Porteous and Neil Bailey. Bergara was very impressed with Dooner in his first outing at York "When a young kid has got to show professionals what passing and enjoyment of football is about, something is wrong. I haven't got wide players at the club so I thought I would give him a chance and he did well. He is well away from having a first team place but at least it is a step forward when you have young players who are prepared to go in and do their best."

He cited Crewe's youth policy which has lifted them into the Third Division as an example. But Bergara does not see the youth policy he inherited as bearing fruit in the near future, saying: "The first thing we have to do now is sort out what we have on the professional side".

It has been a torrid time for the Uruguayan manager since he took over the reins in March, the side drawing five and losing four. Now he is looking to the summer, when he will be chasing "a couple of new faces, I cannot wait for July, when the players come back and we can get the ball rolling again" he said.

The pre-season build-up continued with the biggest clear-out of players in recent history as Tony Coyle, Craig Farnaby, Ian McKenzie, Mike Pickering and Rodger Wylde were released. *(Wylde would stay on at Edgeley Park in a triple role as physiotherapist, coach and emergency player after recently completing his final physiotherapy exams)* **Tony Caldwell, Brian Butler, Mark Payne and Mick Matthews were all transfer listed.**

This left Bergara with only David Logan, Bill Williams, Andy Thorpe, Gary Leonard, Brett Angell, Nigel Hart, John Cooke and Steve Bullock as registered players for the forthcoming campaign.

OW DAN'

OUR MA

ER TO DAN

for Co

Blues' call

By Paul Hince

DANNY BERGERA, Rochdale's Sotuh American-born manager, is to be the new team boss of Stockport County.

He was appointed before tonight's match against Torquay at Edgeley Park.

Bergara succeeds Asa Hartford, who was surprisingly dismissed as County's player-manager last week.

Uruguayan-born Bergara, who took over at Spotland at the start of the season, came out on top of a County short-list, which was understood to have included former Leeds United manager Billy Bremner.

Bergara, who made his name in this country as the England youth team coach, impressed County's new chairman Brendan Elwood with the work he has since done at clubs like Luton Town, Middlesbrough and Sheffield United.

Says Elwood: "I have followed Danny's career with interest over the years and he has done a fine job at every club he has ...

STOCKPORT COUNTY'S new work will be the keynote to the c... And chairman Brendan Elwood for the all-important promotion...

Dibble o

rest of se

AGONY ... City keeper Andy Dibble grimac

ANDY DIBBLE faces an operation that will keep him out of action for the rest of the season and damaging his groin at Walsall on Saturday.

That puts veteran Paul Cooper into Manchester City's front line less than a week after his surprise £20,000 transfer from Leicester.

And the 35-year-old one-time Ipswich goalkeeper ...

Danny Bergara

STOCKPORT COUNTY players met up official... with their manager today - a... found Danny Bergara a... demanding boss, writes Bryan Brett.

A gruelling training session was followed by a face-to-face with all the players who were ...

FOOTBALL LEAGUE DIVISION FOUR

Saturday, 13 May 1989

Pos	Team	P	W	D	L	F	A	GD	Pts
1	Rotherham United	46	22	16	8	76	35	+41	82
2	Tranmere Rovers	46	21	17	8	62	43	+19	80
3	Crewe Alexandra	46	21	15	10	67	48	+19	78
4	Scunthorpe United	46	21	14	11	77	57	+20	77
5	Scarborough	46	21	14	11	67	52	+15	77
6	Leyton Orient	46	21	12	13	86	50	+36	75
7	Wrexham	46	19	14	13	77	63	+14	71
8	Cambridge United	46	18	14	14	71	62	+9	68
9	Grimsby Town	46	17	15	14	65	59	+6	66
10	Lincoln City	46	18	10	18	64	60	+4	64
11	York City	46	17	13	16	62	63	-1	64
12	Carlisle United	46	15	15	16	53	52	+1	60
13	Exeter City	46	18	6	22	65	68	-3	60
14	Torquay United	46	17	8	21	45	60	-15	59
15	Hereford United	46	14	16	16	66	72	-6	58
16	Burnley	46	14	13	19	52	61	-9	55
17	Peterborough United	46	14	12	20	52	74	-22	54
18	Rochdale	46	13	14	19	56	82	-26	53
19	Hartlepool United	46	14	10	22	50	78	-28	52
20	**Stockport County**	46	10	21	15	54	52	+2	51
21	Halifax Town	46	13	11	22	69	75	-6	50
22	Colchester United	46	14	8	24	60	78	-18	50
23	Doncaster Rovers	46	13	10	23	49	78	-29	49
24	Darlington	46	8	18	20	53	76	-23	42

---

recians earn

WE ARE GOIN

TO BE WINNE

Manager's pledge
to supporters

STOCKPORT COUNTY fans will be supporting a winning team sooner rather than later, according to manager Danny Bergara.

The promise comes in an end-of-season week which has seen the County boss give free transfers to five players and make four others available for transfer.

It is now nine weeks since he took over at County, in the wake of the Asa Hartford ...

managerial changes, Bergara continued: "For all sorts of reasons the players who are going were just not up to the pressure of changes within the club and it showed where it matters — out on the field."

The County manager is under no illusions of the enormous task facing him in his rebuilding operation, or of keeping the club's loyal ...

and a lot of patience to get up the league as possible but to earn it. You c... but if you're go... helps. I didn't sp... Rochdale and the ...

"This is going Grand National Right now we have first hurdle. Whateve the past I appreciate those loyal support seeing a winning s will ...

1989/90

Even before the new season had begun, many of Bergara's doubters had altered their opinions of him following a bright pre-season in which his rebuilt side had shown massive signs of improvement on the team that finished the previous campaign. Bergara however was quick to set his new team their target for the season and at the same time ask for supporters not to get carried away: *"We need 50 points by the middle or perhaps the end of January, that will give us a strong foundation and allow us room to consider our tactics for the rest of the season"*

It was a safety first approach by Bergara, who was not prepared to talk about promotion, despite an encouraging warm-up campaign. His side had begun with a win over Vauxhall Conference side Weymouth and then beat a Bournemouth side which included a sprinkling of the Second Division side's most promising youngsters. Then there was a win over Stafford Rangers, a draw with Stalybridge Celtic and a victory over Third Division Walsall which had really got the County fans talking.

Bergara tried to play it all down: *"Beating Walsall got people saying 'We're going up', but I don't like that, I'm optimistic of course I am, and my ambition is to take Stockport County up the League, but you never hear Liverpool boasting that they are going to win the championship - they just go ahead and do it, that's the sort of attitude I want here. Let's forget all the speculation about promotion for a while and concentrate simply on making a good start. If we could reach that 50 points mark in January it would be tremendous, and that is the main objective".*

The Uruguayan had taken his newly built squad away to an Army barracks on the south coast of England, and was relying on the team spirit built during their stay to get his side off to a good start. The players had been put through a tough regime, reporting for duty at the gym at 7-30 am each day before being put through their paces by a super-fit Army sergeant.

The supporters newfound optimism appeared to be justified as the Uruguayan's team began the season in earnest. Within the first two months of the campaign his side had lost just once in the League and also advanced in the League Cup after a two legged victory over Third Division Bury.

Chris Beaumont, another of Bergara's captures from Rochdale along with player/coach Jones, David Frain and Malcolm Brown, had scored the first League goal of the season in the opening day draw at Edgeley Park against Torquay United. Unfortunately the goal scorer was later carried from the field with a shoulder injury that was to keep him out of the side for some time.

Bergara had brought in several players in addition to his four captures from Spotland, including veteran keeper Barry Siddall, George Oghani, Paul Robertson and Garry McDonald. McDonald it was who scored the winner against Bury in the first leg of the League Cup tie. Mick Matthews scoring the goal in the second leg draw against the Gigg Lane side to gain a second round tie against First Division Queens Park Rangers.

A first defeat of the season came at Loftus Road when another new boy, Ian McInerney, gave County hope for the return leg at Edgeley Park. The Hatters were beaten in the League for the first time three days later at Aldershot. The second leg of the Cup tie ended goalless with the top flight side going through, but not

before Bergara's team had made and missed enough chances to win the game. His side were beginning to win over his pre-season critics.

Bergara was joined by another former player of his, this time Keith Edwards, who had been with the Uruguayan at Sheffield United.

The Mail on Sunday reported on the signing of Edwards:

A friendship dating back 13 years influenced the recent move of football's master poacher to Fourth Division Stockport County. Manager Danny Bergara was assistant boss at Sheffield United when Keith Edwards launched his career that was to provide his various employers with a flood of goals. In his subsequent travels to Hull, Leeds and Aberdeen the record-breaking striker never forgot the help he received from Bergara in those early years. And when Stockport joined the queue for the player whose second spell at Boothferry Park had turned sour, Edwards had no hesitation in plumping for Edgeley Park. The 32 year old striker saying: "I had the choice of several clubs but I never forgot how helpful Danny was when I used to go back for afternoon training at Bramall Lane. The fact that Stockport are in the Fourth Division doesn't bother me because they are making a genuine bid for promotion and were prepared to invest their money in someone with a proven record. If I can't score goals in the Fourth Division then I may as well pack it in. It's sad to be leaving the Second Division but I would rather be playing in a successful Fourth Division side than one struggling in the Second"

Edwards hit the ground running notching four goals in his first six games, with Brett Angell, the butt of many supporters jokes the previous season, leading the way with ten goals.

By the end of October the Hatters were sitting proudly at the top of the Fourth Division after Edwards hat struck the winner against Exeter City, the first time County had been top of the League for 13 years, vindicating Bergara's efforts in bringing the striker to Edgeley Park.

Unfortunately a run of only one win leading up to Christmas saw County drop to fifth before wins over Rochdale and Cambridge United put them back in the play-off places. Bergara again raided his former club Sheffield United to bring in centre half Jim Gannon.

Sitting second in the table, in an automatic promotion spot at the start of April, Bergara and his team looked set for an exciting end of season eight game run-in. Two successive draws and then a home defeat by eventual runners-up Grimsby Town, when player/coach Jones was sent off, saw the Hatters drop out of the play-off places.

Of all places it was Spotland where Bergara had to get his team back on track with just five games left, former Dale player Frain giving his side a richly deserved point.

The readers' letters section of the local paper even began to receive positive letters about the new manager:

"I have supported County for 20 years and in all that time our season has usually ended in November when we go out of the FA Cup. I am writing this letter at the end of April with three games to play and we are still in there with a great chance. So whatever happens now I would just like to say well done to all concerned. Thank you Mr Elwood, gracias Danny and to the Stockport public,

*turn out on Saturday and show your appreciation" **(David Laidlaw, Edgeley)***

County then went on a superb run to win their remaining games, including a last day thriller at The Shay against Halifax Town, where they had to win and rely on results elsewhere going their way if they were to claim the last automatic promotion spot. Town had taken the lead against the run of play but County hit back with two late goals from Beaumont and McInerney.

Reports after the game from the home ground PA system told the thousands of travelling County supporters that their team were promoted in third place after rivals Southend United had lost at Peterborough United. The supporters and players alike were as one as they celebrated together on the pitch. Unfortunately this proved to be incorrect information and although the club had reached the play-offs for the first time in their history, the reality was it was going to be very difficult for Bergara to lift his players after their premature celebrations.

And so it proved, as a completely different County team lost both legs of the play-off against a Chesterfield side they had thrashed just two weeks earlier. After the second leg County supporters staged a good humoured pitch invasion at Edgeley Park, standing and clapping in front of the main stand in appreciation of their team's efforts in a season which would live long in the memory and which had brought hope of a new era for Stockport County.

The Stockport Express summed up the feelings of all County supporters:

A Salute to County

A thrilling season for Stockport County has ended in a little disappointment. But County fans celebrated after last week's defeat by Chesterfield in the promotion play-off second leg. They celebrated the club's best performance for 23 years. At long last Stockport folk have a team to shout about, a team that has shocked the cynics and delighted the faithful at Edgeley Park.

Bergara was quick to tell the club's supporters: *"It is obviously disappointing, but you will see that we will go up next season, and with a bloody big bang!!"*

Danny Bergara and Mark Payne

John Sainty, Danny Bergara and
Dave Higgins

Pre Season Training

Danny Bergara and Paul Jones

Stockport County Football Club 1989-90

Brett Angel

Bright St...

STOCKPORT County's newest signing made his home debut on Monday night.
Darren Hope caught the imagination of the crowd with his fast
and skillful play on the wing, and it
was his work that won County an
early penalty.
"I put him in at the deep end
and he didn't let us down," said
Danny Bergara.

...be a very good player.
Stockport's other new signing
from Stoke, Dave Ritchie, made his
mark last week with a hat-trick for
the reserves against Birmingham.
Ritchie had a tough task coming
on for the last twenty minutes
against Hereford, but he is still very
much in the running.

Darren Hope

othing less
han thrilling

...port by Andy Hobson

KPORT COUNTY 1
INGHAM 0
CKPORT County's best
on for twenty years is
ing out to be nothing less
a thrilling.
is vital home win lifted County into
nd place (if only for the night) and
a healthy four point gap between
ckport and rivals Gillingham.
county have managed to survive this season
pite their erratic form, but now the real busi-
s of promotion begins with nearly every one of
county's remaining fixtures being against pro-
ty's remaining rivals through...
And despite looking the stronger team through-
the game County kept the Edgeley Park
nd present.

Skipper Bill back?

SKIPPER Bill Williams is rar-
ing to get back into the County
team for the promotion play-
offs.
And that is despite the fact that
he should be out for another two
months with a nasty facial injury!
He had to have a metal plate
inserted in his cheek after suffering
a fracture during the Grimsby
match, and was ruled out for the
rest of the season.
But Williams has made a good
recovery and has declared himself
available to face Chesterfield.
Says assistant manager John
Sainty: "Bill wants to play and he is
definitely in the running.

"He was training with us last
week, but there could be a problem
if he get another knock on his
cheek.
"But when it comes down to it,
Bill is the only one who can say
whether he is 100 per cent or not.
And the two Stockport lads, Andy
Thorpe and Steve Bullock, did ever
so well at Halifax."
Paul Jones will miss the first leg,
but his suspension will then be over
and he will be available for selection for the return.
● BOTH Chesterfield matches will
be all-ticket, with tickets for both
games hopefully on sale at Edgeley
Park by Thursday afternoon.

The first leg at Chesterfie
Sunday will be a 12 noon ki
not 3 p.m. as reported els
4,000 tickets are expecting
County decided to make th
leg all-ticket to ensure that
fans do not miss out. Seas
holders will be given pr
but under League rules
have to pay for a ticket.
The ticket office will op
a.m. to noon on Sat
there will be no ticke
either at Saltergate or Ed
on either of the match da
● ANYONE wanting
ticket information sho
club on 480 8888.

STOCKPORT
ort

LAD HATTERS

Thorpe, Steve Bul

Page 56 - Th

COUNTY
THE UP?

Danny's boys look
promotion in the fac

KPORT
could be
ely min-
ay from a
the Third
soon.
ns on the
lifted
ack into
set up
doubtedly
biggest
e club's

vel to
turday,
e Shay
club
Third
he in
enty

...our rivals for SIX

	P	W	D	L
FOOTBALL LEAGUE DIVI...				
ETER	45	27	5	13
IMSBY	45	22	13	10
UTHEND	45	21	9	15
OCKPORT	45	20	11	14
RLISLE	45	21	8	16
DSTONE	45	21	7	1
MBRIDGE	45	20	10	1
TERBORO	45	17	17	1
FIELD	45	18	14	
COLN	45	18	14	
HORPE	45	16	15	

DIVISION FOUR

W	D	L	F	A	GD	Pts
28	5	13	83	48	+35	89
22	13	11	70	47	+23	79
22	9	15	61	48	+13	75
21	11	14	68	62	+6	74
22	7	17	77	61	+16	73
21	10	15	76	66	+10	73
19	14	13	63	50	+13	71
21	8	17	61	60	+1	71
17	17	12	59	46	+13	68
18	14	14	48	48	0	68
17	15	14	69	54	+15	66
20	6	20	52	55	-3	66
16	16	14	55	53	+2	64
17	11	18	46	48	-2	62
15	12	19	53	66	-13	57
14	14	18	45	55	-10	56
15	10	21	56	62	-6	55
15	10	21	60	73	-13	55
15	10	21	66	88	-22	55
14	9	23	53	60	-7	51
13	12	21	51	67	-16	51
12	14	20	49	69	-20	50
12	13	21	57	65	-8	49
11	10	25	48	75	-27	43

STOCKPORT County's promotion carnival swings into Halifax on Saturday ... with as many as 3,000 fans expected to make the trip! And the message for those supporters is "Get there early," as there is a limited capacity.

Automatic promotion is a real posibility, but County can thank Shay could see them finish the season as low as TENTH place.

in their difficult visit to Peterborough, and low-
victory, coupled with non-victory for Southend
scoring win for Carlisle at Maidstone, would see
County straight up.

A draw would ensure County of a play-off
place ... leaving them two matches from a great
day out at Wembley on May 28.

A brilliant 3-1 win over Chesterfield on Saturday
kept County on course for an astonishing revival
after their promotion hopes looked dead and
buried three weeks ago.

Three straight wins, with other teams falling by
the wayside, now make County one of the
favourites to go up and had fans streaming on to
the field on Saturday to hail their team's fine
season.

Arrangements...

SHEER JOY at Edgeley Park as t
suffering County fans salute a gr
cess ... and goalscoring golden b
Angell is given a hero's treatment.
carried off after the 3-1 victory
Chesterfield on Saturday.

Fans given an early warning

...ger Friday October 13th 1989

...EY PARK NEWS AND VIEWS - EDGELEY PARK NEWS AND VI

...cial minds
...overtime

...ds have been at work .
...ting to show
...ing a roaring trade with
...kly.

...more support to boost
...lins' and 'County Re-
...ll needed in all areas.
...other Keith Edwards
...0-8888.

...ady and
...to go

BANG BAN
COUNTY ON
RGET

Hereford late
to fall as qui
fire County ta
full points aga

By Andrew Hobso...

QUICK-FIRE County
Hereford standing on Sa
day - going two up after
24 minutes.

The dramatic match at Edgeley
saw three men sent-off and Cou
notch up three valuable promotion
ing points.

Hatters opened well raiding goal again
again with strikers Angell and Edwards
making the score sheet.
However, it looked like Herefo
when a Hami...

FOUR GOAL SALUTE

1990/91

Following the bitter disappointment of the previous campaign Bergara's plans for the new season were dealt a severe blow when top scorer Brett Angell was snapped up by Southend United, the team that had pipped County to the last promotion spot on that last day. Angell had claimed the League's 'Golden Boot' with 23 goals for the Hatters, and would prove difficult to replace. Nevertheless the Uruguayan set about freshening up his squad, bringing in veteran keeper Paul Cooper, youngsters Tony Barras and Lee Todd from Hartlepool United, Neil Matthews, who had scored for Halifax on that dramatic last day in May and central defenders Alan Finley from Shrewsbury Town and former Sheffield United player Paul A. Williams. Strangely Williams played almost from day one as a striker.

The new season started in unspectacular fashion with a goalless draw at The Shay, where the previous season had ended so cruelly, plus an early League Cup exit at the hands of Burnley and a defeat at Rochdale. Bergara's side, in losing just two more games before Christmas, at Northampton and Scunthorpe, had kept themselves in and around the play-off spots without ever looking too impressive.

Bergara's performance since taking charge at Edgeley Park was rewarded early in the New Year with a new improved two year contract. Having witnessed the transformation of the club since Bergara's arrival, Chairman Brendan Elwood said: *"We are delighted to have secured Danny's services on this new long-term basis. He has done an unbelievable job right through the club since he joined us, and with him at the helm, County will begin to rise through the divisions. When he was appointed I already believed that he was the best coach in the business and he has also proved to be an absolutely superb manager. He is a workaholic and we are lucky to have him. We would like him to lead us into the Third Division at the end of this season, of course. But it is not imperative as every member of the board is totally convinced that we will earn promotion under Danny sooner or later. The new contract confirms our faith in Danny, and we felt it only fair that he had his own future settled before he begins to renegotiate contracts with existing players "*

Bergara's latest signing, former England youth international Andy Kilner, who had recently returned from a spell playing in Sweden, made an immediate impact as three wins and a draw at the start of the New Year propelled the Hatters up to the top of the table. The thrashing of Halifax Town at Edgeley Park saw the winger grab his third goal in three games. A poor run of just one win in the next six games saw County drop out of the automatic promotion places, the sole win coming at Sincil Bank when another Bergara recruit, 6' 7" centre forward Kevin Francis, made his first appearance for the club.

The home draw with Scarborough saw the return of Matthews to the side. The former Halifax striker had managed just one goal to date and had hardly featured due to lack of form and injury, but he came off the bench to score both goals and with Francis struggling to make the team, it was an opportunity to stake his claim for a place alongside top scorer Paul A. Williams, the big Irishman having gone about his role of target man quietly but confidently to earn his starting place.

It was Williams who proved to be the catalyst in the superb run-in that Bergara's side had towards the end of the season, his goal against Rochdale in the thumping of Rochdale at Edgeley Park

being his 15th of the season but his last for Stockport County. After the game the big Irishman was the subject of a £250,000 bid from Second Division West Bromwich Albion who were struggling at the foot of the table, Williams' stunning goal sealing his move.

Another example of how Bergara's coaching had improved a player, the son of Nobel Peace Prize winner Betty Williams, Paul had played for four league clubs, predominately as a central defender, before joining County. Having been given a 'free' transfer for the fourth time he arrived at Edgeley Park where Bergara, who had previously worked with him at Sheffield United, successfully switched the Irishman to centre-forward. His early season goal scoring form had been interrupted by an injury that caused him to miss several games. On his return to the side however he set County on their way with the opening goal in a 3-1 win over Darlington at Edgeley Park. The likeable Irishman continued to score on a regular basis, including both goals as the club became the first team to win at Walsall's new Bescot Stadium. With transfer 'deadline' approaching 'Willow' scored the goal that was to rubber stamp a move to West Bromwich Albion.

The goal, which was voted County's 'goal of the season' came at the end of a flowing move and secured a 3-0 victory over Rochdale. With Albion struggling in the 'old' Second Division, and a striker a priority, 'Willow's' wonder strike in front of the Midland club's scouts helped to seal a club record transfer, with County receiving £250,000. Any disappointment at the sale of Williams was tempered by the size of the fee involved for a player who cost the club nothing, just 26 games ago.

As the move came on transfer deadline day, Bergara had no time to react in bringing in a replacement and although his side lost the next two games, his forward line of Francis and Matthews,

186

supported by Beaumont and Kilner, picked itself until the end of the season.

Bergara's team were to rediscover their early season goal scoring form as they won all but one of their final nine games, the only defeat coming at promotion rivals Blackpool (2-3). County notched 25 goals whilst conceding just 9, Matthews leading the way with 10.

Having won at York City on the penultimate day thanks to two Kilner goals, and knowing that rivals for the title Darlington had lost at Scunthorpe United, County faced Scunthorpe at Edgeley Park on the last day needing a win to clinch promotion for the first time in 21 years. Depending on the result at Feethams, where Darlington were playing Rochdale, a County win could see them go up as Champions. However Bergara was well aware that a defeat could see his charges miss out on an automatic promotion place on the last day for the second consecutive season.

Two first half goals, from Matthews and Francis, had calmed the nerves inside the ground but it was clear that the next goal was key, and within minutes of the restart that man Matthews headed home to ensure that the rest of the game was played in a carnival atmosphere. Finley headed home his third of the campaign from a Kilner long throw whilst Francis notched his second and the Hatters' fifth of the day to complete the rout, and at the same time ensure that Bergara's team would finish as top scorers in the Football League.

Darlington had beaten Dale to claim the Fourth Division title, but it mattered not to the County faithful or to their little Uruguayan manager who had delivered on his pre-season promise that his side would come back stronger for their experience of the previous season.

They had indeed gone up with a bloody big bang!!!!

Chairman Brendan Elwood was quick to make sure that the national press knew who it was that deserved the lion's share of the praise for County's promotion after 21 years in the Football League basement:

"We owe it all to our manager, Danny Bergara. The best thing that ever happened to this club was when Danny accepted our offer to become manager of Stockport County. We consider ourselves to be very fortunate to have him as we believe he is the best manager and coach in the business. Before Danny came to Edgeley Park, the highest position the club had reached in more than 20 years, was 82nd in The Football League. Last season he took us to the promotion play-offs and this season he has taken us all the way into the Third Division. Winning promotion on Saturday was one of the greatest moments of my life, but as far as we are concerned this is just the beginning, not the end. Our target is now to bring Second Division football to Edgeley Park within the next five years and we are confident we will reach that goal. My only worry is that bigger clubs will now realise what a brilliant manager Danny is and try to entice him away from Edgeley Park. It might sound like a pipe-dream when I say that we want to give Stockport a First Division team to support, but with a manager like Danny Bergara anything is possible"

Bergara's achievements were also noted by The Northern Football Writers Association as he stood alongside Manchester United manager Alex Ferguson and Oldham Athletic manager Joe Royle to collect a special award for his team finishing runners-up.

Pre Season

Stockport County Football Club 1990-91

Neil Matthews opens the scoring in the 5-0 win over Scunthorpe United that clinched promotion

NER WRECKS ...

GO ... U

by
in
ne
le

ennan
EXHAM 0

dy Kilner
Wrexham
in his first
Stockport

gs for Friday
re a little early
ty of some of the
can't expect a gale-
xpected County against
County Welshmen were

ne or two groans
y of some of the
can't expect a great
mment or such a
itch.

went away content
re three successive
husing about Kilner.
is full debut in spec-

quiet opening, but County moved
smartly ahead in the 19th minute.
  Payne received the ball back after
his corner had been half cleared and
this time his accurate cross found
Kilner storming into the box to
glance a header past goalkeeper

DAVID FRAIN jinks his way past Phil Hardy's challenge... his cross caused the confusion from which Andy Kilner benefited to score his second goal.

CHRIS Beaumont leads anoth... Wrexham defence — this time ... Hardy's sliding t...

CORVISION

ADVERTISER, JANUARY 16, 1991 S

A TOPPING TREA

rain and
big Paul
really on
the ball

by Stuart Brennan

MESSENGER
SPORT

essenger, Friday, February 8th, 1991

County boss
signs on for
another two
year stint...

NEW DEAL FOR
ANNY!

HANDS UP !

FOOTBALL LEA

Pos		Team
1	P	Darlington
2	P	Stockport County
3	P	Hartlepool United
4	P	Peterborough United
5		Blackpool
6		Burnley
7	P	Torquay United
8		Scunthorpe United
9		Scarborough
10		Northampton Town
11		Doncaster Rovers
12		Rochdale
13		Cardiff City
14		Lincoln City
15		Gillingham
16		Walsall
17		Hereford United
18		Chesterfield
19		Maidstone United
20		Carlisle United
21		York City
22		Halifax Town
23		Aldershot
24		Wrexham

But such is the quality
survive and prosper in the
that these two players

Dan
pat

STOCKPORT COUNTY
dan Elwood blesses the
Bergara accepted his invi
manager at Edgeley Park
  For the County chief t
"workaholic" little Ute
will steer the club into
sion within the space of
Says chairman Elw

HAVE a drink, boss!
Stockport County chairman Brendan Ellwood gets a celebration beer — whether he likes it or not — from the players who have won promotion to Division Three after 21 long years. Super County, who had to win their last match on Saturday to make sure, went up in devastating style, putting FIVE goals past rivals Scunthorpe. The team and the fans went wild. And, if you think this is a bit of an indignity for jubilant Brendan, just till you see what the players did to him next. In our EIGHT-PAGE pull-out tribute to the club in the centre of the paper. It was a terrific day for the club, the town and specially for manager Danny Bergara. What an end to the season — and what a way to celebrate National Smile week!

INSIDE: Our eight-page glory special

CURTAIN *Style*

...ESS ADVERTISER, MAY 15, 1991 S...

STOCKPORT
Sport

5 STA...
SHO...

DIVISION FOUR

	W	D	L	F	A	GD	Pts
	2	17	7	68	38	+30	83
	3	13	10	84	47	+37	82
	4	10	12	67	48	+19	82
	1	17	8	67	45	+22	80
	3	10	13	78	47	+31	79
	3	10	13	70	51	+19	79
	8	18	10	64	47	+17	72
	0	11	15	71	62	+9	71
	9	12	11	59	56	+3	69
	8	13	15	57	58	-1	67
	7	14	15	56	46	+10	65
	5	17	14	50	53	-3	62
	5	15	16	43	54	-11	60
	4	17	15	50	61	-11	59
	2	18	16	57	60	-3	54
	2	17	17	48	51	-3	53
	3	14	19	53	58	-5	53
	3	14	19	47	62	-15	53
	3	12	21	66	71	-5	51
	3	9	24	47	89	-42	48
	1	13	22	45	57	-12	46
	2	10	24	59	79	-20	46
	0	11	25	61	101	-40	41
	0	10	26	48	74	-26	40

windor...

MANAGERS AWARDED A RESPITE

ALEX Ferguson and Danny Bergara had a respite from the week's woes at the Northern Football Writers Association Managers Awards Dinner on Sunday night.

The Manchester United manager had a few minutes away from the intense pressure of League and European competitions when he picked up the Barclays Good News and Special Award.

He was given the award for last season's European success in the Cup-Winners Cup and for finishing runners-up in the Rumbelows Cup.

County manager Bergara received his special award for finishing runners-up in the Fourth Division.

Other Northern awards went to Joe Royle of Oldham Athletic, John King of Tranmere Rovers, Ron Atkinson, ex-Sheffield Wednesday, Brian Little, ex-Darlington, Alan Buckley of Grimsby Town, and Alan Murray of Hartlepool United.

Alex Ferguson and Danny Bergara with their awards.

Pensions-n...
PETER RAYNE...

ONE UP.. Neil Matthews opens th...
REPORT...
...94.

...oney.
"To some extent the two other have no way of...
...ubs who have been promoted, players who...

y gets a
n back

DAIRY...
Reddish Electro-Plating...
...rd Division

1991/92

With his side back in the third tier of English Football, Bergara strengthened his midfield by bringing in Peter Ward and Paul Wheeler, the former being a swap deal which saw Mark Payne move to Rochdale after a three year spell with the Hatters, Dale also pocketing £35,000 as part of the deal. Ward was not unknown to the County squad, the tough tackling midfielder had been involved in a post match skirmish with Hatters defender Bill Williams in the tunnel as the two sides had left the field after the Hatters' win against Rochdale on Boxing Day two seasons earlier. Bergara's first job would be to ensure there was no remaining animosity between the two.

Speaking to the press prior to the start of the new campaign: *"I believe that ultimately Stockport County will become a major Third Division force. Having said that I am quietly confident that we can do well in a higher division. You never know what happens from one day to the next in this game. In short, you can't really predict anything. However, we are aiming to do exactly what we did last season by setting ourselves a target of a certain amount of points by a set date. What I am talking about is 52 points by the end of February or the beginning of March. If we hit that target it means two things. Initially it will provide us a base to remain in the Third Division and at the same time provide a platform from which we aim to go much higher. That is why I am not talking about promotion at this stage - just setting and hitting targets.*

"While the first aim is to stabilise in the Third, we are naturally more ambitious than that and want to reach a position as high as is possible. We must tread carefully and must certainly respect the opposition. We know it is going to be harder than the Fourth

Division. In those circumstances we have got to give it our best shot and go out and try to win one game at a time. Then after that, who knows?"

Chairman Elwood had made the Uruguayan aware that funds would be available should he wish to strengthen his squad further. Bergara's response had been typical of his style of management: *"I would naturally like to try and strengthen the squad and what I am basically looking for is another striker, not only to play alongside Kevin Francis, but who can cover for the big fellow when he is either out of form or injured or whatever. But while the Chairman has pledged financial backing, I don't want to rush into anything. I do the same with the football club's money as I do my own at home, where I don't pay £50 for something that I may be able to get at possibly half that amount"*

As with the previous pre-season campaign the Hatters spent time at a south coast Army camp and were also impressive against higher division opposition, beating Second Division Port Vale comfortably with goals from Francis and Tony Barras and drawing against First Division neighbours Manchester City with goals coming from Francis and Jim Gannon.

If County supporters were happy with their side's pre-season form they were positively ecstatic with the Hatters opening performances in the Third Division. If a thrashing of Swansea City on the opening day wasn't enough (5-0), won three more and drew one of their first five fixtures. The Friday night win against Torquay United had seen them go top of the Third Division table for the first time in the club's history. The only black spot on the early season form, being a two legged defeat in the Rumbelows Cup first round against Bradford City after extra time in the second leg at Valley Parade.

Bergara's reward for his side's dynamic opening to the season was yet another improved contract offer from the board of directors, this time a five year deal:

Soar away Stockport have given their manager Danny Bergara a new and improved five year contract. It represents a package deal that could eventually make him one of the best paid bosses outside of the super league bracket. County have rewarded their Uruguayan-born boss following last season's stunning promotion success and rise to Third Division pace-setters this term.

County Chairman Brendan Elwood said: "We are happy to make Danny this offer..even happier that he has accepted it. In fact he has told me there are only two clubs he would leave us for, Liverpool or Real Madrid. Even though his current deal runs to the end of 1993, we wanted to secure his services in case anyone else came in for him. Together we have formed an excellent working relationship and want that to continue as we attempt to take this club to the very top"

Bergara stated at the time: *"I am delighted at the offer and now all I want to do is get on with the job of making Stockport even more successful"*

The first blip in the season came as Chester City won comfortably at Edgeley Park in October (4-0). Around the corner at local club Cheadle Town Brazilian World Cup star Jairzinho was holding a 'soccer school'. He had been invited over to Stockport by the club Chairman Chris Davies whilst the amateur side had played in Brazil during the previous summer on one of their regular international tours.

Chris also worked for the County 'lottery' department and had told Bergara about the former Brazil international being in town. Naturally the Uruguayan had wanted to meet up with his fellow South American and had asked Chris to bring him to the Chester game. Unfortunately after the game the 'post match' inquisition had lasted so long that Jairzinho had retired to his hotel without meeting Bergara.

Chris Davies takes up the story:

It was Monday afternoon and Danny was in his office after taking a training session at William Scholes playing fields in Gatley. No doubt the players were still recovering after an inquest into such a heavy home defeat on the previous Friday night.

I knocked on the door of Danny's office. I was about to explain why I hadn't introduced Brazilian legend Jairzinho to Danny after Friday's game. I was unsure as to what mood Danny would be in. Would he be understanding or would he vent his fury at missing out on meeting the superstar?.

'Come in' came the voice from within. I walked in and stood in front of Danny's desk, an embarrassed look on my face.

Danny looked up, and before he even said a word I feared the worst. If looks could kill. 'Where was Jairzinho?' barked Danny.

I took my time to reply 'He was cold and wanted to go back to the hotel' I blurted.

Those cold eyes stared 'Chris you should have brought him down into my office'

I had already thought of the quick way out 'He wants to come down and watch a training session tomorrow morning'.

'Okay' grunted Danny.

Tuesday morning was grey, wet, windy and cold. It was 10:30 AM and Jairzinho trudged across puddles and mud to the touchline to see Danny and the players going through their drills. John Sainty, the County assistant manager, greeted Jairzinho with a warm handshake. 'Just give him a few minutes, Danny will be with you'

Jairzinho watched from the sidelines as Danny shouted his orders to the players. The cold October wind blew unrelentingly across the wide open fields. Sainty shouted to Danny trying to get his attention. Danny ignored him and continued to concentrate on the training session. Half an hour went by, Jairzinho was shivering, he wasn't used to the cold. Rio de Janeiro on a cold day wouldn't budge below 60°. This felt like being in the Arctic Circle.

'Please can we go' asked Jairzinho. I looked again at Sainty, who tried again to get Danny's attention, to no avail. Once Danny had his players' attention and he was out on the training field nothing else mattered.

It was back to the car for Jairzinho and the warmth of the hotel. Danny never got to meet Jairzinho and relations between Danny and I were strained for some six months afterwards.

Having agreed a new contract, Bergara was to face the toughest spell yet of his reign at Edgeley Park as his side won just four games from twelve in the run-in to the New Year. The Hatters also suffered a heavy first round loss in the Autoglass Trophy at Brunton Park against a Carlisle United side struggling at the bottom of the Fourth Division. Bergara had plucked striker Andy

Preece from Wrexham's reserve side, the striker scoring on his full debut at Swansea but failing to stop his side losing on their travels again as County dropped to sixth in the table.

A superb run in January saw Bergara's side win three and draw one of their four league games and also progress in the Autoglass Trophy with wins over York City and Carlisle United. Francis (6), Gannon (5) and Preece (3) all finding their shooting boots.

The Hatters would continue their assault on both the promotion places and the Autoglass Trophy throughout February and March as they lost just four of thirteen league games, winning against both Hartlepool United and Crewe Alexandra in the Autoglass Trophy to set up a Northern 'Final' against Burnley which would determine if Stockport County could reach Wembley for the first time in the club's history.

Sitting second in the Third Division, an automatic promotion spot, going into April, there were the first signs of nervousness in Bergara's side as they lost at Torquay United. A return to form saw them follow this up with a win at Turf Moor against Burnley in the first leg of the Autoglass Trophy and a home win in the league against Exeter City, midfielder Gannon notching his second hat trick of the season. The icing on the cake coming five days later as goals from Francis and Gannon clinched Bergara and his team a first ever trip to Wembley Stadium to play Stoke City in the Autoglass Trophy Final.

Unfortunately the euphoria of the forthcoming trip to the Capital appeared to hinder the Hatters' progress in the promotion race and, following successive goalless draws against Bury and Stoke City and a defeat at Bradford City, they slipped out of the automatic promotion spots.

However Bergara took his County team into the last game of the season against Birmingham City at Edgeley Park knowing that in their first season back in the Third Division they were at least in the play-offs, a superb feat when considering where the club had been when he took over two seasons earlier.

Having beaten Birmingham City thanks to goals from Gannon and Francis, County would play Stoke City for a place in the play-off final at Wembley. Peter Ward's superb free kick won a tense first leg at Edgeley Park. A Chris Beaumont effort at the Victoria Ground would be enough to see the Hatters earn their second trip to Wembley, where they would play Peterborough United.

Having never played at Wembley in their history, Stockport County would grace the National Stadium with their presence twice in a matter of days.

Upon their historic feat Bergara was quick to praise his 'team of lions':

"They were absolutely fantastic, I'm proud of my team they have worked tremendously hard. If someone had told me 30 years ago when I left my native country Uruguay that I would lead an English team out at Wembley twice in just over a week I would have said they were mad. But this team of mine, with hearts of lions, have done it for me. We may be a small club but we have shown everyone we have what it takes. We have now played 59 games and there are still two more to go. But we are playing better now than all season and remain as strong as ever. I have told my players that they have won nothing yet and now we are going away to prepare for that last assault"

History would show that both games were lost but Danny Bergara had written his name in the football record books as the first ever South American to lead an English Football League team out in a Cup Final at the National Stadium when the Hatters faced Stoke City on 16th May 1992.

Francis had what appeared to be a good goal struck off with the game goalless, whilst Mark Stein, looking suspiciously offside, was allowed to finish clinically to give the Staffordshire side the trophy.

As if to rub salt in his wounds, a week later Bergara again saw his side lose to a questionable goal against Peterborough United, Ken Charlery's first goal being allowed to stand even though it didn't appear to have crossed the line. Francis then had a goal incorrectly disallowed for 'offside'. Charlery adding his second in injury time after Francis had eventually levelled the scores moments earlier.

After the match Bergara called for video evidence to be used to help match officials make accurate decisions:

"It's a crime that you slog your guts out for 61 games in a season and then lose it all on two bad decisions. Something has got to be done"

Television replays showed Peterborough's opening goal and Francis' disallowed effort clearly showed he had a point. Charlery's 51st minute header which rebounded off the underside of the bar appeared to bounce on the line before David Frain hooked it clear. Francis looking onside when he headed home fifteen minutes later.

Nevertheless the little Uruguayan was certainly making his mark, not just in Stockport, but in English football in general. Prior to the end of the season, acclaimed journalist Paul Hince, a former player with Manchester City amongst other clubs, wrote in his weekly column, regarding the fact that Alex Ferguson would more than likely win the 'Manager of the Year' accolade:

There is another local manager who deserves to give Ferguson a run for his money in the Manager of the Year stakes - and his team are not even in the top two divisions. There was a lot of behind-the-hand sniggering when little Stockport County decided to put their future in the hands of the volatile little Uruguayan Danny Bergara three years ago last month. Most of the Stockport County supporters had probably never heard of Bergara. The joke going around at the time was that County had appointed an Irish manager, Danny Begorrah. Well no-one is sniggering now. For this bundle of nervous energy, who needs a packet of Rothmans to get him through a match, has performed what can only be described as a modern miracle in his period of stewardship at Edgeley Park.

Last season a Stockport team, which in turns is inspired, petrified and tickled pink by the little man with the funny accent, at last made soccer sit up and take notice by climbing out of the Fourth Division where they had wallowed for over 20 years.

That in itself was testament to Bergara's passion and commitment to a game that he cheerfully admits dominates his life 24 hours a day. But if lifting County out of the bargain basement was a monumental feat, what he has created since has been well-nigh unbelievable. If the County players and their manager can keep a reign on their nerves over the next month, the unthinkable could become a reality ..... Stockport County in the Second Division and only one step away from the promised land of the Premier League.

Whatever happens between now and the beginning of May, Bergara's side will surely qualify for the end of season play-offs. Given the rub of the green which he deserves, the highly likeable Bergara will have taken a club going nowhere OUT of the Fourth Division, OUT of the Third Division and INTO the Second Division in successive seasons. And if that should happen, perhaps a special medal should be struck for Danny Bergara this summer. Manager of the Year? Manager of the Decade more like!!

Bergara's achievements were acknowledged with 'The Football Writers Association (North)'Special' Award', Barclays 'Good News' Award and The Variety Club of Great Britain 'North-West Sportsman of the Year' Award.

Wembley is a dreadful experience.
flag-waving amateur officials, when so much is at

PETERBROUGH 2, COUNTY 1

But County soared forward searching for a late winner and were hit by a classic sucker punch. Freece dallied a little too long in midfield, and was robbed by Marcus Ebdon. His immediate kick had over the County defence found Charlery in plenty of space.

In the heat and pressure of Wembley, with tired legs from a tough game, nine times out of ten the Peterborough striker would have blazed it high and wide. He didn't.

He struck a tremendous shot which gave goalkeeper Neil Edwards no chance, and the County fans choked on their victory chants in disbelief.

Much of the dejection at the end of the game was personal disappointment — too many County players did not get their game right on the day, players who have performed consistently well all season.

The game had begun ominously for County as the defence struggled to cope with the liveliness of wide men Bobby Barnes and Worrell Sterling. But with Bill Williams and Jim Gannon in good nick, they soon tightened up and as the first half drew to a close were beginning to get on top. The only problem was that, as in the Autoglass Trophy final the week before, they had problems getting their set pieces right.

...Kevin Francis on his equalising goal...
...the winner.

for repl...

so much of ... don't know comment... decisions are decisions
destroyed our and effort of... games has ... you cannot ... linesmen no ... a ... an could see ... d the line in

County · Salute to County · Salute to County

DAY OF PRIDE

by Stuart Brennan

THE pride of Stockport remained intact at Wembley on Saturday as County put on a final show worthy of the stadium's tradition.

If they could only have tucked away one of the chances they created in an exciting and enterprising first half, they could have put the first silver in the newly made Edgeley Park trophy cabinet.

It was not to be and Stoke hit back in the second half to score a winning goal.

The Autoglass Trophy clash had been billed as a "friendly final" but the occasion of the play-off semi-finals being on the same week put paid to that idea.

Twice in the previous six days the two teams had met and in two ill...

Turn to Page 43

Football League Play-Offs 1991-92

Sunday, 10 May 1992

| Stockport County | 1-0 | Stoke City |

Monday, 11 May 1992

| Peterborough United | 2-2 | Huddersfield Town |

Wednesday, 13 May 1992

| Stoke City | 1-1 | Stockport County |

Thursday, 14 May 1992

| Huddersfield Town | 1-2 | Peterborough United |

Sunday, 24 May 1992 - Wembley Stadium

| Peterborough United | 2-1 | Stockport County |

WILLIAM...

OSS SHOULD BE

...rrived from ...ld have im... h he would ...ort County. ...on given to ...ly' image. ...and abu... ...5th man... ...ly from ...the pre...
...ittle to ...rrived

squad. His first full season County's first ever play-off County lost out to Chesterfield months later, Danny become hero by guiding the Club into Division as runners-up.

When the bubbly Uruguay team out to Wembley twice year, the heckling of 1989 was tant memory and was replaced the lovable County boss to be Whilst this may sound a little it does reveal the level of respe by Mr. Bergara in his initial

FOOTBALL LEAG

Pos	Team
1	P Brentford
2	P Birmingham City
3	Huddersfield Town
4	Stoke City
5	Stockport County
6	P Peterborough United
7	West Bromwich Albion
8	AFC Bournemouth
9	Fulham
10	Leyton Orient
11	Hartlepool United
12	Reading
13	Bolton Wanderers
14	Hull City
15	Wigan Athletic
16	Bradford City
17	Preston North End
18	Chester City
19	Swansea City
20	Exeter City
21	R Bury
22	R Shrewsbury Town
23	R Torquay United
24	R Darlington

Salute to C...

Edgeley

by Stuart Brennan

STOCKPORT has its very own twin towers. Kevin Francis and Jim Gannon are two of the biggest reasons County have sent the town Wembley-crazy — ...

tremendous character to and get on with his game. As a consequence he essential part of the team in midfield, tight and when he plays in the defence.

Gannon showed temperament when he to take penalties after season falls even from the has tucked his kicks penalties among ...

WEM-RE

BERGAR...

TED! SAY FANS

WRITTEN BY...

DESIRABLE

As if that success was not enough - County are at Wembley again and in the play-offs, making Danny Bergara the most successful manager in County's long history and one would suspect making him a rather desirable property.

It is Danny's morals and principles that have laid the foundations for success. There are no crazy wages at Edgeley Park and players have to fight hard for their money as well as their place. Danny is a disciplinarian, who demands that the ba...

DIVISION THREE

	D	L	F	A	GD	Pts
	7	14	81	55	+26	82
	12	11	69	52	+17	81
	12	12	59	38	+21	78
	14	11	69	49	+20	77
	10	14	75	51	+24	76
	14	12	65	58	+7	74
	14	13	64	49	+15	71
	11	15	52	48	+4	71
	13	14	57	53	+4	70
	11	17	62	52	+10	65
	11	17	57	57	0	65
	13	17	59	62	-3	61
	17	15	57	56	+1	59
	11	19	54	54	0	59
	14	17	58	64	-6	59
	19	14	62	61	+1	58
	12	19	61	72	-11	57
	14	18	56	59	-3	56
	14	18	55	65	-10	56
	11	21	57	80	-23	53
	12	21	55	74	-19	51
	11	23	53	68	-15	47
	8	25	42	68	-26	47
	7	29	56	90	-34	37

STOCKPORT COUNTY
AUTOGLASS TROPHY SPECIAL

34 TODAY Saturday May 16 1992

BERGARA EYES GLO...

Danny's

...oys

...gh

...ig

...OUNTY heading
... their Barmy A...
...pace of nine days
...laughed at the thou...
...rise above Division
...rank as one of the
...nty
...ay.

Report

...keep their atten...
...on the most imp...
...in the club's his...
..."If it came do...
...we'd give up the...
...Free...

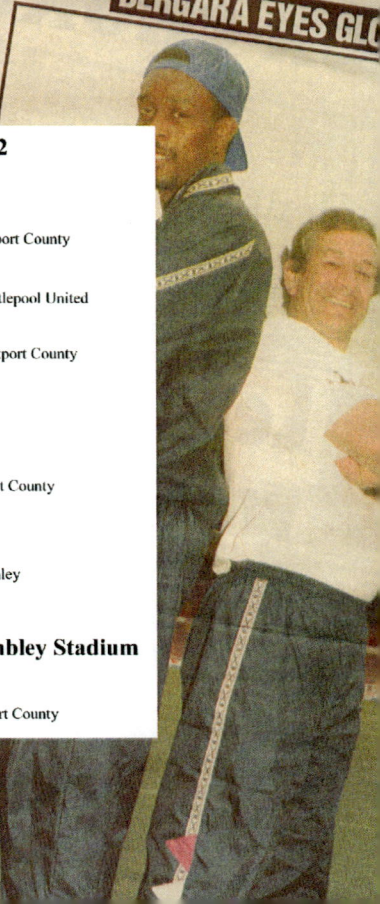

Autoglass Trophy 1991-92

14 January Carlisle United 1 – 3 Stockport County

4 February Stockport County 3 – 0 Hartlepool United

17 March Crewe Alexandra 1 – 2 Stockport County

Northern Area final

7 April 1992

Burnley 0 – 1 Stockport County

15 April 1992

Stockport County (3) 2 – 1 (1) Burnley

16 May 1992 Final - Wembley Stadium

Stoke City 1–0 Stockport County

Sport

...ES

...I FFFFFFF!

**ONE ...
GO...
SA...**

BRAM...
MOAT H...
For further
Information
See Inside for
Details

...evidence that
...signers... arrived that...

...sw, and
...believe in ourselves
...to do it."

Wealthy

...e in the newly-con-
First Division next
...uld be just reward
...improbable chair-
...ger partnership
...County's come-
...wealthy property
...from Sheffield
...rmer Uruguayan
...national from

Pre Season Training

Stockport County Football Club 1991-92

Danny Bergara meets Bobby Moore

Danny Bergara and Brendan Elwood

Alex Ferguson, Danny Bergara and Joe Royle

Stockport County meet the Mayor

Stockport County at Wembley 1992

1992/93

After the heartbreak of the previous campaign had subsided, Bergara set about rebuilding his team's confidence for another assault on promotion to the newly named First Division, so called due to the formation of the Premier League. Although he was frustrated in his attempts to bring in additional strikers and defenders to his squad, his County side once again enjoyed a healthy pre-season culminating in a 4-2 win over Premier League side Oldham Athletic at Edgeley Park.

An unbeaten first month saw County sitting comfortably in the table with the early pace-setters and also through to the second round of the League Cup, Chris Beaumont and Jim Carstairs helping County to become the first visitors to win at Chester City's new home, The Deva Stadium, setting up a tie with Brian Clough's First Division Nottingham Forest.

Carstairs, a former Arsenal youth team player, had featured mainly in his preferred left back role since signing for the club, but had lost his place due to the good form of Lee Todd. With Peter Ward struggling due to a knee injury, Bergara had moved Carstairs up to midfield for the two legged tie against Chester to give Ward a rest. Having played well in both games and scored a superb winning goal he had given his manager food for thought: *"With Jim playing so well I feel I can do without Ward for a time - at the moment his knee injury means he can grit his teeth and play every other game, I am wondering whether to let Ward have an operation and get the problem cleared up for good"*

In the build up to the Forest game County's three-pronged strike force of Beaumont, Kevin Francis and Johnny Muir had bagged in all three games, Francis and Beaumont each grabbing four, Muir helping himself to three. The two legged Cup tie against Forest earned the Hatters great praise from all that saw the games, but ultimately the First Division outfit proved too good for Bergara's team, winning both games by the odd goal to triumph 5-3 on aggregate.

Once again Bergara had seen his team perform well against higher placed opposition and received great acclaim in doing so, Brian Clough being quoted as saying: *"Stockport not only impressed me as a side that work extremely hard, they like to play football too"*

A mixed bag of results in the League before Christmas kept the Hatters in and around the play-offs, whilst wins against Chesterfield and Chester City saw them comfortably through the group stage of the Autoglass Trophy, recalled Andy Preece back amongst the goals with ten on his return to action.

Early in the New Year, with County having dropped to tenth in the table, there was speculation that Bergara was being lined up for the vacant manager's job at First Division Sunderland.

The Daily Mail reported:

Danny Bergara has emerged as a shock contender for the vacant job at Sunderland. The colourful Uruguayan has joined a list of managers who could take over from Malcolm Crosby. Bergara, once briefly manager of Sheffield United, is rated as one of the most innovative men in the game. The Stockport boss has seen his side sink out of the promotion race and after more than three years at Edgeley Park, could be tempted by Sunderland.

Whilst local paper The Northern Echo reported:

Stockport boss Danny Bergara is a surprise candidate for the vacant position at Sunderland following Malcolm Crosby's sacking on Monday. Roker chief Bob Murray has been eyeing managers like Steve Coppell and Dave Bassett but neither are likely to be released by their clubs, and a faction on the Sunderland board regard Uruguayan Bergara as a more realistic target. Bergara who once coached Middlesbrough, has earned praise and managerial awards for his work at Stockport in the last three and a half years.

Whether there was an official approach from the Wearside club is not certain, but Bergara certainly didn't let the speculation affect his own performance. His side were to lose just one of ten League games and also won through to the Northern Final of the Autoglass Trophy. Bergara picking up the 'Manager of the Month' award for January along the way. He had reinforced his side by bringing back Paul A. Williams from West Bromwich Albion for a fraction of the £250,000 he had sold him for. Williams, who had endured a torrid time in the Midlands, scored the second goal of his second spell at Edgeley Park in a 5-1 drubbing of the Baggies at Edgeley Park and made sure the travelling supporters knew how much he enjoyed his strike.

The win against the Baggies took Bergara and his side to within a point of the 52 points target he had set his team before a ball was kicked, and with seventeen games remaining County were in a better position than they had been at the same stage last time out.

March was to be a big month for Bergara and his team. They were to lose the first leg of the Autoglass Northern Final at Springfield Park 2-1 against Wigan Athletic, but then went on a three game winning streak beating Hartlepool at Edgeley Park and winning at Preston North End and Plymouth. New signings Sean Connelly and Peter Duffield both made their debuts at Deepdale. Duffield had arrived on loan from Sheffield United only hours before the game at Deepdale, but that hadn't stopped him grabbing two goals. For the win at Home Park a week later Duffield had been joined by Preston North End players Martin James and Mike Flynn. Winger James had been frozen out by new Deepdale boss John Beck, Bergara snapping him up for £50,000, whilst defender Flynn joined the Hatters for a club record fee of £125,000. Both James and Flynn started on the bench at Home Park, with Flynn playing his part in the win against Plymouth Argyle as his long throw led to Francis levelling the match at 3-3. The big striker would later claim his hat trick with the winner.

Having fallen behind in the race for an automatic promotion place, a poor run of results in April and May almost cost Bergara's side a place in the play-offs too, the only respite coming with a second leg win against Wigan Athletic in the Autoglass Trophy at Edgeley Park as goals from Ward and Francis claimed a third Wembley appearance for the Hatters in a year.

With three League games to play County needed at least four points to guarantee themselves a play-off spot and travelled to Hull City having not won in six attempts since the win at Plymouth. David Miller, with his first of the season and Jim Gannon, with his twelfth, gave Bergara the first three of his target. A drab goalless draw at home to Bournemouth was enough to claim the last play-off spot on goal difference from Leyton Orient, before a last day defeat at Huddersfield Town.

The poor run of form towards the end of the season proved to be the undoing of the Hatters in the play-off semi-final as they struggled to raise their game against a Port Vale side that had finished seventeen points ahead of them in the final table. County were further hindered by the fact that 38 goal striker Francis was banned from both legs, Gannon's goal in the home leg being the only reward as the Potteries outfit won 2-1 on aggregate.

Vale would also be the opposition in the Autoglass Final at Wembley where Bergara was able to call on Francis after his ban, but was unable to use the cup-tied Flynn, by now a permanent fixture in defence. A slow start from the Hatters would see them two goals down early on in the first half.

Backed by a tremendous following from Stockport, County were cheered forward from the start of the second half as 'Danny Bergara's Blue & White Army' was chanted throughout the half, indeed Francis' 65th minute headed goal was accredited to the County supporters by the SKY TV commentators. Unfortunately there wasn't to be another goal despite the supporters and players best efforts and Vale hung on to inflict another Wembley heartache on the little Uruguayan and his team.

Later Bergara would tell the press: *"We are close to what we want to achieve so there will be no big changes. I have to be fair to the players here. Last year I gave them all another chance after coming so close and they did really well to almost get us there again. But I can't keep giving them chances, even though there is not one player at this club I could criticise for lack of effort. The hard truth is I will have to make decisions about some people who are perhaps not quite good enough to get us where we want to go. But for now we have to forget about Wembley and the play-offs and look forward to next season"*

After the season had ended Bergara and his wife Jan had to delay a planned trip to Uruguay after they were invited to dine at 10 Downing Street with the Prime Minister John Major. The irrepressible little Uruguayan was asked to dine with Mr & Mrs Major and special guest The Princess Royal, Princess Anne, and her husband Commander Tim Laurence to mark the State visit of the President of Uruguay Luis Alberto Lacalle.

Bergara had been invited as a mark of respect for his achievements since his arrival in England and was rightfully very proud of his invitation: *"Everything was arranged for myself and my wife to fly back to Uruguay, but once the invitation came I managed to rearrange our holiday. It's very nice to have a little bit of recognition, and it's a great honour for the club as well as myself"*

Jan Bergara: *A call was put through to Dan's office with the receptionist telling Dan that Downing Street were on the line, he thought it was a 'wind-up' and promptly put the phone down. Luckily they rang back!!*

WEMBLEY (AT A C

...again

COUNTY Chairman Brendan Elwood was cock-a-hoop after County clinched their third Wembley appearance in two years.

"It's like an explosion. There was a lull before the game when nobody was talking about Wembley but now we're there it's like a volcano has gone off.

"We took 15,000 last year, this time I think it will be over 20,000. It will suddenly dawn on people that we are there again.

A good crowd for the Autoglass Final could earn the club a figure in the region of £300,000 plus a number of other achievement-related deal with the club's major sponsors, Frederic Robinson Ltd, has already doubled the amount which the company channel

nan
ROM 1
the world
Edgeley

big Paul
arvellous
County

AUTOGLASS TROPHY FINAL

t C 1 Port Vale 2

FOOTBALL LEA

Pos		Team
1	P	Stoke City
2	P	Bolton Wanderers
3		Port Vale
4	P	West Bromwich Albion
5		Swansea City
6		**Stockport County**
7		Leyton Orient
8		Reading
9		Brighton & Hove Albion
10		Bradford City
11		Rotherham United
12		Fulham
13		Burnley
14		Plymouth Argyle
15		Huddersfield Town
16		Hartlepool United
17		AFC Bournemouth
18		Blackpool
19		Exeter City
20		Hull City
21	R	Preston North End
22	R	Mansfield Town
23	R	Wigan Athletic
24	R	Chester City

Football League Play-Offs 1992-93

Sunday, 16 May 1993

Stockport County	1-1	Port Vale
Swansea City	2-1	West Bromwich Albion

Wednesday, 19 May 1993

Port Vale	1-0	Stockport County
West Bromwich Albion	2-0	Swansea City

ACTION MAN. . . County's Kevin Francis causes trouble for Port Vale

County drea

in confett

again left

OMEBA... FINAL SAL...

... February 3, 1993

...ss Sport

...nty battlers
nit boiling poin...

DIVISION TWO

	W	D	L	F	A	GD	Pts
	27	12	7	73	34	+39	93
	27	9	10	80	41	+39	90
	26	11	9	79	44	+35	89
	25	10	11	88	54	+34	85
	20	13	13	65	47	+18	73
	19	15	12	81	57	+24	72
	21	9	16	69	53	+16	72
	18	15	13	66	51	+15	69
	20	9	17	63	59	+4	69
	18	14	14	69	67	+2	68
	17	14	15	60	60	0	65
	16	17	13	57	55	+2	65
	15	16	15	57	59	-2	61
	16	12	18	59	64	-5	60
	17	9	20	54	61	-7	60
	14	12	20	42	60	-18	54
	12	17	17	45	52	-7	53
	12	15	19	63	75	-12	51
	11	17	18	54	69	-15	50
	13	11	22	46	69	-23	50
	13	8	25	65	94	-29	47
	11	11	24	52	80	-28	44
	10	11	25	43	72	-29	41
	8	5	33	49	102	-53	29

Autoglass Trophy 1992-93

12 Jan Stockport County 1 – 0 Hartlepool United

2 Feb Bradford City 3 – 4 Stockport County

23 Feb Stockport County 2 – 1 Chesterfield

Northern Area final
16 March 1993

Wigan Athletic   2 – 1   Stockport County

20 April 1993

Stockport County   (3) 2 – 0 (2)   Wigan Athletic

26 May 1993 Final - Wembley Stadium

Port Vale   2 – 1   Stockport County

...LF SAL...
...rday, 29th May,
...30am - 5pm
...DAY ONL...

...Deliveries:...

tribute Danny

DANNY Bergara has bee
news for Stockport Cour
now Football League s...
Barclays Bank have co
that he is Good News
game.
County's dedicated man
one of the annual award...

BURNLEY 1 COUNTY 1

BURNLEY is a pretty unpleasant place for football teams and their fans to visit writes Stuart Brennan.

So it was to County's great credit that they took on a fired-up Burnley side and their large and noisy support and battled away for a point.

And they were helped through a bad-tempered and frantic match by the magnificent backing of their own fans, an estimated 3,000 of them making the journey.

Dace Danny Bergara's men had gone bound to a Mike Conroy header early in the second half and were subjected to severe pressure and the howling abuse of the home fans, you would not have given them much of a hope.

But they hit back and in the end were perhaps a little regretful that they had not won the match.

Most of the County chances came early in the match, when they made it plain that they had gone to Turf Moor aiming for nothing less than three points.

Chris Beaumont was the main architect. His cross found Kevin Francis unmarked but his first-time volley lobbed a foot over the bar.

Then Beaumont went clear himself from Andy Preece's defence splitting pass and rounded goalkeeper Marlon Beresford only to find full back Ian Measham getting back to clear for a corner.

From that corner Bill Williams' header fell for Preece, but Beresford threw himself in the way of his close-range effort for a fine save.

Burnley started to hit back and Mike Conroy showed his aerial ability, beating Dave Miller to Joe Jakub's cross and nipping the County crossbar with his header.

But Beaumont was away again two minutes later as Miller hooked the ball forward and the County man took advantage of Burnley's amateurish attempt to play an offside trap. He went clear, and with Francis unmarked to his left, slipped the ball past Beresford and beyond the far post.

Francis was a handful, but made none of an impression defending from set-pieces, including a remarkable back-headed goal-line clearance from a Steve Davis effort.

It seemed County would regret missing those chances as, in the 48th minute, Burnley moved ahead. Measham tore apart the County left flank and crossed to the far post where Conroy planted a header
back across... and County were fighting to survive.

David Miller was booked for a body-check on Louis Donowa and Bill Williams' attempts to hack the ball out from under the obstructing legs of Adrian Heath led to a nasty mix-up which earned both players a talking-to.

The niggles continued and Francis was booked for an off-the-ball incident which I certainly did not see and which was also behind the referee, Mr. Cruikshanks turned to see John Pender lying on the ground heard the partisan crowd baying and decided to book Francis, presumably just in case he had done something wrong.

But tempers cooled and County scored at a vital time. Jim Gannon took a free kick from halfway, Francis nodded the ball down and Beaumont took it on his thigh, side-stepped to make a foot of space and hit a low, hard left-foot shot. Beresford seemed to have dropped on the ball, but it squirmed under his body and rolled over the line.

The game had been eventful but it reached a frantic climax when Edwards tipped a scorching Conroy shot over the bar and at the other end Francis and Preece desperately tried to force the ball over the line by an unlaughty scramble but Beresford grabbed it.

There was still time for Francis to blast another chance wide, but the draw was a fair result and pleased manager Danny Bergara.

"It was a pretty good game for the spectators and could have gone either way and, in all fairness I thought we had one or two more chances than Burnley did.

"I was very pleased with the players' approach and attitude because it was not easy to go to Burnley at the best of times, and especially not when they are on a good run.

"Out there, they are real men, out there, brave, real men full of hard work...

CHRIS BEAUMONT – his goal earned County a vital point.

'Great Orme' Mersey be...

LACROSSE Good...

1993/94

As the club came to terms with another heartbreaking end to the previous campaign, Bergara and his backroom staff, John Sainty, Dave Jones, Rodger Wylde and John Bishop all had to work their magic during another hard pre-season. As promised Bergara was going to give his players their chance and hadn't added to the squad apart from keeper Ian Ironside who had joined from Middlesbrough.

Bergara was named 'Manager of the Month' after a blistering start to the new campaign when his side remained unbeaten in the League with three wins and a draw, including a hammering of pre-season favourites Bradford City (4-1) at Edgeley Park. Strangely, considering his success over the last four seasons, this was only the second time Bergara ever won the monthly accolade, although he was more concentrated on the job ahead:

"Obviously it's very nice to get the award because it compensates for the efforts of the players, directors, staff and everyone at the club. I take the criticism when we don't do well so I suppose I get the praise when we do. We have won the award because of the good start, so it won't be a bad thing if we get more awards. There are 41 games to go and we've got to keep winning, but this year I want 52 points by the beginning of February rather than March"

Twin strikers Andy Preece (5) and Kevin Francis (5) had been joined in the early top scorers list by Darren Ryan who had forced his way into the team after a good pre-season. The winger had grabbed three goals in his opening seven games. The following two months saw the Hatters continue their superb form, winning seven of ten League games played, losing only at Hartlepool

United, meaning Bergara's boys sat proudly at the top of the table as they went into November.

The run-in to the New Year saw County lose ground on the automatic promotion places as they lost three games, crucially against Reading and Plymouth Argyle who would become the top two at Christmas. However the Hatters did win three games in the Autoglass Trophy against Wigan Athletic, Bury and Rochdale and won both their FA Cup games, against Rotherham United and Halifax Town, to set up a meeting with Premier League outfit Queens Park Rangers at Edgeley Park.

A win against Barnet and a draw at Brentford nicely set up Bergara's side for their cup clash with a Rangers side that had started the season well and were chasing a European place. The R's featured the likes of Ray Wilkins, Trevor Sinclair and Les Ferdinand in their line-up.

The game itself is one of the best remembered during Bergara's time at Edgeley Park. Not just for the eventual victory, but for the way his side won. The national newspapers had a field day:

Giant Killer - Rangers are flattened by 6' 7" Francis and his Stockport battlers

Kevin Francis at 6' 7" the tallest player in professional football, helped chop the FA Cup legs from under QPR. Francis and his Stockport pals won 2-1 and Rangers' star player Ray Wilkins headed back to London with a parting shot "Next time I want my gutters fixed, I will send for him". Francis was mobbed by hundreds of youngsters after his Second Division workaholics had shamed the Premiership side.

Rangers received a blast from their manager Gerry Francis "If you want to win anything you have to fight, they did, we didn't, we let everyone down". Nobody fought harder than young Francis who, despite a heavy cold, walked away with the man-of-the-match champagne after scoring Stockport's equaliser and intimidating them for most of the afternoon.

The £60,000 signing from Derby County three years ago said "We fancied our chances. Not bad for a Derby reject. I don't like champagne to be honest I will just stick it in the rack. There was some controversy about my goal, Tony Barras was lying injured in their penalty area, but the referee must have decided he wasn't interfering with play"

Rangers were furious at referee John Key's decision. Wilkins said "It was offside. Our players knew the injured man was there so we pushed up". Gerry Francis said "The referee told us before the game that if there was a head injury or clash he would stop the game immediately. We were waiting for him to blow up"

Rangers scored first through Simon Barker, Francis equalised and Andy Preece volleyed the late winner.

High and Mighty - Stockport battlers walk tall to humble Rangers

Striker Kevin Francis, a 6' 7" beanpole who looks like he should be slam dunking into a basketball net, took several giant leaps into FA Cup history and controversy yesterday, as the Premiership men of Queens Park Rangers were dumped out. Rangers could just not hold on to him. His leggy unpredictable work on the ground bemused the Rangers defenders, who were clearly disadvantaged in the air, and his goal, equalising Rangers classic strike from Simon Barker, brought vehement protests from Rangers.

You could understand their fury as Yorkshire referee John Key failed to blow his whistle in the 39th minute. Stockport's Tony Barras was lying injured in the Rangers' penalty area, the ball was in midfield and, as Mr Key ran towards the injured player he seemed to indicate that he was about to stop play. Too late Mike Wallace had already played the ball forward to Francis. Rangers appeared to have stopped playing and the big man controlled the ball and hit it cleanly passed Tony Roberts, the goalkeeper who had come on after just 12 minutes of this tie, when Jan Stejskal injured his groin. All the time Barras was still on the turf and, although he was clearly hurt and taking no part in the move, his mere presence made him a distraction and the referee was clearly caught out.

Rangers' skipper Wilkins protested, chasing the referee to the half way line. Two minutes later, still angry, he was booked. At the interval Les Ferdinand took up the argument and a policeman went on to the pitch to escort Mr Key to the sanctuary of the dressing room. He may however, have felt like telling Rangers something about playing to the whistle. Until that point Rangers were sitting on a 19th minute lead with a goal that was a demonstration of finishing of the highest class, Ferdinand rose elegantly to knock down Clive Wilson's cross as Barker pulled away from his marker and hammered a low volley into the bottom corner of the net.

Maybe Francis' goal rocked the Londoners' concentration. Francis' goal certainly galvanised Stockport. They attacked in swarms, with Francis sending surges of panic through Darren Peacock and his beleaguered defence every time they moved forward. Stockport were a credit to their manager Danny Bergara, the South American football believer who has transformed this little club on the edge of Manchester.

Francis leaped to meet a Chris Beaumont corner and no-one could go with him. Roberts made a brave one-handed save from Barras, but Peacock saved him in the next wave when he headed off the line from Barras. Surely Stockport would score and they did after 74 minutes when Peacock, in desperation fouled Francis. Peter Ward curled the free kick towards Andy Preece whose volley left Roberts without the semblance of a chance.

Rangers were out, they could not match the fire of the Second Division side who were mobbed by hundreds of delighted youngsters at the end.

Preece adds polish as Stockport's gems fashion upset - Bergara sees beliefs vindicated

Danny Bergara, born in Uruguay, played in Spain, managing in england, wants respect. For his beliefs, his players, his team; in any order. At Edgeley Park on Saturday, with victory over Queens Park Rangers of the FA Carling Premiership, he and Stockport County earned recognition on a scale usually reserved for national heroes.

It was not so much an FA Cup third round upset, more a vindication of Bergara's conviction that the beautiful game alone has no place in English football. Yet marry it to the best domestic attributes - strength, determination and the will to overcome adversity - and a potent brew emerges. Mix craft and graft and reap the rewards.

"When I came to this country 20 years ago, my dream was to combine English organisation, spirit and guts with South American skill. If you want to be successful you can't have one without the other. You have to have players who can kick a bit, especially at the back. I don't want players doing nutmegs when they are in danger in their own area. When they are under pressure they should get rid *of it, like Bruce and Pallister do at Manchester United. But when you get in the opponents half that's when you play.*

Whilst Bergara views the blending of power and panache as a necessity when reaching professional level, it alarms him to see the suppression of finesse and flair in those so young: "Kids are not allowed to develop naturally nowadays, they grow big hearts and lungs but have no technique. You should allow a diamond to form, cut it out, polish it and then maybe sell it for £2 million"

Kevin Francis a 6' 7" skyscraper of a striker is Bergara's gem, a £60,000 buy from Derby County - he scored 39 goals last season, surprisingly fewer than half with his head - and now he has 17. He is the fastest player at the club over 40 yards and offers a gangly awkward target for anyone trying to mark him, as Peacock, the Rangers' centre half will testify.

Bergara said: "He is unique, but is not Pele, I say to him keep it simple. To knock it on, get in the box and cause problems. Do what you're good at and don't try to be anybody else"

Andy Preece 6' 2", £10,000 from Wrexham and 20 goals this season, is Bergara's other precious stone. After Francis' equaliser - tinged with controversy as Barras, his team mate, lay injured in an offside position - Preece swept in a 74th minute volley to bring Stockport their first appearance in the fourth round for the first time in 29 years. It was achieved in a manner that produced a huge beam across Bergara's weather beaten face, with his English becoming increasingly fractured as the passion and pride swelled from within. It was a display of style when allowed and force when required. "That proves we are not just a kick-and-rush team" said Bergara.

Rangers, ahead through Barker's precise strike in the twentieth minute, barely deserved a replay. Gerry Francis, the Rangers manager said: "It was Stockport's big day and we always knew we would have to dig in and battle. We should have been able to cope, but didn't"

County Chairman Brendan Elwood said afterwards: *"I thought that Rangers were unlucky, because someone was going to get it soon, unfortunately it was them. We came very close last season losing in the last minute at Derby, we have been beaten three times at Wembley, but today was our day"*

Bergara said of the winning goal: *"It was an unbelievable finish from Preecey, it was as good as Pele, Gullit or even me, and I have scored a few in my time"*

Having brushed aside Rangers, and still awaiting their opponents for the next round as Liverpool took on Bristol City in a replay for the right to travel to Edgeley Park in the FA Cup, Bergara's deadly duo were both on target again a few days later as Scunthorpe United were beaten in the Autoglass Trophy as County set up a semi-final date with Huddersfield Town.

Brighton & Hove Albion were then comfortably beaten as Preece grabbed a hat trick on the day Edgeley Park remembered the manager who had last brought promotion to Stockport. Jimmy Meadows, whose team had won the Fourth Division Championship in the 1966/67 season, had died aged 62. Francis then scored the only goal as Blackpool were beaten as County moved back into the automatic promotion spots.

As well as his managerial skill, Bergara became well known during his time at Edgeley Park for his grasp of the English language when

221

*giving team talks or describing players, one famous occasion came
after Bergara and Jim Gannon had had a disagreement as to the
players best position. Gannon, who Bergara had signed as a centre
half from Sheffield United, but had been used in various positions by
his manager, was attracting the attention of Republic of Ireland
boss Jack Charlton for his defensive displays. Gannon, who had
previously had words with Bergara about not being played in his
best position, had given a 'man of the match' performance in his
side's last game and was aware that Charlton's number two,
Maurice Setters, was at Edgeley Park to watch the next game.*

*Gannon indeed started the game at centre half, but during the
match he had played in a number of positions including right back,
right wing and centre midfield. The player's frustrations got the
better of him after the game and he demanded to know why the
manager had played him out of position when the Ireland scout had
been to watch him play in central defence. Bergara told Gannon
that there were actually a number of scouts at the game who had
all come to watch him, but all wanted to see him play in a different
position.*

*After the game, it was clear in Gannon's mind that his manager was
happy to see him leave the club and soon after he moved to Notts
County on loan. Ironically the Magpies had taken the Irishman to
play at right back!. Gannon's first game for his new club came
against Luton Town, managed by Bergara's old friend David Pleat,
who was impressed by Gannon's performance and gave Bergara a
call the next day to enquire about his availability. Pleat told Bergara
that he was interested in the player but had concerns about his
attitude:*

"I've been told he is volatile"

"He certainly is David, he can play in defence, midfield and attack"
came the reply

Three defeats in the next five games saw the Hatters drop out of both Cups. Bristol City, who had surprisingly won at Anfield, won convincingly at Edgeley Park in the FA Cup thanks to a Wayne Allison hat trick (4-0) and Huddersfield Town, who had lost heavily at Edgeley Park in the previous game, won the Autoglass Trophy match, leaving Bergara to concentrate on winning promotion.

County were to lose only three of the last eighteen games, to promotion rivals York City and more worryingly against struggling Bournemouth and Blackpool. However having beaten Port Vale to leapfrog above them and move onto the same points as second placed Plymouth with two games in hand, Bergara's team went into the last four games with their destiny firmly in their own hands.

Having already clinched a play-off spot, a draw against eventual champions Reading at Edgeley Park was followed by a draw at Bristol Rovers and a win at Exeter City, meaning a last day win at home against Hull City would see Stockport County promoted, but for the first time in months they were relying on results elsewhere to help them out.

Without a goalless draw at Edgeley Park all season, County chose the most important game of the campaign to fire blanks. In an uninspiring display against a Hull City side with nothing to play for, the Hatters failed to get the win they needed, allowing Port Vale, who had won every game since their defeat at Edgeley Park, to take the second automatic promotion spot with a win at Brighton, leaving Bergara to try and lift his troops for yet another play-off semi-final where they would meet York City for a place at Wembley.

Bergara was philosophical about the situation: *"With twelve matches to go, we knew we were in the play-offs, but we did not want to stay there. With six games to we thought we were really in with a chance of automatic promotion. And then we played Port Vale here and beat them. We knew they would really have to pull something special out of the fire if they were to go up instead of us, and they did. York City have beaten us at home, but we have won at their ground so it is going to be tight, but we think we can do it. The players have taken it on the chin and the mood in the dressing room is fine. We've just got to take the bull by the horns and go for it. We have already smashed the club record for points gained in a season so we can't be too upset"*

Chris Beaumont would be the County hero as his solitary goal five minutes before the end of the second game at Edgeley Park settled the tie after the two sides had drawn 0-0 at Bootham Crescent. The striker, who had been recalled for the first leg stated: *"I'm lucky to be in the side, having asked for a transfer back in September I have not had the best of seasons and have struggled o get back in, but I was recalled for the two play-off games against York. One or two people have said I'm looking fit and sharp but I should do because been sitting on the bench in the sun these last few months whilst some of the other lads have had to play six games in a fortnight. Those that have been dropped, like Dave Miller and Andy Preece have been a bit unlucky"*

There was somewhat of a surprise result in the other play-off semi-final when Plymouth Argyle who, like County, had finished 12 points ahead of Burnley were beaten by the Lancashire side. Argyle had earned a goalless draw at Turf Moor in the first leg and were odds on to win the second leg. The Clarets however had other plans and won 3-1 to claim their place against the Hatters.

There was a lot of recent 'bad blood' between County and Burnley, from the supporters right through to the players. The only thing that both clubs would have agreed on before the game was that it was refereed strongly and fairly - the truth was somewhat different.

The facts are simple - County took the lead in the second minute - Mike Wallace was sent off on 13 minutes - David Eyres levelled for Burnley on 28 minutes - Chris Beaumont was sent off on 61 minutes - Burnley scored the winner on 65 minutes.

The reality is that referee David Elleray began the game in poor fashion, allowing a very late challenge on County keeper John Keeley by John Francis to punished by only a yellow card, when it appeared he had at first taken the red card out of his pocket. Keeley was left limping for the remainder of the game.

Ted McMinn and Wallace clashed, McMinn was booked, Wallace was sent off. Elleray having taken the word of the Scot that Wallace had spat at him. Elleray nor his linesman had seen evidence but nevertheless he showed the County man a red card.

With the scores level and Burnley struggling to break down the ten men of County, Beaumont was shown a red card for an off-the-ball incident, later described by Elleray as 'stamping', within five minutes the Clarets had their winner. The brave nine men Hatters almost forced extra time as Francis set up Preece in the dying seconds, but keeper Beresford kept his effort out.

No-one connected with Stockport County, Bergara included, condoned the behaviour of either Wallace or Beaumont, but having been awarded the fair play trophy for the Second Division, it was ironic that County became the first English side to have two players sent off at Wembley for foul play.

The Independent probably summed up the day best:

County fall short as Burnley go up: Parkinson makes the difference

In a play-off final that was full of incident but not of good humour, Burnley overcame a Stockport side who finished the game with nine men, to win the right to play First Division football next season.

County were one player down for all but 14 minutes of the game, and two short for the last half-hour - with both Michael Wallace and Chris Beaumont being dismissed for violent conduct - yet they displayed such determination in adversity that they nearly forced extra time. The Burnley fans, who formed the vast majority of a crowd of 44,806, were demanding the final whistle a full 10 minutes before David Elleray brought the proceedings to a halt.

On a similarly emotional afternoon seven years ago, the Turf Moor club needed a last-day victory over Leyton Orient to avoid the drop to the Vauxhall Conference. They deserved their success here, if only for creating far more chances and maintaining discipline. Burnley finished the Second Division campaign 12 points behind both Stockport and their semi-final victims, Plymouth. Without the play-offs, their season would have been cold soon after Christmas. They were certainly caught cold after just two minutes yesterday when, from David Frain's left-flank free-kick, Beaumont found the net with a neat glancing header.

Playing the game, rather than the man, took a back seat for a while, though. Peter Ward, Stockport's captain, was booked - the first of seven - within a minute for a foul on Ted McMinn. John Francis, whose two goals put paid to Plymouth, was the next to see yellow, for a challenge on County's goalkeeper, John Keeley, which was his last contribution of the day. Before Francis, who has suspected knee-ligament damage, could be replaced, Wallace and McMinn tangled on the touchline. Burnley's wily winger was booked and Wallace was shown the red card by Mr Elleray for spitting, although he also appeared to stamp on the grounded McMinn.

David Eyres, who took over as Burnley's front man, then claimed centre stage. With a cool head he could have had a hat-trick but the strike that counted, in the 28th minute, was good: a run across goal from the right wing finished off by a firm, low shot from 18 yards. Eyres was not the only culprit as the Clarets failed to make further use of their extra man. Adrian Heath, the otherwise outstanding Warren Joyce, and John Deary all missed good chances. County lost another player before the winner arrived: Beaumont taking a walk for lashing out at Les Thompson off the ball on the hour.

Burnley's predictable second goal came five minutes later. The right-back, Gary Parkinson, collected the ball just outside the area after an attack broke down, and his shot was deflected past Keeley.

Kevin Francis, the 6ft 7in Stockport striker, was hampered by a groin strain but was still a constant nuisance to Burnley. He nearly set up a last-minute leveller for Andy Preece, but the Clarets had done just enough to earn the champagne.

'It was bizarre - sheer stupidity,' was the verdict of the Stockport manager, Danny Bergara, on the self-inflicted wounds that contributed to his side's fourth Wembley defeat in three years. He was not wrong.

EDGELEY HERO

SPORT

Ber
turbo-

FOOTBALL LEA

Pos	Team
1	P Reading
2	P Port Vale
3	Plymouth Argyle
4	**Stockport County**
5	York City
6	P Burnley
7	Bradford City
8	Bristol Rovers
9	Hull City
10	Cambridge United
11	Huddersfield Town
12	Wrexham
13	Swansea City
14	Brighton & Hove Albion
15	Rotherham United
16	Brentford
17	AFC Bournemouth
18	Leyton Orient
19	Cardiff City
20	Blackpool
21	R Fulham
22	R Exeter City
23	R Hartlepool United
24	R Barnet

HEAD 2 HEAD with HARDY

MARTIN HARDY meets a manager with rare skills

Danny is pledged

STOCKPORT COUNTY

Football League Play-Offs 1993-94

Sunday, 15 May 1994

Burnley	0-0	Plymouth Argyle
York City	0-0	Stockport County

Wednesday, 18 May 1994

Plymouth Argyle	1-3	Burnley
Stockport County	1-0	York City

Sunday, 29 May 1994 – Wembley Stadium

Burnley	2-1	Stockport County

SPORT

WE'VE GOT TO TAKE
BULL BY THE HORNS.

Second Division
Play-offs semi-final
(second leg)

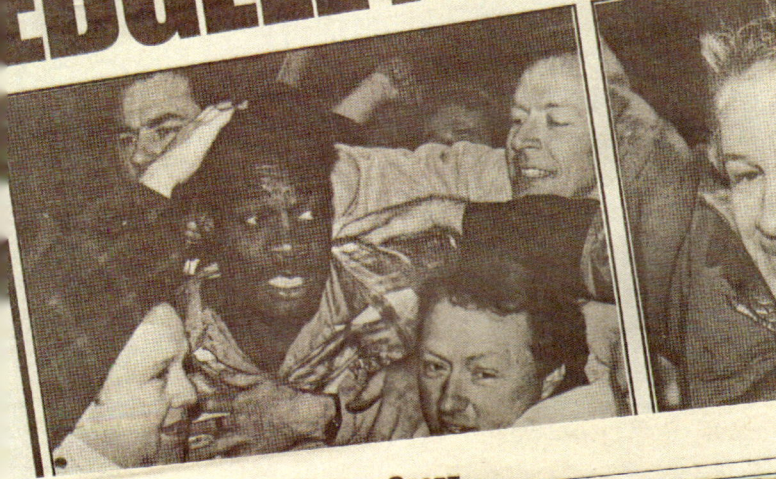

Bergara's boys or

IT'S

salutes his
harged aces

By Peter Gardner

Bergara is
and up and
ort's super-
art to the

ef still warns realis-
well, but don't start

straight up rather than anxiously tread-
ing the tortuous play-off route that has
snared them in successive seasons.

And they are doing so despite the temporary absence of goals from Kevin
Francis, last season's record-breaking hit-
man who set a new post-war mark of 39.

DIVISION TWO

W	D	L	F	A	GD	Pts
26	11	9	81	44	+37	89
26	10	10	79	46	+33	88
25	10	11	88	56	+32	85
24	13	9	74	44	+30	85
21	12	13	64	40	+24	75
21	10	15	79	58	+21	73
19	13	14	61	53	+8	70
20	10	16	60	59	+1	70
18	14	14	62	54	+8	68
19	9	18	79	73	+6	66
17	14	15	58	61	-3	65
17	11	18	66	77	-11	62
16	12	18	56	58	-2	60
15	14	17	60	67	-7	59
15	13	18	63	60	+3	58
13	19	14	57	55	+2	58
14	15	17	51	54	-8	57
14	14	18	57	71	-14	56
13	15	18	66	79	-13	54
16	5	25	63	75	-12	53
14	10	22	50	63	-13	52
11	12	23	52	83	-31	45
9	9	28	41	87	-46	36
5	13	28	41	86	-45	28

■ DARREN RYAN ... target man

ckport's
s fashion upset

port have profited from three
Wembley finals — one in the
old third division play-offs,
two in the Autoglass Trophy —
during his tenancy. Though
losers on each occasion, the
Cheshire club refuses to dwell
on what might have been and
continues to push for success
in the Endsleigh Insurance
League second division. They
lie third in the table.

But while Bergara views the
blinding of power and pa-
nache as a necessity when
reaching professional level, it
alarms him to see the suppression of finesse and flair in

basic instincts. Bergara said:
"He is unique but he is not
Pelé. I say to him to keep it
simple. To knock it on, get in
the box and cause problems.
Do what you are good at, don't
try to be anyone else."

Andy Preece, 6ft 2in,
£10,000 from Wrexham and
20 goals this season, is
Bergara's other precious
stone. After Francis's equaliser — tinged with controversy
as Barras, his team-mate, lay
injured in an offside position
— Preece swept in a 74th-
minute volley to give Stockport their first

Preece and County are bang

■ ABSOLUTELY FABULOUS ... County's Andy Preece (above) volleys the winner against Queens Park Rangers then turns (right) to celebrate what he called 'The goal of his life'

FA CUP THIRD ROUND DRAMA

High and mi

Stockport battlers walk tall to humble Rangers

STOCKPORT 2 QPR 1
BY JAMES MOSSOP

STRIKER Kevin Francis, a 6ft
7in beanpole who looks as
though he should be slam-
dunking into a basketball net,
took several giant leaps into
FA Cup history and controversy as the Premiership men
of Queens Park Rangers were
dumped out.

Rangers just could not hold
him. His leggy, unpredictable
work on the ground bemused the
Rangers defenders, who were
clearly disadvantaged in the air,
and his goal, equalising Rangers'
classic strike through Simon
Barker, brought vehement protests from Rangers.

Controlled

You could understand their
fury as Yorkshire referee John
Key failed to blow his whistle in
the 39th minute.

unty...1
ork......0

brink of First

EMBI

Stockport County Football Club 1993-94

On the road to Wembley...again!

Francis and Preece celebrate winner against QF

Danny enjoying another great County win

Play Off Final heartbreak against Burnley

Big Kev in tears at final whistle

1994/95

Following the huge disappointment of yet another Wembley defeat, the beginning of the end of Danny Bergara's reign was about to unfold. Having sold one of his star strikers, Andy Preece, to Premiership Crystal Palace, the little Uruguayan's reputation for spotting talent was to benefit the club financially once again. Having picked up Preece from Wrexham's reserve team for £10,000 he sold him for £350,000 just two and a half seasons later.

Bergara set about bringing in several new faces, amongst them Geordie pair Alun Armstrong and Tony Dinning from Newcastle United, whilst several of the 'old guard' were allowed to leave, including Tony Barras and Bill Williams.

The campaign started in fine style with Armstrong netting in both the opening day rout of Cardiff City and a fine away win at Cambridge United, indeed at the end of October the team were sitting in second place in the table. Five defeats in five games, with no goals scored, during November signalled a dramatic downturn in the club's fortunes. County won only five games from 21 played through to the end of February, plummeting from second to thirteenth in the table.

Also during this run the County fans said farewell to a 'living legend', Kevin Francis, who was sold to First Division Birmingham City.

Ask any non-Stockport supporter to name a County player, past or present, the majority would name Kevin Francis. It could be argued that the Big Man, through his deeds on and off the pitch, gave

Stockport County a lasting, national image, perhaps for the first time in their long history.

Francis joined Derby from his local side Mile Oak Rovers in February 1989 but with first-team chances limited at the Baseball Ground he moved to Edgeley Park two years later in a deal that was worth £45,000, initially. Under the expert tutelage of manager Danny Bergara, Francis emerged as, possibly, the most-feared striker in the lower divisions. He grabbed 5 goals from 11 starts, helping the Hatters to escape from the bottom division for the first time in 21 years. And the step-up in standard didn't faze the 'Big Man' as he, affectionately, and understandably, had become known.

Francis scored in both legs against Burnley in the Autoglass Trophy Northern Final to help County reach Wembley for the first time in the club's history. Then, eight days after losing to Stoke in the Trophy Final, Francis became the first County player to score in front of the twin-towers when he netted in the 2-1 play-off defeat by Peterborough.

Francis hit 28 league goals the following season and then matched that total twelve months later in a campaign that saw his strike partner Andy Preece score 21 of his own. Led by the dynamic duo Bergara's men reached two more Wembley finals but couldn't break their duck, losing first to Port Vale and then to Burnley. Francis scored his second Wembley goal against the Valiants.

After the departure of Andy Preece to Crystal Palace, for a club-record £350,000, in the summer of 1994, Francis was joined in attack by an 18-year-old Alun Armstrong who will be the first to admit that the Big Man helped his first tentative steps in his Football League career immeasurably. By now Francis had scored his 100th County goal - only the third player in the club's history to achieve this honour.

For more than 12 months a move to his beloved Birmingham City had been muted. It finally happened in January 1995 when Blues' boss Barry Fry broke County's transfer record by paying £800,000 to take him back down the M6. Francis' final Hatters appearance was, like his first, as a substitute, this time against Bradford City. County lost the game 2-1 but perhaps inevitably, and poignantly, Francis scored. It was his 88th County League goal scored from just 156 appearances. Speaking 24 hours before joining Birmingham Francis said: "Edgeley Park has been like a second home for me. Most people who get up for work say, 'Oh no, another day and I've got to face so and so,' but for me coming in for training and playing for County has been a pleasure. It has never been a problem."

The Manchester Evening News summed up Bergara's transfer dealings:

<u>Mr Goldfinger</u>

Bargain hunter Danny Bergara has sustained Stockport with a staggering £1.7m pot of gold. That's the financial windfall County have reaped in sales since Bergara took over at Edgeley Park almost six years ago. His super selling has embraced just four players, all strikers, that has provided solid Edgeley Park foundations for a once ailing club.

Bergara's biggest sale was the £800,000 package deal that took record marksman Kevin Francis to Birmingham City last month. Prior to that, County unloaded Andy Preece to Crystal Palace, a deal that will eventually be worth £400,000. And two earlier outgoing transfers saw Paul Williams sold to West Brom for £250,000, he was later bought back for a knockdown £25,000, while Brett Angell went to Southend in a £260,000 deal.

Bergara acknowledges: "Without the sort of foundations that money has helped provide, we would not now be building a new all-seater stand." Bergara, who completes six years as manager next month, has also taken the club to an unprecedented four Wembley visits that have helped lift average attendances from a crippling 1,500 to a more balanced near 5,000. It is a track record any manager would be proud to announce on his CV, particularly in the lower divisions.

Francis' replacement, Ian Helliwell, signed from Rotherham for £20,000, scored twice on his debut in a four goal thrashing of Hull City. Unfortunately it was to prove a false dawn for the new County number nine as he struggled to find the net over the next few months. With his side struggling, some County fans believed that Bergara had lost his magic touch, although it must be said that most teams would struggle to cope with the loss of two players that had notched 62 league and cup goals between them during the previous campaign.

Bergara celebrated his upcoming sixth anniversary in the Edgeley Park hot seat with a home win over Cheshire rivals Crewe Alexandra, thanks to goals from two of his most recent signings Martyn Chalk (2) and Armstrong. It was one of the old guard who was given special praise afterwards from the supporters. Chris Beaumont, Wembley villain, was now playing in the central role instead of Helliwell had impressed all with his all-action display as County claimed only their second win in ten games.

On transfer deadline day Bergara made his last signings for the club as he brought in veteran Peter Davenport from Scottish side

St. Johnstone and Marc Lloyd Williams from Welsh outfit Bangor City. Helliwell returned to the side ten days later for the win at Plymouth Argyle. Goals from Deniol Graham and Dinning giving Bergara a win in what was to be his last game in charge as he was to be sacked a couple of days later following an 'alleged' incident between the Uruguayan and the club Chairman at a function.

The fact that the team were well off the promotion places, sitting just below half way in the table, appeared to be extremely convenient for the club to part company with a manager who had performed near miracles in his six years at Edgeley Park and though Stockport County were to gain promotion to the First Division a little over two years later, under the guidance of Bergara's replacement Dave Jones, the majority of County fans will always be convinced that it was the little Uruguayan that put the club on the football map.

FOUR-MIDABLE

STOCKPORT COUNTY hit four goals for the third time in four matches on Tuesday night as they swept into the Coca Cola Cup second round.

A second half ...

Express/Advertiser sports editor Matt Horn

JMAES
accoun
mer
(above
cess i

all have been different if any
of their rivals had turned up!

Jackie Newton, Senior Ladies' race winner

Race report - Page 84

inning double!

Kev and Alun clinch points

again although he was a bit disappointed with some of his footwork on Saturday.

"Alun is a strong lad, only 19, and he has got a great chance if he keeps trying and working hard. I hope the pair keep doing it."

Elsewhere at County a hamstring injury has prompted ... to let Kevin Brock go. The boss admitted: "He's a good player and I gave him a chance but we are well

equipped with players of a similar type.

"I have made Dean Connelly available and Dave Miller has joined Wigan on loan. A couple of clubs are interested in David Frain and there could be ... development in the next few days."

A tribunal yesterday told County they must pay £30,000 to Stoke for Paul Ware, half the amount now, £5,000 after 25 games, the rest after 50.

Match report - Page 86

COUNTY AR

...PORT COUNTY
N ACTION,
...LEY PARK,
...UNTY
V
...UTH ARGYLE

Ring 480
4491 ext. 2
or fax us o
480 4847/

Sport

...RT
...ress
Advertiser

...ked
...ace

...WITH A DIFFER-
...ce striker Kevin
...his way round the
...oal with his shirt
...face after he had
...y goal with a diving
...minutes from time
...nemouth at Edgeley
...rday. Joining in the
...f three vital points is
...rtyn Chalk.

A RELIEF!
...match report
...ture - Page 86

...HIS WEEK

...win..win

...pairs of seats for
...County v

WITH
GOL
TOU

GO

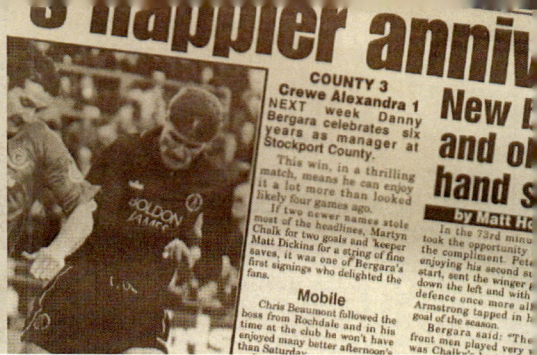

COUNTY 3
Crewe Alexandra 1

NEXT week Danny Bergara celebrates six years as manager at Stockport County.

This win, in a thrilling match, means he can enjoy it a lot more than looked likely four games ago.

If two newer names stole most of the headlines, Martyn Chalk for two goals and 'keeper Matt Dickins for a string of fine saves, it was one of Bergara's first signings who delighted the fans.

Mobile
Chris Beaumont followed the boss from Rochdale and in his time at the club he won't have enjoyed many better afternoon's than Saturday's.

DIVISION TWO

W	D	L	F	A	GD	Pts
21	12	6	71	40	+31	75
22	7	9	69	31	+38	73
19	10	6	66	27	+39	67
19	9	10	57	44	+13	66
17	12	7	59	33	+26	63
16	14	7	51	36	+15	62
18	6	13	62	60	+2	60
17	9	11	58	46	+12	60
17	8	14	57	55	+2	59
16	10	12	54	51	+3	58
17	7	14	53	43	+10	58
14	12	11	59	54	+5	54
16	6	17	54	53	+1	54
12	13	14	45	44	+1	49
12	12	15	50	54	-4	48
10	16	12	47	63	-16	46
11	12	15	47	50	-3	45
8	13	18	46	64	-18	37
8	11	20	38	65	-27	35
9	6	22	34	71	-37	33
7	9	22	39	64	-25	30
6	8	23	27	58	-31	26
4	9	26	32	77	-45	21

Danny Bergara Stockport County Statistics

League Games

	Played	Won	Drew	Lost	GF	GA	Diff	Points
1988/89	9	0	5	4	8	14	-6	5
1989/90	46	21	11	14	68	62	6	74
1990/91	46	23	13	10	84	47	37	82
1991/92	46	22	10	14	75	51	24	76
1992/93	46	19	15	12	81	57	24	72
1993/94	46	24	13	9	74	44	30	85
1994/95	39	16	6	17	54	53	1	54
Totals	278	125	73	80	444	328	116	448

THANK YOU BERGARA!

Saint and

THE last few days have been amongst the most...

THE SACKING OF DANNY

March 28, 1989 to Mar

Stockport Express Advertiser

SIX... AND O

AXE OVER BURY BOSS

SOCCER

dfinger

Most succes in County's

by Matt Ho

WHEN Kevin Francis left Edgeley Park it was accepted a legend was leaving.

If so where does that leave the now departed Danny Bergara?

The man has enjoyed phenomenal success as well as phenomenal disappointment in a six-year reign during which he has transformed the club from a

Four trips to th Towers and four defe some magical memori the way as well as gen income for the club.

That income, adde successes in turning so into silk purses, have h transform the club's fina

When it came to find bargains that club fi

The End

Jan Bergara remembers the fallout from the last days of Bergara's reign at Edgeley Park: *Dan is and always has been a man of his word and expected the same from others. The most honest guy you could ever wish to meet. So when the Chairman phoned to say he was thinking of stopping his expenses of £50 per week (of which the maximum Dan ever claimed was £32 per week) with a view to Dan moving to Stockport, as Dan was busy with transfer deadline and the Chairman was going on holiday, Dan asked if they could discuss it on his return from holiday, or at the end of the season, to which the Chairman agreed, Dan expected that to be the case.*

But on returning from the Plymouth game in the early hours, Dan stayed in his digs overnight as there was a sponsors' dinner at the Alma Lodge Hotel the following evening, and to Dan's surprise, with no warning, the club suddenly stopped his expenses. This was just before the sponsors' dinner leaving Dan out of pocket for cash for the evening, which would have come from his expenses. It also left him with a very nasty feeling of a broken agreement and the question what was going on! This was followed by blatant and outrageous dishonesty on the part of the club, surrounding his dismissal. A gentleman's word is his 'bond', and it always was with Dan!

I remember Dan saying on his dismissal "Whatever I say now will be exactly the same in 5, 10, 20 years time, because the truth does not change!. One of his favourite quotes was "Lies have short legs, they can't run far!".

It seems the club weren't wanting to continue paying him, earning too much plus percentages on players he was improving, when sold.

But being a fair man, if there were financial difficulties, he would have taken a pay cut, if needed, to help Stockport's cause, if they had suggested it! But with a legally binding contract it seemed they were trying to provoke a reaction from him so they could dismiss him without paying him. Justice and truth would come through.

The first to phone Daniel after his dismissal were David Pleat and Alex Ferguson, who were both shocked at the news! The essence of the man was his absolute fairness. When the Chairman chose, to Dan's surprise, to increase his salary, Dan's immediate concern was for his coaches and told the Chairman it was only fair to give them a rise too! The Chairman wasn't of the same view at the time so Dan had to push for it! I remember telling him at the time "You really are a fair man" but I knew that already! He proved it time and time again

Stockport lost their case and their appeal was thrown out. Dan told the Tribunal with hand on heart and conviction "Sir, I loved Stockport and they loved me!" Dan was only penalised for swearing and told the Tribunal if he had been given the opportunity he would have apologised. He apologised to his coaches and the hotel manager, Mr Hudson, the next day. It's funny he learnt to swear in English at football, where it seems to be common place to this day!

Following a Board Meeting on March 31st 1995, Danny Bergara had been dismissed following allegations of assaulting the club Chairman, Brendan Elwood at the Alma Lodge Hotel after a club function, it was also alleged that the Uruguayan had made a false expenses claim.

What followed was a long, drawn out and painful couple of years for the Bergara family as, having been sacked from the job he loved, Bergara had no option but to claim unfair dismissal, taking

239

his case to an Industrial Tribunal. The case was first heard in November that year, the Tribunal finding in Bergara's favour in April the following year.

Summary

Taken from the official Industrial Tribunal notes

Applicant: Mr A D Bergara

Respondents: Stockport County Association Football Club

1. The Tribunal, on the balance of probabilities based upon the facts, found that Mr Elwood sought to unilaterally alter the terms and conditions of employment pertaining to the applicant by withdrawing the accommodation allowance without any agreement. The tribunal was satisfied on the facts as found that and it was agreed that the clause concerning expenses allowance would be reviewed at the end of the 1994/95 season, but that if there was a proposal to vary it at an earlier date there would be a further discussion between the applicant and Mr Elwood after he had returned from holiday abroad. Such additional discussion never took place and therefore the terms of clause 19 remained in force and the decision by Mr Elwood to withdraw the expense allowance was a decision was taken unilaterally.

2. At the Board meeting on 16th March Mr Elwood incorrectly advised the Board that there had been an agreement reached with regard to the expense allowance and the Board reached a decision in the absence of the applicant. The minutes record that this matter appears on

240

the team manager's report rather than on an agenda for financial matters.

3. The Tribunal was satisfied on the evidence that the applicant was not informed of the Board's decision between the 16th and 29th of March 1995.

4. The Tribunal satisfied that the applicant was abusive to Mr Coxon and about the directors and specifically Mr Elwood and Mr Jolley to Mr Coxon, Mr Jones, Mr Sainty and Mr White. The Tribunal however was satisfied on a balance of probabilities that swearing was commonplace in this workplace as shown by Mr Elwood in his conduct in the foyer of the Alma Lodge Hotel and that of Mr Jolley in the conference room also at the Hotel on 29th March.

5. The applicant did not misbehave in any way during the dinner or during the after dinner speeches and function at the Alma Lodge on the evening of 29th March 1995.

6. The applicant did not behave aggressively in the foyer of the Alma Lodge Hotel that evening and it was Mr Elwood who was the aggressor and sought to strike out at the applicant.

7. It was Mr Jolley who behaved aggressively in his dealings with the applicant in a conference room at the hotel that night

8. The respondents did not seek an explanation from the applicant for his actions in expressing himself the way he did to Messrs Coxon, Jones, Sainty and White on the night of 29th March 1995.

9. The members of the board did not carry out an independent investigation into the events upon the night of 29th March 1995 at the Alma Lodge Hotel which were plainly inaccurate on the findings of the tribunal and in replying upon those matters permitted Messrs Elwood and Jolley to be both judge and jury in the investigation. The picture painted by Mr Elwood and Mr Jolley they knew it would be inaccurate on the tribunal findings

10. The tribunal was not satisfied that the respondents had a genuine belief that the applicant was guilty of misconduct warranting dismissal based upon reasonable grounds the independent evidence called before the tribunal from Messrs Scraggs, Miller, Hudson and Beales in various central aspects of the case show the allegations which were ranged against the applicant of events at the Alma Lodge Hotel to be misconceived and inaccurate. If there had been a proper investigation conducted by board member who had not been present on the night and able to bring an independent mind of these matters, a reasonable investigation might have been carried out.

11. The tribunal was driven to the conclusion that whatever reason Mr Elwood and Mr Jolley wished to terminate the applicants contract of employment. In meeting this conclusion, the tribunal reminded itself it was its function to impose its own decision on matters, but to investigate whether the respondents acted reasonably.

As far as the procedure was concerned with regard to the handling of the dismissal, the Tribunal concluded that this was not fair or reasonable. The applicant was not offered an opportunity

to present his case to the Board of Directors on 31st March 1995 or have it presented on his behalf.

He was not afforded an opportunity to discuss matters with any member of the Board and was not warned that his employment was at risk. The Tribunal accepted that the first he knew about the possibility of his dismissal was as a result of what a journalist informed him.

It is claimed that there was independent evidence available amongst those who attended the Alma Lodge Hotel on 29th March which would've presented a clearer picture than the partisan approach that was adopted.

As far as the minutes were concerned in relation to the Board meeting the Tribunal found that there were two matters which caused great anxiety. In addition to the matters which were relied upon in concluding that dismissal was appropriate was resume of conduct by the applicant during the preceding six months. This formed no part of the evidence called before the Tribunal and was at best to be regarded as mischievous.

As far as Mr Coxon was concerned he advised the board of an incident of abuse following the dinner about which no evidence was called at the Tribunal. Once again the Tribunal concluded that this was a mischievous matter and was inaccurate.

The Tribunal concluded that there was a measure of contributory fault on the part of the applicant and this was a percentage of fault which should attach to both the basic and compensatory award of compensation. The Tribunal had been advised by the parties that the applicant sought compensation as the preferred remedy, the Tribunal considered that:

1. The intemperate derogatory and vulgar remarks made to the respondents 'officials on 29th March 1995 was significant, the most serious of those was the derogatory terms used by the applicant to his subordinates Messrs Sainty and Jones in referring to the Chairman and Financial Director of the football club, and also the terms used by him to Mr White in relation to the same two individuals.

2. The Tribunal was satisfied that the applicant was invited to a meeting in Sheffield on 30th March 1995, notwithstanding the vulgar way in which Mr Jolley expressed that request, the applicant was aware that he should attend the meeting in order to discuss other financial matters or his alleged conduct during the previous evening.

The Tribunal concluded that it was appropriate to make a deduction therefore in any award of compensation which might be made and in exercise of its' judicial discretion considered that the appropriate percentage was 25%. Since this was an issue of conduct the Tribunal considered that it was appropriate to make this deduction in respect of all aspects of the award of compensation might otherwise be made.

In closing the unanimous decision of the Tribunal was that:-

1. The applicant was unfairly dismissed

2. The Tribunal concluded, on a balance of probabilities, that there was a measure of contributory fault which attached to the applicant was assessed at 25%

3. The Tribunal stood adjourned for consideration of the question of remedies and directed that in the absence of

agreement being reached between the parties within 14 days of the issue of the decision to the parties the matter be relisted for remedy forthwith.

Chairman Brendan Elwood did not accept the tribunal's findings and launched an immediate appeal to have the decision overturned: *"I was gobsmacked that they could come to this verdict, that he was only 25% responsible. It was more like 100%. I don't accept any responsibility at all".*

The subsequent appeal was rejected at the end of June 1997, the case summed up with the following statement:

It appears this is a decision which is full of common sense, understanding and correct direction at every point. In many ways it comes close, if we may respectfully say so, to being the model decision. However that may be, we are entirely satisfied that no error of law is shown either by the football club or by Mr Bergara, in the decision which was reached and therefore follows that, notwithstanding these submissions that have been made to us, we are obliged to dismiss the appeal and cross-appeal.

The Club's failed appeal even made the headlines in The Times annual end of year awards in the law section. On Tuesday December 30th, the paper ran with the following:

Sadism, silly suits and Stockport County

Sadism, silly suits and Stockport County - A review of the best, the worst and the oddest in the courts during the past year. The past year boasts strong contenders for the awards of most optimistic submission by counsel, most ridiculous lawsuit, most injudicious judge and most unsatisfactory juror - among other hotly contested honours.

Optimistic submission of 1997 was made on behalf of Stockport County Football Club, which was appealing against an industrial tribunal decision that the club's manager had been unfairly dismissed. The Finance Director had told the manager to come to a meeting the following day at which the Finance Director would "Tear up his contract and shove it up his arse". The employment appeal tribunal noted that "it is suggested on behalf of the club that this was a very proper invitation to a disciplinary committee at which these matters would be fairly heard". The club's appeal failed.

Bergara's dismissal featured in the book 'Scams, Scandals and Screw-ups' in an article written by David Conn:

The plan to turn Stockport County around had begun with what might be termed the infrastructure, as Bergara remembers: "The dressing rooms were disgusting, filthy, there were nails sticking out. I said I wanted them repaired, painted. The players had too little respect for the club and themselves; they were walking around the showers barefoot and I insisted they wore flip-flops to stop them slipping."

He had introduced changes to the playing methods, training practises, and tactics. Briskly, defiantly, he insisted that Stockport County was not a suburban dumping ground in the shadow of its Manchester giant neighbours but a club with its own history, dignity and a few thousand loyal supporters who deserved self-respect too.

He had, though, salvaged the self-respect of Stockport County and its fans. One lifelong fan told 'On the Line': 'He is a hero of mine. There are people here who would give their right arm to save Danny. He was held in such high esteem by a lot of people here.'

But not, ultimately, by the people with most reason to thank him, the Chairman and directors. By 1995, Bergara, according to his contractual entitlements, was being paid close to £90,000 a year. He still lived near Sheffield and so had agreed with the club that he could stay in modest digs near Edgeley Park on odd late working nights.

The club made available an accommodation allowance of £50 per week. As an arrangement for a successful football manager it was painfully unextravagant. In March 1995 Bergara agreed with Brendan Elwood that at the end of the season they would review the accommodation allowance. (With a view to Bergara moving to Stockport)

Shortly afterwards, on 16 March, Stockport had a Board meeting. Bergara was not there. He had asked if he could be excused from it (with the transfer deadline approaching) and asked the Chief Executive, David Coxon, to speak on his behalf about playing matters. At that meeting, Elwood told the board, falsely, that Bergara had agreed that his £50 weekly accommodation allowance would 'cease forthwith'. Quite apart from the fact that this was untrue, nobody, according to Bergara, communicated this to him. Two weeks later he put in an expenses claim for the heartbreaking petty sum of £64 (being the total of his previous two week's worth of claims) with no idea that he was about to lose his job.

The romantic involvement of the man from Uruguay with the club down the A6 ended in a foul split, an industrial tribunal hearing the evidence, the tribunals reached their conclusions about what had happened. The club refused to pay the expenses claim, and Bergara lost his temper. He was abusive to Coxon and said that Elwood and David Jolley, the Finance Director, were 'bastards' for withholding his expenses. He referred to the two directors 'again in bad language' when speaking to his deputies, John Sainty and Dave Jones. (Jones subsequently replaced Bergara as manager on a third of his salary). The club's vice-chairman, Grahame White, testified that when he met Bergara in the car park on their way to attending a sponsors' dinner, Bergara had explained what had happened and described the Chairman and Finance Director as acting like a couple of 'f**king gangsters'.

Jan Bergara: *This description was probably borne out of an article in the press when Dan first joined Stockport County saying that he had joined the Sheffield 'mafia'. I found it quite unsettling when I read the article. Dan and Grahame had a very close relationship and Grahame would always call Dan after games as he loved nothing better than chatting at length about the game.*

Bergara accepted the Tribunal's judgement that the swearing was 'out of order' and said that if he had been given the opportunity he would have apologised for it. But he had not been given the chance. However, the Tribunal found that at the sponsor's dinner, at the Alma Lodge Hotel, Bergara had behaved 'quite properly' in spite of statements to the contrary put forward by witnesses for the club. But Elwood did not do the same in the foyer after dinner: 'He swore at Mr Bergara, he sought to assault him by striking at him on two occasions and told him not to bother to turn up for work as he no longer had a job.'

The record of Finance Director David Jolley's behaviour was equally damning: He poked Mr Bergara in the chest and issued him with a tirade of swearing and abuse which he, Mr Jolley, described as a 'Sheffield volley' and then Mr Jolley said that Bergara was to come to a meeting at his office the following day and at that meeting he would 'Tear up his contract and shove it up his arse'.

The Tribunal further noted that 'It is suggested on behalf of the club that that was a very proper invitation to a disciplinary committee at which these matters would be fairly heard,' but dismissed this explanation. Had the consequences not been so serious for Bergara, the whole shabby story would have had its comic elements.

On 31 March Elwood told a Board meeting that Bergara had assaulted him. The Tribunal came to the opposite conclusion, but the story that Danny Bergara had hit his Chairman went round the footballing world like wildfire and is the single biggest reason why Bergara has struggled to find another manager's job ever since.

Here is a coach with rich experience, who has spent most of that time unemployed at home in Sheffield. Yet the tribunal was unequivocal about what has since been accepted as a true piece of gossip: 'That was clearly an untruth. It was Mr Elwood who tried to assault Mr Bergara.'

Acting on Elwood's version of events, which followed Elwood misleading the Board about Bergara's expenses, the Board voted to sack Danny summarily. In the end the Industrial Tribunal judged Bergara to have been 25 per cent to blame, for his 'intemperate, derogatory and vulgar remarks' and for not attending the meeting at which Jolley had promised to 'tear up his contract and shove it up his arse'. Bergara stated at the time "I didn't quite fancy that, would you?"

This meant that they considered the club to be 75 per cent to blame, declaring them to be 'an employer who, so far from being reasonable, had treated his employee, this manager, with a complete lack of frankness, in a disingenuous way, which must have been exceedingly provocative to him'.

Bergara won his case, and was paid damages, but not until August 1997, nearly two and a half years later. When 'On the Line' saw him, he declined to talk about it; the papers were there to see, he had won, he had nothing further to say. He talked only about football, about his record at Stockport and his work on the technique of the raw players he had brought to Edgeley Park, whom the club had sold on as lower division stars.

A career great in its unique way. And it all effectively ended with a seedy piece of out-manoeuvring over £64 living expenses, an attempted assault by Elwood and chest-poking and foul abuse from Jolley.

An employee of the club told 'On the Line' that she laughed ruefully even at the 25 per cent fault attributed to him for the intemperate remarks made in the maelstrom: "Danny is a gentlemen, a lovely man, totally opposite to the people running that club. The fact is that he had to learn to swear to fit into English football, which is a crude and brutal place to work. It was just so laughable that he ends up being criticised for a way of behaving and language that, as a foreigner, he was taught by the English".

We learned that Bergara was not the only Stockport County employee who had felt the need to make a claim to an Industrial Tribunal for unfair dismissal. Three others, accounts assistant Lyn Porter, lottery manager Tony Constance and safety officer Philip Collister, brought cases to the Tribunal and had them settled by the club. Four instances in five years for a club that employed fewer than 20 non-playing staff is a record that David Cockburn, a solicitor and vice-president of the Employment Lawyers Association, told us indicated a nasty regime at the 'friendly club': "I'd say that is a high number but it's not only a high number. I think it discloses an approach to a style of management which has little to do with modern management techniques. It's more a macho management where they will hire and fire at will, where they think they can develop more obedience than team spirit"

This is not an image of the 'Friendly Club' that Stockport have sought to portray under Elwood's chairmanship.

The local press featured several reports:

<u>**Why Bergara got the Boot**</u>

A clash over expenses was behind the flare-up which led to the sacking of Stockport County manager Danny Bergara. The bust-up between the Chairman of the "Friendly Club", Brendan Elwood, and the most successful manager in County's history happened at a sportsman's dinner at the Alma Lodge Hotel last Wednesday. Then, on Friday afternoon, came the shock announcement that the six year reign of the 52-year-old County boss was over.

Bergara was the man with the midas touch in the transfer market, especially with the selling of ace striker Kevin Francis and Andy Preece for over £1m profit. He also brought success on the playing field, gaining promotion and taking County to four Wembley finals in three years.

Ironically it was Elwood who brought Bergara to Edgeley Park in March, 1989, from Rochdale. He once said of Bergara that he is so good Stockport were resigned to losing him, but whoever lured him away would have to pay a fortune in compensation. Now Elwood and County have lost that chance of a fortune... by sacking Danny!

Bergara Boulevard

Street sign scheme to honour County's sacked manager, Danny Bergara Boulevard could be one of the latest additions to Stockport's street names if the borough's Deputy Mayor gets his way. Labour councillor Max Jones wants the ex-County manager's achievements to be marked forever with a road sign, "I think it would be a nice touch considering what he has done for the club," said the councillor.

Uruguayan Danny was sacked almost two weeks ago after a six year spell at the club which made him a hero of the Edgeley Park fans. The top tactician transformed the team from a laughing stock to one of the best in the lower divisions. He took the Hatters to Wembley four times, suffering four defeats, but made major triumphs in the transfer market to boost the club's purse.

One of the roads to benefit from the celebrity status suggested by Councillor Jones could be on the Bridgehall Estate building scheme. Councillor Jones said: "I think we should be looking into this, providing the area committee and technical services committee consider it."

Dave Espley the editor of the popular County 'fanzine' The Tea Party wrote the following:

Thank You Bergara!

The last few days have been amongst the most sensational in all my 23 years of watching county. There I was, sitting at work and idly wondering how we could fill two more issues this season, when the phone rang. It was a reporter, "Have you heard? He said, kicking off a crazy couple of days which ended with one of the most successful managers in County's history sacked after a late night fracas with the Chairman.

As I write, the details of the incident are too clouded to be debated here. However, what is indisputable is we have lost an excellent manager, whose team gave more pleasure to County fans in the last six years than any other manager in living memory. It's extraordinarily sad it should end this way. Most decent County fans wouldn't have begrudged Bergara leaving the club amicably en route to managing a higher division team.

Many of us half expected such an eventuality. But to leave under a cloud, ignominiously fired, is too incredible to comprehend. He deserved better. Danny Bergara's principle achievement during his years at Edgeley Park was not reaching Wembley four times. The frequency with which Wembley is used for all manner of competitions these days, including the play-offs, means that, although still an achievement, it is easier.

No, Danny Bergara's greatest accomplishment was in transforming a joke team, one which had only finished in the top half of the bottom division twice in the previous 18 years, into an established and successful side, widely seen as a major force in the lower divisions.

It would be as well not to forget Bergara's influence in the area of County's finances also. I doubt whether the enormous construction behind the Cheadle End would have progressed further than being a gleam in an architect's eye had it not been for the money which flowed into the club as a result of Bergara's eye for unproved talent. A profit of £500,000 from the sale of Kevin Francis, over £300,000 from the sale of Andy Preece and an amount nearly double that selling the two Paul Williams' and Brett Angell.

253

Even offset against his spending, that still represents an enormous chunk of income which has placed County on a far more secure financial footing than could ever have been dreamed of in the 70s and 80s. I take some consolation in the fact that, surely, Bergara won't be out of work for too long. While his achievements prior to his time with County weren't particularly striking, his record since appointment at Edgeley Park has been nothing short of breathtaking.

One minor blemish at the end should not be allowed to spoil that and if English football can't see fit to employ Danny Bergara again, then it's English football's loss. It's not overly dramatic to say that any County fan who had followed the team since before Bergara arrived had their life changed by the little man. My own hope is that we're are not forcibly reminded by results over the next season or two, just how much of a debt we owe him.

Not surprisingly, the events of last week tended to overshadow the game at Shrewsbury on Saturday. I didn't go, as it was my son Christopher's third birthday, but by all accounts, it wasn't much of a match. Our last six games offer Dave Jones the chance to prove the right man has been appointed but before hearing that the appointment was permanent I had thought that Brendan Elwood might bring in an outsider once more.

The very first issue of "The Tea Party" carried an interview with Elwood in which he stated the three candidates he had in mind to replace Asa Hartford six years ago. Bergara was first choice, the late Cyril Knowles was another, and Billy Ayre, then at Halifax, the third. Amidst recent speculation about Sammy McIlroy, Graham Barrow, Howard Kendall and Phil Neal, no-one has picked up on the fact that Billy Ayre is out of work. But we should all give Jonesy and the team our support.

Whatever happens, however, let's remember that all County fans owe Danny Bergara a massive amount.

A Very Sad End

So the "Soccer Sleaze Express" finally hit Stockport. County's Manager and his Chairman were in a fracas that ended with police being called to a local hotel. Within 36 hours the most successful boss in the club's history was out of the job.

This being Stockport the story did not cause the headlines reserved for Merson, Cantona, Graham et al, but for those connected with the club it was a very painful experience. It is unbelievable that it should end in this most acrimonious and public manner. But end it has and the substitution now is clear. County did not hesitate in appointing Dave Jones to replace Danny and, no matter what the loyalty to the former gaffer, it must be hoped that fans are equally quick to get behind him. He has had an excellent grounding in football management. He has a lot of support around him and, to judge by recent performances, a side that can do better next year.

So adios, buena suerte and gracias Danny and good luck Dave. As the saying goes, the king is dead long live the king.

Danny Plans for a Future in the Game

"I'm down, but I'm not dead," said an emotional Danny Bergara on Monday morning. Speaking from his Sheffield home he explained that as the team he had built was in action at Shrewsbury on Saturday he was clearing his den. He continued to refuse to be drawn on the circumstances surrounding his dismissal, but added: "Most importantly of all I want to thank my family for their support through thick and thin."

He admitted he was eager to get back into the game he loves as quickly as possible. He said: "I am sure something will come up. As a football manager the older you get the wiser you get." Of Dave Jones he said: "I rang him on Friday night, Saturday morning and Saturday night. He was pleased with the performance and the result and I was pleased for him. I have wished him all the best."

Matt Horn of the Stockport Express summed up Bergara's reign in his column:

Six and out: Most successful boss in County's history

When Kevin Francis left Edgeley Park it was accepted that a legend was leaving, if so where does that leave the now departed Danny Bergara?

The man has enjoyed phenomenal success as well as phenomenal disappointment in a six year reign during which he has transformed the club from a laughing stock into one of the most respected in the lower Leagues.

This season has been a rare island of mediocrity in a sea of success and it is the first time since he took over that County are not going to finish in the top of the table play-off places. He has done it all on limited resources through tireless hard work and a devotion to the club. His triumphs in the transfer market have provided the club with much-needed money.

An examination of his record speaks for itself:

1989/90 4th in Division Four - lost in the play-off semi-final

1990/91 2nd and promoted from Division Four

1991/92 5th in Division Three - lost in the play-off final at Wembley. Also lost at Wembley in the Autoglass Trophy

1992/93 6th in the new Division Two - lost in the play-off semi-final. Lost again at Wembley in the Autoglass Final

1993/94 4th in Division Two - lost in the play-off final at Wembley

Four trips to the Twin Towers and four defeats, but some magical memories along the way as well as generating income for the club. That income, added to his successes in turning sow's ears into silk purses, have helped to transform the club's finances. When it came to finding the bargains that club finances required he undoubtedly had the midas touch, just look at the figures:

Kevin Francis - bought for £60,000 sold 116 goals later for £800,000

Andy Preece - bought £10,000 sold 54 goals later for £350,000

Paul A Williams signed on a free transfer and sold for £250,000

Paul R Williams another free transfer sold for £150,000

Just those four deals represent outstanding business for the club and when he did spend money he certainly spent wisely. Few would argue that at £150,000 Mike Flynn was a real bargain. Similarly Jim Gannon £70,000, Neil Edwards £10,000 have more than proved their worth. He leaves the club with a number of other players that will surely one day command high fees. Tony Dinning and Alun Armstrong have shown enough already this season to suggest that they are the latest diamonds to be mined and polished by Bergara.

His undeniable success must've seemed light years away to the Edgeley Park faithful when he arrived. His first twelve games in

charge did not bring a single victory, but it didn't take him long to stamp his style on the club and results quickly started to improve. His record was such that when things started to go wrong this season, most notably the nightmare months of November and February, it was much harder for the fans to accept. But he never lost faith in either himself or his players and only days before he was sacked, after the unlucky defeat by Huddersfield Town, he was promising "You wait until next season things are going to be a lot different then"

The fans, who have shared his frustrations throughout this season, were starting to share that optimism. Even in mid-March the excited talk was of anticipation as to what lay ahead in August. Richard Harnwell, the club's historian, admitted "I have been supporting Stockport County since the mid 1960s, all I remember was the highlight of any season being when we avoided re-election. In the early part of the season all we have to look forward to was a cup draw against a top club before another season going nowhere. When Danny Bergara linked up with Brendan Elwood all that changed. For the first time we had a Chairman supporting the manager and the manager responded. I have spoken to many players, past and present, who say that he is without doubt the best coach that they have ever played for. He was a breath of fresh air. He gave me things I thought I would never have - the joy of promotion, four trips to Wembley for starters. It has been the most successful period in the clubs history"

Danny enjoying using extended metaphors in his programme notes, and one of his favourite ones was to look at the club as a house. The prize of promotion was like moving from a semi to a detached house. He wanted to build a garage and get a garden in the hope of getting closer to palace's like Manchester United. Last week the demolition men moved in and his County dream home was flattened. But Danny would be the first to admit that he was the focal point of a close-knit team, he may have gone but Dave Jones, John Sainty, Rodger Wylde and Dave Philpotts all remain. Perhaps his greatest legacy will be leaving behind the men who can build on the foundations he has laid.

In the same paper, some of the squad had their say:

Scandalous, says sad skipper Flynn

Stunned County players expressed their sadness when the news of Danny Bergara's sacking was broken to them on Friday afternoon. Skipper Mike Flynn, Bergara's record signing, claimed "It's scandalous. He spoke to the players before training, but he didn't say much. The news is a great shock. We don't know what happened because only a couple of the players were at the hotel. I think the club might have acted hastily because in six years hard work the gaffer has never brought the game down. The players would like to hear the other side of the story".

Peter Ward who was at the Alma Lodge Hotel on that fateful Wednesday night said "I left early to look after my children and if there was a problem, it was being well hidden. It had been a good night and everyone had enjoyed themselves. I am shocked and disappointed. We have heard the gaffer's side, and it is up to the Board whether they want to tell us their side. After all the success of recent seasons, it is a sad way for it to end"

Chris Beaumont, who followed Bergara from Rochdale to Stockport said "I am really shocked, he was loyal to the core to the club, and even when he spoke to us before training, he told us to go out and win at Shrewsbury, whether he was there are not. He wanted us to do well for Stockport County"

Danny Bergara Stockport County Statistics

League Games

	Played	Won	Drew	Lost	GF	GA	Diff	Points
1988/89	9	0	5	4	8	14	-6	5
1989/90	46	21	11	14	68	62	6	74
1990/91	46	23	13	10	84	47	37	82
1991/92	46	22	10	14	75	51	24	76
1992/93	46	19	15	12	81	57	24	72
1993/94	46	24	13	9	74	44	30	85
1994/95	39	16	6	17	54	53	1	54
Totals	**278**	**125**	**73**	**80**	**444**	**328**	**116**	**448**

Sheffield Wednesday FC

Following his departure from Edgeley Park, Danny Bergara had already been linked with several managerial posts, most notably Plymouth Argyle, Chester City and Darlington. However the call that changed his thinking came from one of his oldest contacts in the English game, David Pleat.

Bergara's old partner in the Luton Town youth department had also made a name for himself as a first team manager, and had recently been appointed as the new manager of Premier League Sheffield Wednesday and he had offered the Uruguayan a role in his new backroom staff. Bergara had been offered the position of head coach where he would work with the first team alongside Pleat and player-coach Chris Waddle.

Pleat told the press: *Danny was successful at Stockport on limited resources. But he can maximise the players available and likes playing imaginative, enterprising football. He had a long-ball reputation at Stockport but this was a result of the demands of the lower divisions and his need to make the best of the players he had. I know that Danny can coach short-ball as well. In his Stockport days, he was a victim of the system. I will give him his head to work with senior players, players who are more talented than those he has worked with before. As a coaching team, myself; Danny and Chris Waddle, we shall try to produce imaginative, exciting football. I know that Danny has the ability. He has just needed the platform. We had a coaching relationship that was stimulating at Luton for the two years before Harry Haslam took Danny with him to Sheffield United.*

Like Bergara, who was still in dispute with County, Pleat had left his former side Luton Town under somewhat of a cloud as the Hatters were unhappy with the level of compensation Wednesday had offered for their manager. Town were considering legal action against Wednesday with Gordon Milne, the new Chief Executive of the League Managers' Association, hoping to persuade League chairmen to adopt the team managers' charter. He hoped that the wrangle over a compensation fee for Pleat should not be repeated once the charter is in place: *"Football by its nature is a game of change. Players, managers and chairman move about and you need to handle these changes as smoothly as possible. Once the charter is in place, there will be a procedure that everybody will think about in order to avoid adverse publicity".*

The local press covered the news of Bergara's appointment:

<u>At Close Range</u>

Danny Bergara's appointment as David Pleat's new Sheffield Wednesday assistant may have surprised the wider world but not this particular corner of it. Or, at least, not those with longish memories. Above all, Pleat never forgot the young Uruguayan with whom he worked at Luton early in both their careers. And so it was that, 22 years on, Bergara got the call from his old pal to link up again at Hillsborough.

But, of course, many of us remember, too, how they almost paired up in Sheffield some 17 years ago. When Bergara joined Harry Haslam in moving from Luton to Sheffield United, Pleat was invited to follow suit. But he stayed at Kenilworth Road, progressing to Haslam's management job, and it has taken the best part of two decades to complete the reunion at the other end of Sheffield.

"I'm grateful that David appreciated the way I worked with the youngsters all that time ago at Luton," says Danny, back in football just a few months after his sudden departure from Stockport. "We've kept a close relationship ever since. Whenever I was out of work he always asked me to look at players for him. Now I'm delighted about his confidence in me and the chance to prove myself here. I'll do my utmost to show that I'm good enough to justify that faith. I believe Sheffield Wednesday will get very good value for money from David and myself. This club belongs in the top five in the Premier League and I'll do everything I can to help David get us there."

Bergara regards the Hillsborough invitation as the pinnacle of his career and "a chance I've fully deserved after 22 years hard work in this country." The genial 52 year old, who became English football's first foreign coach in joining Luton, has constantly defied the widespread impression that he was merely an outsider looking in.

When Rochdale hired him in 1988 Bergara achieved another 'first' - as the only South American to manage a League club. And his work with the England Under 18's under Ron Greenwood's tenure was another pioneering move.

But it was Bergara's success with Stockport that really silenced the sceptics. One promotion and four Wembley appearances, two play-offs and two Autoglass Trophy finals, represented an outstanding record for an unfashionable club. Now Bergara is looking to bring to Hillsborough what he calls "a combination of South American skill and the English style.

He added: "We were wrongly labelled a long-ball team at Stockport. You don't get to Wembley four times playing that way. People got it wrong because we used the ability of the players *available by hurting teams in their half. Once the ball was there you saw the skill in the Stockport side. Here I'm hoping, with the players at Sheffield Wednesday, we can maybe go through the middle a bit more."*

An Old Pals Act

Danny Bergara and Sheffield Wednesday have something in common - they've both been to Wembley four times in recent years without winning a trophy there! But now they are together and striving for success, with Bergara taking up his job as head coach after returning from a Mediterranean holiday. Bergara managed Stockport to two promotion play-off finals and two Autoglass finals - and he took the Lancashire club up once. He left Stockport in March and was delighted when his old pal David Pleat offered him a chance to get back into the game quickly. "I'm just pleased that David thought of me," says Bergara, who came from Luton to Sheffield to join United in the 1970's and has lived in the same Bradway house for 17 years.

"David and I kept in contact since I left Luton. I picked the phone up if I needed a bit of advice when I was manager with Rochdale and Stockport, and likewise if David wanted any information about the lower divisions, he always knew where I was. We have a lot of respect for each other. I think we'll do well. If we can match at this level what I did at Stockport, I'll be happy. And if we get to Wembley, I want to win something!"

Bergara talks of the importance of modesty and respect between a coach and his players, and of the need to play in a way that suits the players that a club has. He added: "I will do what David wants. He will be looking at the situation, together with myself and the staff, and we shall do whatever needs to be done. "I hope we have a successful time. We won't ask for 101 per cent from the players, but 99 per cent will be short."

There was a quick response to the above article in the readers' letters page:

<u>**Realistic Owls can be Winners**</u>

After reading Paul Thompson's article 'An Old Pals Act' in the Green 'Un, July 8, I felt quite pleased and comforted when he quoted Danny Bergara who speaks of the importance of modesty and respect between a coach and his players and the need to play in a way that suits the players that a club has. Over the past two seasons, I have repeatedly read in the local papers praise of Wednesday's attractive football and of the team being a 'passing team'. I have attended matches where they have had possession of the ball for two-thirds of the game, but they finished up losing the match.

When attractive football is mentioned, in relation to Sheffield Wednesday, I always think back to the time of Vic Buckingham and the team that Wednesday had in the mid-sixties. They played attractive football but they didn't win matches. Buckingham inherited from Harry Catterick a strong, purposeful team, in my opinion the most successful team Wednesday ever enjoyed since the war years, and he tried to turn it into a 'passing team' with drastic results.

Wednesday supporters are hungry for success, they want security in the Premier division and no more yo-yo teams, they are tired of repeatedly fighting against relegation, but deserve a string of victories leading to winning one or two trophies. If David Pleat and Danny Bergara can achieve this and still play the 'passing game' so much the better. However, I do detect a degree of realism creeping into their philosophy and perhaps an intention to play to their strengths. I would suggest if this policy is carried out then there is hope for the future. (B Parkin, Sheffield)

Wednesday had entered the Intertoto Cup and with the qualifying group stages being played during the pre-season schedule, it was an early introduction to competitive football for the new management team.

Wednesday, who were to play their two home games at Rotherham's Millmoor Stadium, were drawn in the same group as Germany's Karlsruhe, Swiss team Basel, Denmark's Aarhus and Poland's Gornik Zabrze. Wednesday lost their opening game in Switzerland 1-0 to Basel. Winning the next game at 'home' against Gornik Zabrze thanks to an own goal and further strikes from Mark Bright and Chris Waddle. Bright scored his second goal of the competition when Wednesday drew in the next game away at Karlsruhe. The result was a good measure of where the squad were at, as the German football season had only just ended and the Owls were only a week into their pre-season.

Early Effort is Big Booster for Danny

Owls head coach Danny Bergara, taking charge of the team for the game, saw encouraging signs for the future in the way the team performed in Karlsruhe.

"The lads responded well," he said. "Obviously we need to consider that we are only one week into our pre-season work. There will be a lot more to come. We have shown we can already last 90 minutes. It was a great effort. I'm more pleased because after they have

responded to me in this manner, I'm sure there will be an even greater response for our manager. We did a job."

Pre-match planning was influenced by a video of Karlsruhe in action, and Bergara was aided by chief scout and coach Mick Mills. Added Bergara: "It was a beautiful ground, a beautiful pitch, and a good crowd for this competition, the lads did themselves some kind of justice by fighting to the last minute. It got us a point". Mark Bright commented: "This game came at the end of a reasonably hard weeks' training. We knew it was going to be a tough one. German teams are technically and physically very good. They had six or seven people over 6ft. It was emphasised that this was a fitness exercise for us. But we still didn't want to lose. This was Germany v England, after all."

Wednesday were to play their last group game at Millmoor against Aarhus knowing that they needed to win and hope that the Germans lost in Poland for them to qualify for the knockout stages. The Owls kept up their side of the deal by claiming a 3-1 win thanks to two more goals from Bright and another from Dan Petrescu. Unfortunately Karlsruhe won comfortably 6-1 to claim the top spot in the group and knock Wednesday out.

The League campaign began with three very tough fixtures for the Owls, with games against title 'fancies' Liverpool, Blackburn Rovers and Newcastle United. A second half Stan Collymore goal had brought an opening day defeat at Anfield whilst goals from Waddle and Mark Pembridge had been enough to bring a win against Rovers in the first game at Hillsborough.

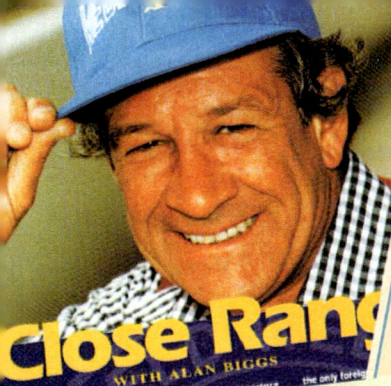

Close Rang[e]
WITH ALAN BIGGS

[C]an't get fair chance -Dann[y]

In off the POST

[re]alistic Owls [ca]n be winners

SHE...

SHEF...

SOCCER

Pleat calls Bergara

[Al]an Appleyard

DAVID PLEAT has asked former Stockport manager Danny Bergara to join him at Sheffield Wednesday as part of the club's eventual backroom staff.

Uruguayan Bergara, 53, is expected to accept the position of head coach and work with the first team alongside manager Pleat and player-coach Chris Waddle.

Both Bergara and Waddle are on holiday thinking over the respective offers.

Pleat said: "Danny was successful at Stockport on limited resources. But he can maximise the players available and likes playing imaginative, enterprising football.

Bergara, who worked alongside Pleat at Luton in the late 1970s, has also managed Rochdale and had two coaching spells at Sheffield United. He left Stockport towards the end of last season after a dispute with chairman Brendan Elwood.

Gordon Milne, the new chief executive of the League Managers' Association, hopes this week's compensation dispute between Sheffield Wednesday and Luton Town will be one of the last.

Having succeeded Jim Smith as the third full-time LMA chief, he hopes to persuade Endsleigh League chairmen to adopt the team managers' charter.

He said this week's wrangle over a compensation fee for David Pleat should not be repeated once the charter is in place, especially if Endsleigh clubs sign.

■ Football by its nature is a game of change. Players, managers and you need to handle these changes as smoothly as possible. Once the charter is in place, there will be a procedure that everybody will think about in order to avoid adverse publicity.

■ Manchester United's Paul Ince yesterday insisted

[I]t had always been his intention to return from Italy without signing for Inter Milan in order to mull over his proposed multi-million pound move.

The England midfield player dismissed as "nonsense" suggestions that the delay in moving came because his wife, Claire, could not find anywhere she wanted to live.

United's chairman Martin Edwards said: "We are not banking on Paul going. If he stays, it just means we will not be in a position to spend heavily on the transfer market over the short term."

■ Crystal Palace's winger John Salako's proposed £2m move to Newcastle has been delayed.

The former England man, who had travelled to Tyneside for talks and a medical, was due to complete the signing yesterday afternoon, but the club's chief executive Freddie Fletcher announced: "John has gone back to London to discuss the move

the mid-Sixties. They played [bu]t they didn't win matches [inherit]ed from Harry Catterick, [so, i]n my opinion the most su[ccess] may have ever enjoyed since I [wan]t to turn it into a "pea[ceful]" [res]ults.

[Play]ers are hungry for suc [in] the Premier Division ar [the]y are tired of repeatedly [bu]t deserve a string [...] [...] one or two trophies.

[Dann]y Bergara can ach [...]ing game is much th [...]a degree of realism [...]n and perhaps an in [...]

[...] this policy is carri [...]ture.

[...] Sheffield S12.

...a lot

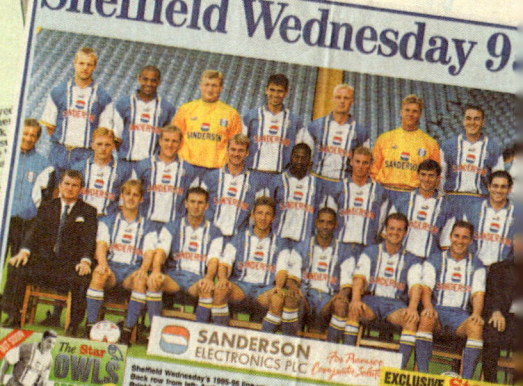

Sheffield Wednesday 9...

SANDERSON ELECTRONICS PLC

EXCLUSIVE Star POS[TER]

The Star OWLS SPECIAL 30p

Sheffield Wednesday's 1995-96 line-up:
Back row from left: Andy Pearce, Mark Bright, Kevin Pressman, Peter Atherton, John Sheridan, Michael Williams, Lee Briscoe, Ian Nolan, Guy Whittingham, Richie Barker. Centre row, from left: David Pleat (manager), Mark Pembridge, Paul Atherton, John Hyde, Marc Degryse, Dan Petrescu, Des Walker, Andy Sinton, Des [...], Richie Barker (manager's assistant).

taking th[...] and Kev[...] towards [...]

"Basi[c...] mitment [...] lacking [...] come ho[...]

"Alan [...]

"Well, [...] about W[...] by the a[...]

Po[...] p[...]

DAN Petr[escu...] player tha[...] cultured [...] passing an[...]

The man[...] Dan's stren[...]

"I don't [...] try better or [...] ing full-back [...] run," [...]

There we[...] Liverpool an[...]

For exam[...]

An early report in the Green 'Un:

That's more like it

Under new management and doesn't it show. Wednesday have looked a different side in their first two games, compared to last season. There seems to be a sense of unity and commitment on the pitch. Players appear to know exactly what they're doing and what they are expected to do. There is a shape, a pattern, and quick and incisive football within that framework.

The new boss and his head coach Danny Bergara are clearly doing everything to try to make the most of talented individuals. That means welding them into a team, not the club's strong point during their underachievement of previous years. Pleat, for his part, can only have been pleased by the willingness of players to learn and work hard. The team have looked fitter, sharper. No doubt their desire to impress a new boss has been another beneficial factor. Getting it right in every game is a different matter of course. Wouldn't it be typical of football if the Owls were brought down to earth by Newcastle tomorrow!

But, so far, fans couldn't ask for much more as Pleat and his staff begin to transform the club. The new system at the back has generally coped pretty well against formidable opposition, even if Stan Collymore and Alan Shearer did both get free to score. Fullbacks Ian Nolan and Dan Petrescu are both suited to the attacking fullback roles. Des Walker, Peter Atherton, and the re-emerging Julian Watts have formed good understanding in the centre-back positions. John Sheridan, working from deep and directing operations, remains the team's midfield general. Already there has been tactical variation. At Anfield, Pleat chose two midfield battlers, Mark Pembridge and Graham Hyde, and had Chris

Waddle playing off Mark Bright. Against Blackburn, it was the old partnership of Hirst and Bright up front, with Waddle linking play behind them, and no place in midfield for Hyde.

Pleat has sought to add to the armoury by sending Watts forward at set pieces, and by adding in-swinging corners and long throws from Mark Pembridge, whose hit and miss first two games ended with a determinedly taken winner against Blackburn. Watts, without a senior goal for the club, has already had one header cleared off the line at Anfield, and another hit the bar against Blackburn (from Pembridge's throw). Bright and Hirst looked something like their old selves and had a real battle with Blackburn centre halves Colin Hendry and Ian Pearce.

Hirst wasn't making a fuss about it, but he suspected that Pearce should have been sent off for the swinging hand that caught him in the face: "I don't go down for nothing," he said. Pleat has already shown himself willing to make decisions that could raise eyebrows among fans, Hirst being on the bench at Anfield, for example. It helps when the boss knows exactly what he wants and does what he feels is best for the team. Pleat notably decided not to throw Marc Degryse in after his injury, some managers would have felt compelled to field a big new signing, but eased him in as a sub. It was good management too when Pleat chose not to give Degryse an outing in the second half against Blackburn if he felt that it might upset the balance.

There are bound to have been a few long faces when Pleat made his selection known to the players, but not everyone can play, and they all have to fight for places. Andy Sinton, one of those disappointed to miss out, responded with a useful stint as a sub taking over from Chris Waddle in the role behind the front two during the Blackburn game.

Pleat hasn't finished yet. He will strive to improve the side, and there could be exciting times ahead.

The Owls were indeed brought down to earth in their next game as Newcastle United claimed top spot in the table, a position they wouldn't give up until March the following year, thanks to second half goals from David Ginola and Peter Beardsley. Early problems for Pleat and his management team were the lack of goals from his side and with a forthcoming tricky League Cup tie against Division Two leaders, Crewe Alexandra, Bergara had warned his players of the risk of a cup upset.

<u>**Under-Dogs with Real Bite**</u>

Danny Bergara spent enough time in the lower divisions to know what will be going through Crewe's mind before their Coca Cola Cup clash with Wednesday. His experiences carry an obvious warning for the Owls, underestimate the opposition at your peril! Bergara was boss of Stockport when they knocked QPR out of the League Cup at home in the fourth round: "It was the furthest we had got in 20 odd years; our attitude was right, theirs wasn't," he says. "That's what lower teams are banking on when they play teams from a higher division".

Bergara and David Pleat were back at Crewe this week to watch next Tuesday's Coca Cola Cup opposition beat Brighton 3-1 in Division Two. It put the Alex top, with only one goal conceded at home. Says Danny, who also managed Rochdale: "David and I have both had experience in the lower divisions. Our team's attitude must be right on the night. I always say that you've got to be well organised and must want to win more than the other side. Then your ability will come through. If you think 'We'll slaughter this lot', then you've got no chance".

The Wednesday head coach had many a battle with Crewe: "We were always enemies! It was always a local derby. I think we usually got the better of them, and we beat them at their place on our way to Wembley in the Autoglass Trophy. They have a neat and tidy ground, and a neat and tidy team, but when I saw them this week their side had changed quite a bit. I think they are a bit more direct in certain ways. They like to knock the ball about. Sometimes in the past they were known for being a terrific keep-ball team, who were not so positive in getting forward quickly. Against Brighton this week, they did well. They scored three and could have scored more. Brighton scored one and could have scored more, as well."

The Owls comfortably saw off the threat of the Railwaymen and indeed Division One outfit Millwall in the next round, with new Dutch striker Marc Degryse finding his feet early in his Wednesday career with four League and Cup goals. The lack of goals was still proving to be a concern in the Premier League with only three scored in an eight game run pushed the Owls down the table. They were also to lose at Arsenal in the next round of the League Cup.

A five match unbeaten run towards Christmas, the best of the campaign, saw Pleat's team finally discover their shooting boots as David Hirst (5), Bright (5), Guy Whittingham (3) and Degryse (3) earned points against Everton, Coventry City, Manchester United, Leeds United and Southampton.

Having won on the opening day of the New Year against Bolton Wanderers, Wednesday travelled to Division One Charlton Athletic in the FA Cup where they were to suffer a surprise defeat. This was to set the tone for a dreadful run of results as the Owls picked up just fifteen points from their last seventeen games, a win against Arsenal and draws against Chelsea and West Ham

United in the last month just enough to see them finish two points above the relegation places. Following an end of season Board meeting it was decided that there needed to be radical changes to the coaching system at the club. Pleat was to keep his job but the majority of his coaching staff were dismissed.

The Sheffield Star reported on Bergara's dismissal:

I Didn't get Fair Chance - Danny

Sheffield Wednesday's axed head coach Danny Bergara today claimed that he didn't get a fair chance at Hillsborough. He was manager David Pleat's first appointment, as first-team coach, but was fired by the club after 11 months.

"I am very sad to leave a great club," said Bergara today. "It was some experience. The Chairman (Dave Richards) listened to my claims and agreed that I had not had a good chance to fulfil my coaching and managerial abilities. But that's how it goes in football. I don't point fingers at anyone. I wanted to stay, in any capacity, but I take the decision on the chin. The Chairman has been very good with me. We have parted on good terms, and I have probably gained a friend."

Bergara refused to elaborate further but is likely to have been given too little responsibility and authority for his liking. From an early stage in the season, first team coaching was being spread amongst a large back-room staff, with Frank Barlow in particular becoming more heavily involved. And I believe that the Board felt that Bergara's appointment had not worked out, and that a change was required. A backroom clear-out is part of the changes about which Dave Richards spoke only recently in The Star. Barlow, a popular personality at Hillsborough, has joined Arvel Lowe and Mick Mills at Birmingham City, and Richie Barker, like Bergara, has left the Owls.

Darlington

Having been one of several of Sheffield Wednesday's backroom staff to have been released from their contracts, Bergara was soon back in work as he joined Jim Platt at Darlington in time for the 1996-97 campaign.

Darlington had been beaten in the play-off Final by Plymouth Argyle at the end of the previous season with Platt at the helm, although he had previously been joint manager with David Hodgson. With the expected return of Hodgson as manager for the new season, Bergara was employed as assistant director of coaching.

The Quakers appeared to have recovered from the hangover of losing the play-off Final and had begun the new season in steady if not spectacular form. By mid-September they had already thrashed eventual champions Wigan Athletic at Feethams, to remain in the play-off spots with the early pace setters. Four days later Hereford United were also beaten at home in what turned out to be Bergara's last game at the club.

Rotherham United

With Rotherham United suffering their worst start to a season since 1933, joint managers Archie Gemmill and John McGovern left the club by mutual consent. The Millers appointing Bergara as Chief Coach the same day. John Breckin was promoted to become the Uruguayan's number two, with both men solely in charge of first team affairs.

The Millers had also been at Wembley at the end of the previous season, where they had won the Autoglass Trophy Final against Shrewsbury Town thanks to two goals from Nigel Jemson, however the run to Wembley had papered over the financial problems that the club were suffering from. Several players had moved on including Jemson and his strike partner Shaun Goater.

With his side sitting bottom of the table and without a win to their name, Bergara set about bringing players in on trial including former England international Neil Webb, who he knew from his days as England Youth coach.

Bergara also had a look at Aly Dia, who had been the subject of a much publicised 'scam' which had earned the player a one month contract at Premier League Southampton. Having played in the German Second Division, Dia was looking for a club in England where his wife was studying. A friend of his phoned Graeme Souness and claimed that former 'world player of the year' George Weah had recommended Dia, adding that he was a cousin of Weah's. The Saints' boss offered Dia a one month contract and, having had no opportunity to watch him, named him on the bench against Leeds United. Dia replaced Saints' legend Matt le Tissier in the first half but was replaced himself early in the second half after it became obvious that he wasn't ready for that level of football.

Bergara didn't offer the Senegalese player a contract, with the striker going on to sign for non-league Gateshead.

Youngsters Jimmy Crawford and Mark Druce joined on loan from Newcastle United and Oxford United respectively, former Sheffield United player Brian Gayle was given a one month contract, whilst Neil Richardson, Darren Garner, Paul Hurst,

Martin James, Steve Slawson, Steve Farrelly, Andy McIntosh and Craig Davis were made available for transfer.

The win against Peterborough United at Millmoor gave Bergara his third win in seven games to lift his side off the bottom for the first time but a heavy defeat in the return fixture against the Posh a month later and a home defeat against Stockport County saw the Millers drop back to the bottom.

As well as being bottom of the table Bergara was struggling with several off field issues, mainly financial, as he was tasked with lowering the wage bill. He also had a football problem as two players, Shaun Goodwin and Darren Garner, refused to be substitutes for the home game against Millwall. Goodwin demanding a transfer whilst Garner had walked out of the ground. Bergara stated that unless he received an honest apology, neither would play for the club again. Both players earning a two week fine for their actions.

Early in the New Year several members of the squad agreed to an early release from their contracts as Bergara continued to trim the club's wage bill. As if to prove how difficult the juggling of finances became, Bergara brought in striker Earl Jean on a short term contract after he had impressed during a trial. The former St Lucian international would go on to notch six goals to become the club's top scorer before Plymouth Argyle offered him a permanent deal, meaning he left the club without the Millers making a penny.

Early in March 1997 The Rotherham Independent Supporters Club held a forum which was attended by 500 fans. The panel included club representatives Phil Henson and Bergara. The main points of discussion being the financial struggles that the club were suffering, including the fact that the Millers were losing £10,000 per week and that, Ken Booth apart, none of the other directors were able to support the club financially. The club was up for sale with no interested parties, the other problem being that even though Millmoor was in a poor state, they had to remain there as there were no funds available from the Football Trust.

All in all Bergara used over thirty players as he attempted to keep Rotherham in the Third Division, a hard earned draw at eventual runners-up Stockport County, where he received a hero's welcome from the home supporters, as the familiar chant of 'Danny Bergara's Blue & White Army' rang around Edgeley Park for several minutes, and back-to-back wins against Shrewsbury Town and promotion chasing Bristol City being the only real highlights after Christmas.

On April 8th 1997 the Millers became the first club to be relegated after the defeat at Wrexham, Bergara's side still had four games to play but he was sacked before the last of those having been in charge for eight months, with Mick Hennigan taking over in a caretaker role.

Doncaster Rovers

Bergara's next venture into the manager's hot seat saw him at Belle Vue for a very brief spell as Doncaster Rovers manager. The 1997/98 season is remembered by Rovers supporters' as the worst ever in the history of the club but considering that Bergara became the fourth manager that season when accepting the role in November, just four months into the campaign, it would be no surprise.

Darlington F.C. 1996/97

ROVER THE MOON . . . Danny Bergara is the last surviving member of Doncaster's coaching staff after cost-cutting

Ex Chelsea striker Kerry Dixon, who had controversially replaced manager Sammy Chung just two hours before the first game of the previous season, lasted just three games of the new campaign. Having suffered an opening day defeat at Shrewsbury Town, his side lost 8-0 in the League Cup to Nottingham Forest before another heavy defeat to Peterborough United. Dixon then resigned stating that his team selection was being influenced by Chairman Ken Richardson.

September saw Rovers name Colin Richardson, who wasn't related to the Chairman, as the new manager. Eight games and four points later and Richardson was gone, to be replaced by popular youth-team manager Dave Cowling. Cowling was in charge for just three games, all of which ended in defeat before Bergara was brought in.

A draw in his first game against Cardiff City was followed by another draw at Barnet but his next three games ended in defeat. At the end of the month after suffering abuse and threatening behaviour from a section of the Rovers' supporters, Bergara resigned from match day management but stayed on as Director of Football, General Manager Mark Weaver naming himself as manager until the end of the season. The long awaited first win of the season came as Rovers won against Chester City in December.

The Local paper summed up the state of the club:

Danny's Doncaster Challenge

In Uruguay they have a saying that 'You cannot make rump steaks out of tripe'. Ironic really because that is exactly what Danny Bergara has tried to do with the worst team in the Football League this season. Doncaster Rovers are a shambles, rock bottom of

Division Three with just four wins from 41 games, in which they've conceded a staggering 105 goals. If they do not win at Chester today and Hull avoid defeat against Hartlepool, Donny will be relegated to the Vauxhall Conference after a run of 75 years as a League side.

Never mind money to buy players, they do not have enough cash even to paint over the burn marks left by the fire that wrecked the main stand almost 2 years ago, nor will they until someone buys the club from current chairman Ken Richardson who, as many of Rovers dwindling band of diehard fans will tell you, is the most detested man in town. Poor Bergara is not far behind in the hate stakes, he cannot understand why, and frankly neither can I.

Bergara, 55, and a man showing dedication beyond the call of duty, is Donny's first team coach. Correction he is their ONLY coach. And his duties stretch to even driving one.

"I had to get behind the wheel of our 16 seater the other day, to drive our kids to a game at Leeds. The youth development officer, David Dew used to do it, but he upped and left last Friday. Same as most everybody else really.

"So it's just me and the physio now, he looks after the injuries and I do the rest - coaching the first-team, reserves and kids. I also do the school of excellence every Thursday night as well.

"I think I'll stick to the football now though, I had a bit of trouble driving the bus - smacked into a wall at the petrol station and scratched one side. I just hope the damage is covered on the insurance"

There have been times over the last few months when Bergara felt he needed extra insurance cover too. That is because a section of *fans launched a vicious hate campaign against him from no apparent reason*

"I came in last November after the team had been stuffed 4-0 at Scarborough. They had been getting beaten regularly by fours and fives and Forest put eight past them in the Coca-Cola Cup.

"I turned things around, despite taking over a bunch of players who were clearly not fit or organised enough. We drew my first two games in charge against Cardiff and Barnet. Then we lost by the odd goal in five at Preston in the FA Cup and away to Lincoln in the League. And that's when the fans started turning on me and hurling abuse. I can take the flack but it got to the stage where I feared for my safety.

"These so-called supporters had already threatened our General Manager Mark Weaver with violence, twice he had to be escorted from the ground for his own safety, and had to change his home and mobile phone numbers because of the threats.

"I did not deserve the stick I was getting, so after a month I told Mark I was no longer prepared to sit in the dugout on match days. I could handle the verbal abuse and the spitting, but there was no way I'd lay myself open to physical attacks. So I carried on coaching the lads during the week, but did not turn up for matches"

But Danny was forced back into match day action two weeks ago after the rest of the coaching staff were wiped out in yet another cost-cutting exercise. Bergara admits "I had no choice. I had to come back and run the team because I'm the only one left. It was a case of doing the job on match days, or risk being out on my ear. I decided to carry on for two reasons. Firstly I need the income because I have a family to provide for. But, secondly I'm a football man, I have been in the game for 41 years and, despite all the aggravation, heartache and problems I'd rather be with Doncaster than not involved at all.

"Of course it's bloody hard. It's the toughest job I've ever had, especially when you have fans protesting at every game. Especially too, when you only have nine full-time pros on your staff, actually make that eight because one of them is serving three months in prison for driving while disqualified.

"Last Saturday I had to throw in seven under 19's against Hull. We still beat them 1-0 which means we're not dead and buried yet. Where there is life there is hope and, if we win at Chester, there will still be hope for us. But our game after that is at home to Notts County on Easter Monday, and they are so far in front, they've already won promotion.

"Realistically we haven't had a chance of staying in the League, but I really do pray that this club finds a buyer and stays in business. As daft as it sounds, after all I've been through, I'd consider staying on in helping them next season"

Even if it means continuing to try and make rump steaks out of tripe......

Having lost that game against Chester City at the Deva Stadium, Rovers were relegated with four games still to play. Rovers had seen five different managers take on the role during the campaign and used forty five players during the campaign, it came as a surprise to no-one connected with the club that they would lose their Football League status at the end of the season. Both Weaver and Bergara left the club in the summer.

Grantham Town

Bergara's last spell as manager came at Grantham Town for the 1998/99 season where he once again linked up with his former Sheffield United Chairman, Reg Brealey. The Gingerbreads had won promotion to the Southern League Premier Division from the Midland Division at the end of the previous campaign.

Manager Gary Mills had resigned following budget cuts put in place by Brealey after the businessman had taken over the club in the summer. Bergara was happy to step in and help out his former Chairman but unfortunately the side struggled with the step up, and a string of poor results saw Bergara become the club's Director of Football & Chief Scout with Tony Kenworthy becoming manager. The team eventually finishing 17th.

Scouting

After a spell out of the game, Bergara resurfaced as a scout for his oldest friend in the English game, David Pleat, who was by now Director of Football at Tottenham Hotspur.

Bergara then began a working relationship with Mick McCarthy, who had held the Uruguayan in high esteem from his early days as a young manager finding his way in the game. McCarthy had never forgotten his early meetings with Bergara or the fact that he had been able to call on him for advice but most importantly he knew that Bergara could spot a player.

McCarthy, who had recently taken over at Premiership side Sunderland after a spell as Republic of Ireland manager, gave Bergara a scouting role for the Wearside club. Bergara remained with Sunderland for three years until McCarthy moved to Wolverhampton Wanderers in 2006. Once again the pair linked up as Bergara became a scout for the Championship outfit, a role he held until his death the following year.

During his long career in the English game Danny Bergara has been used as a scout by some of the best managers in the game. Whilst at Luton as a coach learning his trade he would often be asked to look at players. Years later as an established coach, either in spells between management roles or employed by a club as a full time scout, he would often be asked to provide reports on potential signings. Below are some of the players that over the years Bergara has recommended his employers to sign:

Mark Hateley - Leeds United Res v Coventry City Res (September 1981)

19 Years old, good acceleration and pace, fairly good in the air, good movement off the ball, good turning ability (he turns as he collects the ball - in one move he is away) - can play either side although he is very much left footed. He did put in a very dangerous ball with his wrong foot, which means to me he can use either foot if he has to (all good natural skilful players can do that) He gets into very good positions 95% of the time but didn't have good service. His first touch wasn't as good as I would've expected from a good player and he did lack concentration at times but that can all be worked on. He did have three chances and I would expect him to score at least one of them but I could improve him. I like him, and once he's learned to finish who knows!!

Hateley established himself in the City first team over the next two seasons before beginning a long and successful career with Portsmouth, Inter Milan, Monaco and Glasgow Rangers. The big striker scored almost 200 goals in a career spanning 500 games, he also won over 30 caps for England.

Kevin Ratcliffe - Everton Res v Man City Res (October 1981)

21 years old, a very strong player with a good left foot, didn't do particularly well in the air and allowed forwards to turn him but he is very quick and made a couple of great forward runs through the middle, although he didn't always take the chance, he does like to play safe and make his distribution very straightforward. He certainly looked good when moved to play left back where he showed more determination and tackled opponents with no hesitation. Having only seen him once I've seen enough to say that, specifically in a position that is not his, he does look very good bet to me.

Ratcliffe forced his way into the Goodison Park first team the following season and remained a permanent fixture for the next ten years, making almost 350 League appearances and also earning himself over 50 caps for Wales.

Mick McCarthy - Leicester City v Barnsley (December 1981)

Danny had actually gone to watch Larry May and the following report was about Mick McCarthy:

At 21 years old I think he's a better footballer than May but does make some mistakes including giving away silly free kicks in and around his own box. He does have a nice touch and needs to work on his tackling. It is apparent he wants to do everything 'very beautiful' with regards to his passes. He can deliver a good long throw-in which is good at the end of the day. He is not yet top-class for me but May isn't either. It all depends on what you're looking for, they are both good defenders though I think you would get more out of him going forwards when required.

McCarthy moved to Manchester City two years later, ironically May replaced him at Oakwell, winning promotion to the Premier League in his first season. Two successful seasons with Glasgow Celtic were followed by short playing spells with Lyon and Millwall before the former Irish international moved into a successful management career. He would later use Bergara as a scout.

David Speedie - Darlington (March 1982)

Bergara watched 22 year old Speedie three times in the month as Luton Town appeared keen to sign the lively forward:

Mansfield v Darlington - in absolute terrible conditions he showed some good touches, a little bit of pace and scored an excellent diving header. I'm not too sure about his thinking at times, he did not play to the conditions, however I was pleased with what I saw. His reading of the game and basic priorities need working on.

Rochdale v Darlington - I hope by the time you receive this report we have had a chat on the phone and you have the deal wrapped up. The lad was superb and although not aware of what goes on when losing possession, (this is something we can teach him) he has a lot to offer to a team in a higher division. He might have problems against better defenders but after seeing him twice I have no doubt YES!! At £25,000 we should get him before somebody else does. He scored twice, one was again another beautiful header, and should also have been awarded a penalty.

Stockport County v Darlington - This is the third time I've seen the lad and I think once again he's a good player and would be very useful with better players around him (therefore better service). Again did excellent in the air. Only had one chance that he created for himself, the keeper made a superb stop.

Whilst other clubs pondered, Chelsea nipped in to buy Speedie for £80,000. The Scot also had successful spells at Coventry City, Liverpool and Blackburn Rovers amongst others. He accumulated over 500 league appearances scoring almost 150 goals in his professional career. Speedie also earned 10 caps for Scotland.

Gary Lineker - Rotherham v Leicester City (August 1982)

21 years old. Didn't play from the start, was named as substitute. Came on after 66 minutes and could not have had a better spell. Worked hard when defending and did so when required. Played wide on the right and gave full back Breckin a hard time, showing pace, skill and that he is not chicken. Did well in the air and showed good control of the ball, can come forward either way, down the middle or on the outside. Finished off a good appearance with a good goal, from a fairly difficult cross, but finished it well after a clever diagonal run. I would follow him David, he is a good bet.

Lineker went on to make almost 200 first team appearances for the Filbert Street club before moving to Everton. Having scored 40 goals in 57 appearances he moved to Barcelona. On his return to England he moved to Tottenham Hotspur before finishing his career in Japan. Lineker scored 48 goals in just 80 appearances for England, winning the Golden Boot at the 1986 World Cup.

Chris Waddle - Leeds United v Newcastle United (October 1982)

22 years old. A strong and powerful runner, has a lot of skill. He played mainly on the right side and likes to switch to the left occasionally. On the day I don't think he was as positive as he should've been, but showed he has a lot to offer. I like him. He was by far the most skilful player on offer. As I have said before he likes to move around looking 'not involved' in a very unorthodox manner before bursting into life. He is a very good footballer. How much would he cost though David??

Waddle established himself in the first team at St James' Park over the next two years before joining Tottenham Hotspur in 1985 for £590,000. The unorthodox winger went on to enjoy a

great career, making over 350 appearances over the next ten years for Spurs, Olympic Marseille and Sheffield Wednesday. Waddle also earned over 60 England caps.

Brian Marwood - Hull City v Peterborough United (November 1982)

This is the fourth time I've seen 22 year old Marwood this season. He had an excellent game scoring twice, one was a beauty, and he made the other two. He was, on the day, a class above the rest. I don't know how much you want to buy him but I don't think you would be getting him for less than £100,000 at this moment in today's prices. I would say yes - he excited me and not many players do that to me

Marwood went on to play top flight football for Sheffield Wednesday, Arsenal and Sheffield United. His transfer fees totalled well over £1,000,000. He won the First Division title twice whilst with Arsenal.

Steve Bruce - Bradford City v Gillingham (January 1983)

23 years old. Bruce didn't do as well as I expected him to, but still showed things to make me believe he is as good a proposition as any. He kept Bobby Campbell quiet all afternoon and when it came to tackling it was no messing. Did well in the air and could've scored (probably should of, heading a free kick in the first half wide). Going forwards he did not do as well as I would have liked him to do but the conditions were not favourable for coming out from the back playing accurate football. When I spoke to you after the game I had no doubt about this player, and I still haven't. I would like to see him again definitely.

Bruce moved to Norwich City at the end of the following season for a fee of £125,000. His form over the next two and half seasons, in winning the Second Division and the League Cup earned him an £800,000 move to Manchester United where he would win almost every honour available apart from an England cap. Bruce is still rated by many as the best English centre half not to be capped.

Micky Adams - Bradford City v Gillingham (January 1983)

At 21 years old David I have no doubt YES!! What a good little player. If I was the Liverpool scout I would be recommending Kennedy be replaced tomorrow. I can't find anything wrong with him - skill - guts - awareness. I think he has the lot to make it big. An excellent little player.

Adams moved from Third Division Gillingham to First Division Coventry City and went on to make over 300 top flight appearances for the Sky Blues, Leeds United and Southampton before moving into management.

Joleon Lescott - Sheffield Weds v Wolverhampton Wanderers (December 2000)

The player I came to watch was ok (see report) but Joleon Lescott for Wolves at 18 years old is well worth having another look at, he did well in the air (6' 2" and still growing) - good awareness - good feet and anticipation. I think he is definitely a player we should keep an eye on and should definitely be watching again.

Lescott played over 160 first team games for Wolves over the next six seasons, his form earning a £2,000,000 move to Premier League Everton. Having become a regular in the England squad he

was sold to Manchester City three years later in a deal reported to be £22,000.000.

Phil Jagielka - Sheffield United v Crystal Palace (September 2001)

19 years old, played both midfield and later left sided centre back (his best position). Didn't have the best game but I can see the lad going on to climb up the ladder with good advice and good coaching work . Showed his versatility playing in two demanding positions and looked ok against experienced strikers Freeman and Morrison. I would say he is well worth following.

Jagielka established himself in Sheffield United's first team, playing 250 games during which time he was the subject of several transfer bids. He eventually signed for Everton in July 2007 in a deal worth over £4,000,000. He has also become an established England international with over 20 appearances.

Nigel Reo-Coker - Sheffield United v Wimbledon (October 2002)

Aged 18. Good strength - also good engine (one that will run for 90 minutes) - two good feet - good aerial power - very good awareness for his age (plenty of room for improvement as he gathers experience) - as a young lad new in the first team perhaps a bit raw - as above as he gathers experience the lad will get enough confidence and could become a super player. He should be watched by senior staff, and needs to be followed by another scout as based on what I have seen this player would definitely have a 'sell on value'.

Eventually Reo-Coker moved across London to West Ham United for over £600,000 where he helped them regain their Premier League status. 120 games later he moved to Aston Villa in a deal

worth over £8,000,000. The midfielder made over 250 Premier League appearances.

James Milner - Bradford City v Leeds United (November 2002)

At just 16 years old he is a very good player and will get better. Two terrific feet, mainly left. Good dribbling skills. Excellent awareness for one so young. I was very impressed with the lad. All the lad lacks is some more strength and power but he will get there as he grows naturally. That will also help with his aerial power. Could be another Wayne Rooney in the making. I would recommend he is watched by senior staff. This player would definitely have a 'sell on' value.

Milner played almost 50 games for his hometown club before being sold to Newcastle United for a reported £3,600,000 after their relegation from the Premier League. Almost 100 games later Milner was on the move again this time to Aston Villa where he spent some time on loan before signing permanently for £12,000,000. By now an England regular 100 games for the Villains later and he was sold again, this time to Manchester City for £28,500,000.

Rickie Lambert - Sheffield Weds v Stockport County (September 2003)

21 years old. The lad had a pretty good game especially when he was moved from midfield to a position behind the front two. His awareness was excellent and he made some clever runs into the box and also wide areas causing a lot of problems to the Owls rearguard. Average pace - right footed but could use both feet - some good first touches - Awareness excellent (his best quality perhaps) - Good all round passing - adequate crossing (mainly from set pieces) - tackling is not his favourite way to win the ball, but did well when he had to - plenty of room for improvement with his heading (with his height and strength he can improve with good coaching) - his finishing also needs working on (but that's what we're able to do). I think we should definitely keep an eye on this lad 8/10.

After a drop in form Lambert actually moved down a division to join Rochdale where he rediscovered his goal scoring touch. A move to Bristol Rovers proved successful leading to a move to Southampton who had recently dropped into the third tier of English football. Back-to-back promotions with Lambert scoring over 80 goals saw the rejuvenated striker playing in the Premier League. His form since has seen him earn national honours, scoring the winner on his England debut against Scotland.

Chris Brunt - Sheffield Wednesday v Leicester City (January 2006)

At 21 years old there is room for improvement in various departments but I'm sure we can help the lad a lot. Although mainly left footed, he can use is right one whenever needed. He scored a 25 yard absolute screamer, playing mainly on the right wing, which suited him perfectly, as by going inside onto his left foot to score. A fair bit to learn but overall YES!! He's a player we should be looking at - excellent awareness - excellent shooting - good pace - great with both right and left foot - good heading ability - good control and passing - would just need to work on his stamina.

Eighteen months later, by which time he was the club's most experienced player, Brunt moved to West Bromwich Albion in a deal worth over £3,000,000. Brunt was named in the Championship team of the year as he helped the Baggies to the Premier League in his first season.

And one that Bergara wasn't too keen on:

Paddy McCourt Rochdale v Swansea City (October 2003)

21 years old. The lad went on as a substitute on the hour mark and did not justify his introduction to his team. In my view the lad has some problems with his attitude (it would take a manager like Mick McCarthy to put him on the right path) The way he went about it when he was brought on wasn't good. Didn't do much and only one or two crosses were his best contributions on the day. He has good pace and can use both feet. Passing not good on the day and he didn't have a shot in the 30 minutes he was on. He didn't go anywhere near a tackle and didn't win a header as he wouldn't want to damage his fancy hairstyle. His marking would be better suited to helping the groundsman. All in all an 'I love me' type of player who is nowhere near ready for our first team.

Having seen Patrick in February last year, when he also came on as substitute and looked a good prospect on the day, I have spoken to my old landlady (from my days as Rochdale manager) and she tells me his attitude has changed dramatically from being a modest, dedicated young player to one of bigheaded and arrogant. I would suggest we try to get him on a month 'loan' to get a better look at him or perhaps take a risk a very very low price.

Having attracted interest from several clubs that season, but with no offer made, McCourt struggled to command a regular place in the team at Spotland and eventually moved back to Ireland where he rebuilt his career with Derry City. A five year spell at Glasgow Celtic followed but the winger made only 66 first team appearances before leaving Parkhead.

The Man from Uruguay

His name was Danny Bergara, the Man from Uruguay
He came to us from Rochdale, we all wondered…why?
It didn't take too long for us to understand the reason,
as he took us to the 'play-offs' at the end of his first full season.

And then the following year, with all the wheels in full motion,
a truly memorable campaign, ended with promotion.
We had a team to be proud of; and were always on a high,
He put Stockport County on the map, the Man from Uruguay.

Our team was always in the news, both in print and on TV,
And soon he took us to a Cup Final for all the world to see.
Danny led his team out at Wembley; the sun was blazing in the sky,
The 1st foreigner to do so, the Man from Uruguay.

We went to Wembley, twice that week, both games ended in defeat
Danny took us back twice more, the taste was bittersweet.
Even though County lost all four games, he told us not to cry,
He made us all believe in him, the Man from Uruguay.

His six years at Edgeley Park were the best many had ever seen,
He gave us a new sense of pride in our 'little' football team.
He laid down the foundations for the club to aim up high,
He will always be Sir Daniel, the Man from Uruguay.

And now we mourn his passing, a time of sadness and great loss,
To those who will regard him as the club's greatest ever 'boss'.
He will be remembered as a 'legend' as time goes by and by,
We will always be grateful for our time, with the Man from Uruguay.

PB 2007

Memories

David Pleat (Luton Town/Sheffield Wednesday)

Danny came, he saw, he conquered. He made a lasting impression on all his friends and colleagues as a canny football coach in a foreign country. He climbed a ladder fraught with difficulties and reached his goal.

I was first introduced to Danny around 1979 when I joined the Luton Town coaching staff. We used to listen to Harry Haslam's combination of mixed metaphors and unique humour, Danny was bright but he didn't understand some of the jokes - neither did I. He laughed - as I did.

I once went to say something to Dan and prefaced it with 'Well Danny boy'. Danny gave me an icy stare "I'm Uruguayan, not Irish"

He picked up English so quickly considering that since leaving his home country in his teens he had spent his footballing career in Spain. We used to compare notes, discuss and stimulate each other with our coaching views.

He was a great demonstrator of the skills of our game. He could trap, he could volley, he could shoot - he could bend the ball years before Beckham did.

Danny's pride in Uruguay was incredible , he used to tell me "Only 6 million people, the great Schiaffino and Santamaria, wonderful footballers. The 1950 World Cup win in Brazil in São Paulo and his own achievements as a goal scorer in Sevilla and Majorca.

He was a great enthusiast who helped the youngsters develop the game. I can tell you of at least two Luton players who had wonderful careers who came to us as 16-year-old bright boys and who Danny worked with and coached and developed. They listened and they believed in him. and one of them went on to be a full England international - Ricky Hill.

I admired how he dealt with the occasional prejudice that unfairly but inevitably surfaced, he was made of tough stock, he was strong, he was athletic.

When we played in charity football matches, we used to joke that we would have to bring an extra ball because Danny needed one on his own. My word he could dribble, and his ability to shield the ball from his opponent was tremendous, fantastic strength, and his tricks that he had to dribble. He was a master of ball skills.

When England looked for a 'support' coach for the under 18 team, we recommended Danny to the FA, but we didn't need to as they were all already aware of his abilities from his work and coaching sessions at Lilleshall where he had earned his FA coaching certificates. He went on to help John Cartwright with England Youth, the first, the very first foreign coach to achieve this recognition. I know how much the late Brian Clough and Peter Taylor enjoyed his company, they were fascinated by his words and his achievements.

When Danny left Luton to accept the offer to go with Harry Haslam as his assistant at Sheffield United, it was a new adventure and he quickly adjusted to the warmth of his neighbours and down to earth mentality in Yorkshire. He continued to gain a reputation as a good coach culminating in his major breakthrough as manager of Stockport County.

Others will have closer and greater affinity with his devotion and deeds at that club. What a wonderful record - a golden period. When Danny had full license to put all his ideas into practice. The leader of the pack, I knew that Danny was achieving against all the odds, and he also knew that on occasions that he had to battle an undercurrent of prejudice.

But he defied the odds, strong willed, focused and opinionated he was a driving force. A man of simple tastes, he stayed in digs beside the ground, he never did join the celebrity managers club, he was a muck and nettles man, a worker. and Danny kept winning.

He spoke glowingly of his men, players who would never have even dreamt of Wembley were now visiting regularly. He was as proud of Stockport as they were proud of him.

We were reunited many years later, if only briefly at Hillsborough. It was a difficult period, outstanding players that were in the twilight of their careers and not able to come to terms with that, clearly on the wane and making it a difficult dressing room. Danny, like many of his coaching colleagues, found the recent soccer hype and rampant commercialism a negative for all those who love the game for what it is.

I miss him, we all miss him, but we were all proud to know you Danny boy, you will never be forgotten, because you were a Champion.

Peter Mead (Luton Town)

I have to say it was no surprise to me that Danny went on to be a success in the managerial merry-go-round in English football with his outstanding personality, tactical knowledge and coaching techniques. In putting some information together about our time *together at Luton it has made me quite emotional thinking of past playing memories and that he is no longer with us. It was an honour and privilege to have known him and be coached by him because without his and Dave Pleat`s guidance at youth and reserve team level I would not have gone on to play league football for Northampton Town. I Still have the same passion and commitment as he had for the game now still at 57 years of age working on the scouting circuit for different clubs (Bolton Wanderers at the moment) and often bump into ex players Andy King and Lil Fuccillo. Danny`s name often crops up about our days at Luton Town and both players hold him in a high regard and remember what he had done to help them on in their careers.*

Andy King (Luton Town)

I started out at Tottenham but having been released I joined my home town team Luton Town about the age of 16. Having spent some time being coached by Danny I was soon in the first team, making my debut aged 17.

As well as being coached by Danny, I also played in a few games with him as he often appeared in the Combination League side. He could do things with a ball that none of us could do. I remember a time when I was coming to the end of my contract and was struggling for form, Danny put me at sweeper in a reserve game against Tottenham Hotspur and told me to watch the game develop in front of me. I had the game of my life, the confidence I gained from that one game soon earned me a place back in the first team and having played about thirty games I moved from Luton to Everton. The fee was £35,000 which was eventually worth £60,000 after I had played fifty games.

Years later, when I had retired and Danny was in charge at Stockport County, he told me that there was a job coming available at Edgeley Park that would suit me - working with the youngsters. Unbeknown to Danny the job had already been offered to Dave Jones, who was a close friend of Mark Higgins, the son of the club's General Manager, John Higgins. Even though he hadn't actually promised me the job, Danny actually took the trouble to ring me back and apologise for the fact that it had gone.

Having moved into coaching and management myself over the years, the one thing that I have always kept from my days working with Danny is that I like my teams to express themselves in the opponents half of the pitch, as that is where to hurt them most.

Tony Kenworthy (Sheffield United)

I first met Danny when Harry Haslam brought him to Sheffield United as first team coach in 1978. Both Harry and Danny had previously been successful at Luton Town. The first thing that I noticed about Danny was his attention to detail. He was a stickler for one touch football. If you took two touches he let you know about it. He was a workaholic, we'd watch hour after hour of videos before a match studying our next opponents, then he would ring me in the evenings inviting me round to his house to watch the video of the last game we'd played, stop starting the game showing me where I was going wrong and how to put it right. I have many, many football stories about Danny that I wouldn't dare put down on paper. Danny was a winner a brilliant coach and a genuinely lovely man.

He once described to me in great detail the best way to kill a snake, fortunately I've never needed it...YET. He was a great lover of golf, although I would hate to have been with him when he missed a

301

putt. I once wore his training kit under my track suit as a joke without telling him. He stormed into the dressing room "We have a thief in the club" he said "I'll get to the bottom of this". When he turned his back I lifted my track suit top and showed Dave Gilbert (ex West Brom) Danny's top under my track suit .Danny turned on Dave accusing him of taking it...then stormed out... I never did tell him.

Harry Haslam tried to sell me to Leeds but Danny talked him out of it. After leaving Sheffield United I was due to sign for Mansfield Town when the phone rang it was Danny, "Come and have a chat with Bruce (Bruce Rioch) at Middlesbrough he's looking for a left back" I drove up and had a chat but Bruce wanted me to move up there and I was settled in Sheffield with Mansfield 30 minutes down the road it was the obvious choice. Danny was a true football man, football is a quieter place without him, football needs characters and we lost one when Danny left. Football will miss him, I certainly do.

Keith Edwards (Sheffield United/Stockport County)

I was really saddened by Danny's passing, he was the best coach I have ever worked with. I was never one for extra training with anyone until Danny arrived at Sheffield United. But then I often stayed voluntarily to work with him because what he did was worth doing. He was a lovely bloke and a regular in a golf foursome along with myself, Emlyn Hughes and Dane Whitehouse.

Phil Henson (Sheffield United/Rotherham United)

Danny was a hard working manager and coach. We worked together at Sheffield United, coaching the reserves, junior team and the school of excellence on Thursday evenings.

It was a seven day a week job. One day Danny announced that we must have a day off to re-charge our batteries, however finding the time was a different matter. The season was well under way and Danny got in to a routine of taking the next day off after reserve team matches to relax.

I was taking a training session following a reserve team match, at Norton Lees training ground, which involved the reserves and juniors, when I heard someone shouting my name. It was Danny, not joining us for the training session as I thought, but about to 'tee off' on the adjacent golf course. Golf was always Danny's way of relaxing.

Danny was an excellent coach and a good friend and we continued our working relationship when he was appointed manager at Rotherham United some years later.

Alan Biggs (Sheffield United)

He wasn't the new manager. He was "only" the coach. But this was the first – and still only – time in my reporting career when the coach has stolen the show from the new boss.

That, I imagine, is the impression Danny Bergara made on everyone meeting him for the first time in 1978. He had been appointed alongside Harry Haslam in a new management team at Sheffield United. Haslam, nicknamed "Happy Harry," was an established boss after six successful years at Luton Town. His young sidekick with the foreign name was an unknown quantity. Yet it was Bergara who, by sheer force of personality, captured the imagination.

Danny was 36 at the time. It seemed from the first meeting that he was in perpetual motion. This was a guy who could whip up more energy sitting in a chair – a position he only adopted under extreme *sufferance – than most could generate by pacing a room. His swarthy, youthful face engaged you by being so expressive, whether genial, excitable or intense. All the while his hands and arms would be working in synch with a torrent of words. As for his legs, how he kept them still long enough to sit remains a mystery.*

Not all of the words were intelligible. Sadly, there was less tolerance in those days for those who struggled with our language. Today we happily accommodate Premier League managers speaking through an interpreter – even an England boss in the early days of Fabio Capello. Danny was a pioneer in going on to become the first Football League manager not to speak English as a first language. The Uruguayan went the extra mile to learn it, unlike so many who have followed him. Yet he was given all too little credit for that.

Danny's mode of expression and his effervescent nature led many to regard him as an eccentric character. Yes, he had unusual traits that were part of his charm. But this only blinded some people who should have known better to his brilliance as a coach. Some players, and maybe the English game itself, discriminated against him – not in any racial sense but in regarding him as something of an oddity. Well, he was that all right – but in an entirely different way.

Danny could not only teach technical skills to a much higher level than most domestic coaches, he could also demonstrate them at will.

To those players and clubs open-minded enough to see this, Bergara was inspirational in word and deed. I was astounded at his brilliance with a football while working with him on a pilot television coaching series that sadly never saw the light of day. But it didn't have to be a ball. He would show me his party trick at the drop of a hat – or shall we say a coin. He'd take one out of his pocket (any size), drop it from his hand, flick it back up with the outside of his heel and land it smack in the centre of his forehead. I've seen performing seals do less!

What wouldn't English football give now for a few Danny Bergaras? The metaphorical penny has finally dropped. Attitudes have changed. As a nation we need new tricks. Who better than someone like Danny to teach them? He was the right man in the right place at the wrong time. A man ahead of his time.

Coming to these shores in an earlier era, Danny had to adapt to the pragmatic realities of the English game. He demonstrated his tactical nous and adaptability by working with players of, at best, basic ability. His wonderful achievements with Stockport County, where he became the first foreign manager to lead out an English club at Wembley, need no embellishment here. But allow me to indulge in a personal favourite memory of a lovely bloke who became a friend during and after his time at Bramall Lane. It was the night when Danny masterminded one of the shocks of the season as Sheffield United dumped a mighty Liverpool out of the League Cup. Afterwards, as the beer flowed in the press room he demonstrated just how to an assembly of goggle-eyed reporters – by marking out his tactics on a desk top and using bottle tops for players!

I must add that it wasn't only players who were inspired by him. Danny was also hugely encouraging to me in my career, following my work in radio and newspapers and instilling a sense of self-belief that at times I lacked. I was honoured when his lovely wife Jan asked me to speak at Danny's funeral following his untimely passing in 2007. It turned out that the service was held in my local church where Jan was also often among the congregation. Let me tell you the congregation that day was the biggest that church has ever known. The place was filled well beyond capacity and the proverbial gates had to be locked as an army of Stockport supporters crossed the Pennines to pay homage.

Yes, they worshipped Danny Bergara that day. As did all who had the pleasure of knowing him.

Anonymous Rochdale fan

I remember on January 2nd 1989 we had lost at home to Leyton Orient 0-3, and Dale were losing their momentum after a fantastic start to the season. During this game there had been a few muffled chants of 'Bergara Out' in 'The Sandy'. These were immediately shouted down by the wiser Dale fans who were appreciating firsthand the work Danny was doing.

Later that night I was shuffling into The Ratcliffe Arms for a swift half to be met by Bergara leaving the pub hanging onto a cig if I remember rightly. I felt sorry for him having seen us well beaten by The O's and also with him having to bear the brunt of some stick from the crowd. So, I said to him, "Hard lines today."

He turned round to me sharpish, and in the voice akin to Manuel from Fawlty Towers snapped, "Hard fooking lines! Never mind that. Those b*stards shouting for my head had better watch out. I'm not standing for that sort of sheet. My boys did their best and will always do their best with me in charge. I'm not fooking standing for 'Bergara Out' when I'm in the dugout. They can all get fooked!"

It was the first time I'd spoken to somebody in the game and to say I was a little amused was an understatement. But his latino passion for the game and his job at Dale shone through in that chance encounter.

Kevin Francis (Stockport County)

The day I met Danny Bergara was in his office for a discussion regarding the possibility of signing for Stockport County. It was a shock to actually be sitting there as the call to travel to Stockport only came the night before. The journey took me 3 hours from Derby to Stockport due to bad weather. I had no idea who or even where Stockport was. Late the previous night my wife Sharon and I looked at tele-text to see where Stockport was in the league table. We scrolled down each division and they were nowhere to be found. We thought it was too big a drop from Derby County (in the old First Division) to Division Four.

I left home with the impression it would be good experience to talk to another club but had no intention of dropping down so many divisions so early in my career. Little did I know that dropping down would have elevated me to such heights? Danny helped mould me into the player that I became and the man I am today. My honest first impression of Danny was 'this guy is crazy' but after being in his company for about 4 hours I realised he was not crazy just infected. By that I mean infected by the love of the beautiful game. His love and passion for football and Stockport County was contagious.

I am sure the players already at Stockport were already infected but once I signed it soon became apparent Danny had spread the infection to everyone at Stockport County. Resisting Danny was futile…. when I got home and told Sharon I had agreed to sign for Stockport that took some explaining. I took Sharon with me to sign the contract a few days later so she could also see the magic of Danny Bergara.

I can honestly say that in the four years at Stockport County I had some of the most memorable times of my entire football career. They were filled with every range of emotion from elation to despair. During those years anything Danny asked of me I would have done and then did without question. He instilled a belief that spread throughout the whole club and not just on the pitch. Danny had a personal touch to his man management that seems to be lacking in football today. He believed in every one of us and made us feel like we could beat anyone and achieve everything. Alas a Wembley victory still eluded us. That memory still sucks ass!!!

As I look back on some of the videos it's not just the goals, crazy celebrations and hairstyles that bring back happy memories. For me it is the look of sheer joy on my team mates faces and one occasion that stands out the most to me would be the first Wembley appearance. As Danny led us out onto the pitch he had the biggest shit eating grin on his face. The pride on his face was priceless and we wanted to win for him that day.

Even after leaving Stockport Danny and I maintained contact. We would exchange Christmas cards (well Sharon would!) and Danny and I would have a long phone conversation guaranteed at Christmas. The phone calls took us back to when Danny used to call me at home the night before a game. If you have ever spoken to Danny on the phone you would understand it was never too long before he would have you rolling around in laughter with his unique grasp of the English language.

All of my memories of Danny are fond. The world is a sadder place without him but when his name is brought up and I reminisce it's an excuse to use one of Danny's catch phrases as he would say 'Get the whisky out' - Cheers boss.

John Sainty (Stockport County)

I was at Stockport County with Eric Webster helping to coach the first team when the Chairman & directors decided to appoint a new manager - enter Danny Bergara. Although I had been around football for most of my life - my path and Danny's had never crossed.

Eric Webster introduced us, explained my role at the club and Danny asked me to stay on for a couple of weeks to show him around. Meanwhile, he brought in Brian Green to be his assistant, having previously worked with him at Rochdale. At that time, the manager's office was in a basement off of the main corridor and quite pokey with only two desks for three people! We all got on well together, but after six weeks, Danny seemed undecided who he wanted as his assistant. However Brian decided to leave so it was just myself and Danny. He took full control of players, staff and coaching and although money was tight, Danny seemed to have a good rapport with the chairman (Brendan Elwood) and most of the directors, all of whom were Sheffield based as was Danny.

Danny's work at other clubs (mainly Luton) was with the younger players and one of his favourite sayings was 'If the foundation of a building was correct, then the rest of the building would progress and improve' and with this philosophy, Danny wanted a good youth set up, enter Dave Jones who was brought in as youth team coach. Danny's foundation ideas began to take place.

Players came and went, as far as I remember, all down to Danny. The man had unbelievable ball skills and in training, his touch and control was brilliant. He would do things with a football that most players would not be able to emulate in their life time.

309

After a while Danny recognised Dave Jones's ability as a coach could be better used with the first team so Joe Jakub was brought in as youth team coach, Danny's team was now complete. He was manager, I was assistant, Dave was first team coach and Joe responsible for the younger players. The success Danny achieved with Stockport was possibly the most successful period in their history, apart from one promotion, we did miss out on a lot of finals and play-offs all at Wembley.

Danny was a workaholic. Travelling back and forth to Sheffield every day proved difficult so Danny took digs locally, first just 20 yards walk from his office and his second about 20 minutes walk away. This meant Danny spending endless hours in his office which the problem for Dave and I was, he expected us to stay along with him and invariably we never left before 7pm in the evening. It was not quite so bad for me as I lived nearby but Dave had to travel to Liverpool - sometimes it seemed we were never away from the place.

Dave and I would never really work out why, with Danny's skill and his South American roots, his concept of playing the game invariably was a long ball game for which he always opted for a big striker. Danny brought in Kevin Francis who was the biggest and whose goal scoring exploits for County were brilliant. Also brought in was Paul Williams - the Chairman's son-in-law, another big striker.

Both Dave and myself learnt an amazing amount from Danny - he was a character and the game definitely needed people like him. I can never work out why Danny was relieved of his managerial position - it was definitely nothing to do with the footballing side. Something just got a bit out of hand and neither side, Danny or one of the directors, were prepared to say "Sorry, I was out of order" but knowing them both that was never going to happen and sadly there was only one casualty and that was Danny.

I have met many people in football and it was an honour to have known and worked with someone like Danny who was so good for the game of football in his own inimitable way.

Stuart Brennan (Stockport County)

I have been lucky enough to have met and interviewed some of the biggest names in sport, from Ian Botham and Ricky Hatton, to Eusebio and David Beckham.

But none of them has left me with the kind of memories, and anecdotes, that I gathered when I was covering Stockport County from 1989 to 1994, and dealing with the inimitable Danny Bergara.

It was clear from the first day I met him that Danny was different – fiery and foul-mouthed one minute, the next minute animated and laughing as he ran through a moment from Saturday's match, or recalled a funny story from his playing days.

He was a tremendous character and will never be forgotten by anyone who worked with him, or alongside him.

He made his name as a deadly striker and a brave one. I remember him telling me a story about his early days at Racing Club, when he was a teenage striker and came up against a gnarled brute of a centre half. The game followed a pattern, of the defender kicking Danny up in the air, and Danny getting up and shaking his hand in front of him, making a clucking noise, as if offering feed to an animal. The defender got more infuriated, and kicked him harder each time, but Danny tormented the life out of him and helped his team win the game.

Danny was proud of his Uruguayan roots, reciting the 1950 World Cup winning team at the drop of a hat, but he was also an Anglophile, and argued strongly that, as he had spent more of his life in England than he did in Uruguay, he was an Englishman.

The stories are too many to recount here, but my lasting image was of Danny on the team coach, heading to a game up at Hartlepool.

As we drove along a dual carriageway, a confused old lady was heading the wrong way, coming straight towards the coach before realising her mistake and swerving through a convenient gap in the central island. Those of us at the front of the coach, including the driver, were all a little shaken by the moment, but Danny sat in his front seat, serenely puffing at his pipe.

One of the directors jokingly suggested that maybe the lady was Uruguayan, and thought she was on the right side of the road. Danny took a long draw on his pipe and said calmly: "They cook peas in all countries of the world …"

I have no idea to this day what he meant, and no-one was composed enough to ask!

Danny eventually banned me from the team coach after I laid into the team when they were top of the table and lost 5-0 at bottom club Hartlepool. But there were no hard feelings, and he continued to either scream down the phone at me one day, then greet me like a long-lost friend another.

He called me a "Judas" and a "Camelon", as I "Changed colours" – he couldn't quite grasp that the reporter's job was to say it as he sees it, and not just toe the club line all the time. But he didn't bear grudges, so that was never a problem.

Then, of course, there was the football. Danny's teams got unfair stick for being big and physical, which they undoubtedly were. But to get out of that old Fourth Division, you had to be prepared to battle – but when you think back, he also brought in good footballers like David Frain, Peter Ward, Andy Kilner.

I still sometimes watch the highlights and goals tapes from those days with fondness – there were some great goals, and some marvellous moments. The memories Danny gave to County, and my personal memories of him as a man, and as a manager, will always remain with me.

Stuart White (Stockport County)

Anecdotes are often personal things. I guess sometimes they only mean something to you and their impact doesn't necessarily remain the same when you try to convey them to a wider audience. So many things have been said about Danny Bergara over the years and anything I might add to any list of tributes could never be the funniest or the most profound but to me and my family, the memories of all that he was and all that he did for Stockport County Football Club, for Stockport as a community and certainly for me as an individual will always be cherished.

I don't actually have any one memory of Danny that stands out above any other. I was 20 when he took over and while I had always been proud to support my club, all I'd known at Edgeley Park was years of meandering failure and half-hearted dreams of mid-table mediocrity. Looking back, perhaps the biggest thing he did was to challenge that malaise and instil a belief that we could actually achieve something decent.

For some reason, I regarded one great Monday night in October 1989 as pivotal. After hammering Gillingham 3-0 away on the Saturday, we beat Southend United 1-0 with a Brett Angell goal in front of a crowd of over 6,000. I was at University in Sheffield at the time and after driving over for the game, I arrived quite late and wasn't able to park anywhere near the ground. That increased interest was down to Danny and that was probably the night when his impact really started to become tangible. Even though we'd already hammered Hartlepool 6-0 and run QPR close in the League Cup, that was arguably when the real belief kicked in and if there is anything I associate with Danny apart from the much-vaunted funny tales of malapropisms and the four glorious defeats at Wembley, it's that quality. He was enthusiastic, he was dedicated, he was a fantastic coach and he was a great manager...but above all else, at that point, it was clear he was a winner as well. 'Never give in' was something I remember him saying with some real passion several times over and I know from his daughter, Ellen, that even to the end, he never did.

I was lucky enough to grow up with my Dad on the Board of the club I supported. That meant I was able to be in and around the place every now and again and when Danny breezed in and my Dad introduced me to him for the first time he looked me up and down and asked if I could head a ball? Before I had chance to muster any reply, my Dad killed it for me by butting in with: 'Not well enough for you!' Cheers, Dad.

Still, embarrassment aside, being my father's son, meant I could be in Danny's company every now and again and that meant occasionally being invited into the inner sanctum of his office down beneath the main stand, just off the players' corridor. I remember being there one afternoon when in mid-conversation, he walked round from behind his desk, shifted his stride to one side, rolled a random stray golf ball back under his foot, flicked it up and dropped it effortlessly into his shirt pocket. As if it was something everybody did every day of their lives. But how good did it look? I was just gobsmacked at the momentary casual display of incredible skill.

Then there was the Sunday afternoon he phoned and asked for my Dad. While I waited for him to come to the phone I asked Danny about our defeat at Doncaster the previous day. I asked how this player had done, how that player had done and then we got on to Kevin Francis, who probably hadn't had his best game for us. "Big Kevin?" came the questioning reply. "He was nothing but a bloody whitewash!" OK, so I'm pretty sure he meant 'washout' and not what you might coat a shippen wall with but I had neither the balls nor the bad manners to laugh at what I'd heard.

He'd visit our house every now and again as well and he came up one Boxing Day evening after we'd drawn 1-1 at home with Wrexham. He was staying over at his digs near to the ground as we were playing Blackpool away the next day and after having dinner and a glass or two of whiskey, he started talking about some of our players...and in particular about how Tony Dinning could be a great player for us, if only he'd stop 'riding the horse' so often? I knew what he meant. My Dad knew what he meant. I'm not so sure my Mum did but she smiled politely anyway and went to make the coffee! The conversation subsequently turned to our game at Blackpool the next day and how we were going to be better than we had been that day, even though it was only a 24 hour turnaround. Blackpool were always decent and somehow they always seemed to do well against us at that time and being a natural pessimist, I wasn't sure how we'd get on...but suffice to say, *we followed the disappointing home draw with a 2-1 away win and everything he said came off. As ever, I was in awe of him.*

In the end though, quite apart from being fantastic for our club, Danny eventually shaped my career in a way I could never have predicted. While I was never going to be good enough as a player, I had always loved football and when I was at University in Sheffield, as well as watching reserve games at Bramall Lane and Hillsborough, I'd also drive to the likes of Rotherham, Barnsley, Chesterfield and Derby just to pay my couple of quid and watch a game. I would then speak to my Dad and mention this player and that player as having done well and he would then mention those players to Danny when he spoke with him...which was pretty much every day and often for hours at a time.

In the end, after our double Wembley disappointment in 1992, Danny invited my parents and I to go out for dinner in Hathersage with him and Jan. It was then that he asked me if I'd like to become a part time scout for him and rather than pay to watch the games, get the tickets put on and watch them in a more 'official' capacity. Obviously, I accepted the invitation and started going to games as a representative of my club; often going with him to Barnsley, Rotherham and Sheffield United for reserve team games as well. That experience was utterly invaluable to me. He'd talk me through games, telling me what to look out for, asking me what I thought of this player and that player, explaining why they would or wouldn't be a fit for our club. He was patient, he was always endlessly enthusiastic and he was, perhaps unwittingly, a great teacher.

I've since been lucky enough to scout for some great managers and am currently working full time at a level I never thought possible. All of that stems back to whatever Danny saw in me and the trust placed in the opinion of a then 23 year old, by my Dad aside, perhaps the biggest personal hero I've ever had. When I was given my first full time job as Head of UK Recruitment at West Bromwich Albion in 2009, I only wish I could have thanked him personally for his input all those years ago. One of the first people I did tell, though, was his son, Simon, when he and I went to a game together at Blackburn Rovers one afternoon. That was the next best thing.

Danny had a massive impact on the careers of some fantastic Stockport County players such as Alun Armstrong, Tony Dinning, Kevin Francis, Andy Preece, Paul Williams (both of them!) and more besides. My development as a scout was something and nothing in the grand scheme of all that he achieved but that doesn't stop me appreciating all that Danny did for me and on a less glamorous level, I hope he would have taken a little bit of pride in it. One thing is for sure, though, he made me and thousands like me ridiculously proud of Stockport County. And for that, I could never thank him enough

Aiden Casey (Stockport County supporter - written shortly after Danny's death)

When I heard Danny had passed away my eyes began to water. But most of the sadness I've felt has been mixed with pride and amazing memories. I am 29 now and have been going to County with my dad and brother since I can remember. For years County where a laughing stock. My Dad used to force me to go and told me it was our duty as a family and that one day County would reward us for our loyalty. He said if there were more loyal families like ours, then County wouldn't struggle so much.

We were made fun of at school. Laughed at in the streets. Every other little kid had a United or City shirt on. We were mocked because we were different. Dad told us we should be proud to be different. "You can't change your religion" he would say. We had to accept what we were.

Danny Bergara made us proud of what we were. He finally gave us something to be proud of. We started to really want to go to County. He made all the kids at school want to be different, just like me. The bullying stopped.

He made all the years of pain seem so worth it. He gave us highs and took us to places we'd never dream of going. He made all my Dad's stupid beliefs, suddenly seem not so stupid. He was the prophet my dad had always promised. He gave me a feeling I never thought County could give me.

Danny was a simple man. He came from a humble background, but he had the heart of a Lion. If the size of your heart was a measure of how good a manager a man was, then Danny would've been Real Madrid's greatest ever manager, not just Stockport County's.

Thank you for everything Danny. We will always love you

Ged Gibbons (Stockport County supporter)

We all have our memories of 'The Man', mine was Fulham away in November 1991 and I took my son Mike away for a birthday treat (he is 30 next month so it must have been his 7th birthday) anyway he wanted to get the players' autographs on his programme but he could not get near to the pitch to see the players due to the fences that they had around the ground to keep the hooligans at bay.

After the game, which we won 2-1, he asked if we could wait until the players came out after the game so they could sign his programme, so being his birthday I agreed, the players started coming out in dribs and drabs and he mentioned to one that it was *his birthday, so they then took him into the dressing room where Danny made a big fuss of him and he got all the players to sign his programme – needless to say it made his day – but not mine as I wasn't invited and they left me outside the ground when he was took into the changing room !!*

Andy Preece (Stockport County)

Growing up I was an Aston Villa fan and had a season ticket. I used to go when they won the First Division Championship and European Cup and I always used to look up to Peter Withe. He was a great player and one of my heroes. Then when I became a professional myself I suppose Danny Bergara at Stockport was the first person who got the best out of me. I really looked up to him and hung on every word he said. He was a great coach and I had total respect for him.

It's very hard to say what it was about him. He had a great accent and even when he was saying something serious you'd be laughing inside because it did sound a little funny. But he had such a passion and a drive for the game that it made a big impression on me. He never spent much money but every time he did the players repaid him so many times because he always got the best out of them. Danny gave me a massive belief and I think every other player who went to Stockport County improved .

Mike Flynn (Stockport County)

Danny was the official starter of all the good things that happened at Stockport County and the club and myself owe a lot of thanks to him. He had his own ways and some of his English was not the best but we had a good few laughs and he was great for me and the club

Chris Beaumont (Stockport County)

In life you come across a few gents. Danny was a true one. He treated me like a son, gave me belief and everything I achieved in my footballing career was down to this true gent. God Bless Danny and Thank You.

Phil Brennan (Stockport County)

Danny gave me so many good memories during his time at Edgeley Park, winning promotion from the Fourth Division and that first ever trip to Wembley being stand out moments, but the thing I remember most was that there was always laughter. I suppose when the team is winning far more often than it is losing, it is easier to enjoy yourselves, but I believe that Danny made the place enjoyable just by being Danny, his use of the English language had me in stitches at times. I know from speaking to the players he did the same to them.

My favourite line from Danny came as he was being interviewed after a game that County had come back to win. The team had been below par in the first half but gave a tremendous second half display to blow away the opposition.

One of the first questions asked was: "Danny, it was like a different team had come out for the second half. That must have been one hell of a half time team talk. What did you say to them?"

Danny replied "I just told them to stop being frightened of the other team. They are just eleven men, just like you. They all have two arms, two legs and one cock"

Jon Keighren (Stockport County)

It was the morning after the night before: 31st March 1995. It was the morning after Danny Bergara had allegedly punched his Chairman, Brendan Elwood. I was working on the Breakfast Show on the local radio station Signal Cheshire in the centre of Stockport when the tip-off came in from a County fan – I don't remember who it was, but he was very clear: "Danny Bergara has been sacked."

At first I couldn't believe it, given that County were on a decent run in Division Two and looked to be a good bet for the Play Offs once more. I managed to get hold of County spokesman Steve Bellis, who was able to confirm that Bergara had indeed left the club following an incident at the Alma Lodge Hotel during a function for sponsors just a few hours earlier.

Piecing together the bits of the story, it became apparent that Danny entered into an argument with club officials who apparently challenged him over his accommodation expenses. After a few drinks, the argument became more heated, whilst Danny became more agitated, and the whole incident ended in a fracas witnessed by many of the invited guests. Regardless of who threw the first punch, there could only be one possible outcome.

The story began to emerge that Danny had assaulted Chairman Brendan Elwood, leading to his immediate dismissal, but it would take Danny another four years – and an expensive Tribunal – before he was cleared of the allegations in a case of wrongful dismissal. The Tribunal heard that the argument arose over an expenses claim of £64 and that the 'assault' never took place.

To try and corroborate the story on that morning in March 1995, I decided to keep ringing the manager's direct line at the ground on the off-chance Danny might return to collect his belongings, and eventually the phone was answered by that distinctive, recognisable voice. I began by expressing my regret and told Danny how sorry I was that he had lost his job, but I explained that, as a journalist, I needed to get the story right and asked if I could record an interview with the great man.

Danny was clearly still in shock, his voice trembled and he sounded more fragile than I could ever have imagined. He said he didn't feel it was appropriate to do an interview, but he would read out a prepared statement for me to record. Danny took my number and agreed to call me back. In all honesty, I assumed I would never hear from him, but Danny was true to his word and called back within a few minutes. I transferred the call to the studio and proceeded to record the most moving bit of radio I have ever heard in my life. Here is the full text of Danny's emotional statement:

"Sad news, after six great years of continuous achievements and success, building great foundations at the club in most departments, I'd like to thank my staff, the players and the fans especially for the tremendous support during my time at Stocky.

"I can leave holding my head high and I am proud of what I have done at the club. I would also like everyone involved or attached to the club not to look at my dismissal as a step back, but to look forward for even better times to come.

"The only two regrets I have is that at Wembley we did not manage to win an Autoglass Trophy or promotion to the First Division. Most important of all, thank you to my family that supported me through thick and thin. God bless you all x Bye Bye."

Arguably the most fascinating part of his statement was his prophetic phrase urging everyone 'to look forward for even better times to come' – Danny must have swelled with pride to see his former first team coach Dave Jones lead County to promotion to the Championship, as well as the semi-finals of the League Cup, just two years later.

By the end of the recording, we were both in tears, and it was clear that Danny was finding it hard to get his words out, but I let the tape roll and finished recording Danny's prepared statement. Afterwards, I turned off the tape and we had a brief chat, thanking each other for mutual support over the years, but it would prove to be the last time we ever spoke.

It was only recently in a conversation with biographer Phil Brennan that I learned Danny had written the statement out himself on a series of Post-It notes before reading it to me down the phone. I was even more amazed when Phil showed me a copy of those Post-It notes – Danny had kept them until the day he died in 2007, which made the whole episode all the more poignant, and in an instant it took me back almost twenty years to that darkest of days.

As for the tape recording, that was lost many years ago during one of the many changes of ownership at Stockport's local radio station, but thankfully Danny was much more fastidious about maintaining his football archive, and it is truly remarkable that his scripted statement can still be seen to this day.

In all honesty, I cannot say I knew Danny particularly well, because I never got as close to him as I did to later managers such as Jim Gannon, Gary Megson, Carlton Palmer or Alan Lord.

A few years previously, whilst working on the Stockport Express, the Sports Editor Stuart Brennan asked me to write a double-page profile of Danny, looking back at his amazing upbringing and his nomadic football career. We examined in depth his humble beginnings, herding goats in Uruguay, before embarking on a playing career which saw him take to the field with the likes of Ferenc Puskas and Alfredo Di Stefano, and I loved those interviews, listening to Danny talk about his experiences in the game.

But my fondest memory has to be interviewing Danny on the pitch as we walked out together at the old Wembley Stadium a couple of hours before kick-off in the Autoglass Trophy Final of 1993 against Port Vale. He spoke so brilliantly and so passionately about the club that held a special place in his heart and his eyes welled up as he talked about his love of the fans and his pride at taking 'little Stocky' back to the Twin Towers once again.

Perhaps the saddest aspect of Danny's dismissal from Stockport County was the immediate aftermath, as he sought new employment. It quickly became apparent that 'mud sticks', and it would prove difficult for Danny to get his career back on track, because the allegation that he 'punched his chairman' made other clubs wary of offering him a job.

Thankfully, time has been kind to both Danny, as well as Brendan Elwood, and with so much water under the bridge, it was a fitting tribute to see the Main Stand at Edgeley Park named after Danny Bergara in 2012. There will surely never be a more iconic figure at Stockport

Mick McCarthy (Sunderland/Wolverhampton Wanderers)

As a player I played many times against teams managed by Danny and always enjoyed the battles. Once I had made the move into coaching I would often meet Danny at games as he was always scouting for one club or another. What struck me was that he always had time to talk to me and other coaches and scouts. Unlike some managers and scouts he never refused to offer help, he loved to discuss the finer points of the game and his depth of knowledge of players at all levels was incredible.

When I first became a manager, I was one of the youngest at just 33, Danny was one of the first people to ring me and offer his congratulations, I remember thinking that it was a superb gesture from an established manager.

When I took on the Sunderland managers job in 2003 I offered Danny a scouting role, which I am glad to say he accepted. He was with me for the three years I was at The Stadium of Light and also stayed with me when I moved to Wolves in 2006, working for me right up until he was taken ill.

I would like to say that I really liked Danny as a man first and foremost, I thought he was one of the best people I have ever worked with in football and it goes without saying that he had a real talent when it came to spotting a player

Early Days

Wedding Day

Ellen's Christening

Simon and Danny - with the ball from the Seville v Real Madrid game

Silver Wedding

Ruby Wedding

Simon Bergara

One of my earliest memories (if not THE earliest) was of my Dad walking me up to collect my 'gift' on the Three Kings Day (Spain's equivalent of Christmas day held on 6th January). The man-made stage in one of the goal mouth/penalty areas in the Estadio Sanchez Pizjuan in Sevilla occupied by three footballers dressed up as the kings gave the occasion an extra buzz. Although I was too young to sense this at the time ,receiving this gift in such a revered arena could have introduced me to the fact that I would be blessed and brought up in a family that was quite unique, as Alberto D Bergara was no ordinary Dad and Sevilla football ground no ordinary venue.

My later memories, of which there are many, was that I had a Dad who was honest, fair, loving and generous in all ways especially of his time although in his jobs in professional football, his time was always in demand. I was massively proud to have him as my Dad.

This admiration also extended itself to the wider community of his extended family, friends and within football.

Wherever we went his natural passion and enthusiasm for life and football (football was life!) drew people to him like a magnet. Family occasions and re-unions alike he would be submerged within a circle of people all hanging on his every word!

On the many occasions I attended matches with Dad when he was scouting it was the same. Before the match, at half time and after (if we didn't have to set off early to "Beat the traffic") everyone loved his company and I would often sit patiently alone eating a sandwich and a nice piece of cake in the 'scouts and guests room' until we sat in our seats, watching the match, when I could have him back to myself! These were priceless memories especially listening in on conversations with some famous football managers where Dad would come out with things about "Earning the right to play" and "In my country we say - in the land of the blind the man with one eye is king" which were priceless!

So I would not have swapped Dad for the world even if it meant sharing him with his incredible passion for football. In later years, especially as his success grew at County, I had an incredible pride, as his Son, for what he was achieving, not only as the pioneering first foreign manager in English football (and the incredible number of hurdles he had to overcome to get there) but the humble way he took success and failure in his stride.

As a player, coach and a manager I was proud of the fact he was a man of the people always giving of his time to everyone and if this meant I would have less time with him to myself then so be it.

I remember (with a very heavy heart) a Dads v Lads match at Prae Wood primary school in St Albans in the mid 70's. These were supposed to be a walkover for the mighty school team against grown-ups who hadn't kicked a ball since their own school days. But not this particular year. I lost count at 8-4 with Dad scoring 'at least 5 of them' putting all my pre-match "We're going to do you lot" bravado firmly in my place.

It used to make me laugh how every situation or conversation would come back to football. Discussions starting around teaching, politics or about my job in the Skipton Building Society would always end up back at Big Kevin Francis or how Dad scored 7 goals in three games against Spain's number one! Even the famous barbeques he would cook on Sunday afternoons had sausages, kidneys, burgers and ribs set out in a 4-5-1 or 4-4-2 formation on the grill!

So I was proud to have ADB as my Dad from a child to his final days and beyond and that pride remains as strong as ever today.

His never say die attitude for which he was renowned at all the clubs he worked for was further illustrated to me in October 2012 when my wife and I visited Sevilla for an emotional return. When President of Sevilla FC, Jose Maria Del Nido presented us (at half time of the Sevilla 3 Mallorca 2 match) with a historical picture frame of a famous goal Dad had scored against Bilbao in 1970 he said to me "Su padre, que siempre marcó en los últimos 20 minutos " ("Your father he would always score when we needed in the final 20 minutes") . Wow I thought - over 5 years after his passing and over 40 years since wearing the great white shirt of Sevilla with distinction he is still remembered with such inspiration.

At that moment I could feel the hairs on the back of my neck and that my Dad was smiling down again from up above.

Ellen Bergara

YOU SAY - "The Man from Uruguay"

I SAY - "My Dad's from Uruguay".

I am so proud to be the daughter of Alberto Daniel Bergara! I always have been. And not just because he was an awesome footballer and manager! But because he was my teacher, my encourager, my winner, my Dad.

TEACHER and ENCOURAGER

Just as he taught his players to believe in their potential and to simply give their best he taught me to do just that through school, through dance college, through Uni, through life! He would always be there, no matter what. His love for me was clear. Ever providing, ever supporting, ever encouraging.

As Dads do - he taught me to swim without armbands and to ride my bike without stabilisers. As I grew older he taught me how to polish my school shoes, how to cook an omelette, how to change the oil filter and how to trim the edges of the lawn! He even taught me how to putt a golf ball in the mini golf course he created in our perfectly mowed (football pitch style!) back garden. He painted a line on the side of the garage wall - above the giant daisies (las margaritas)- so we could practise playing tennis in the summer. Dad loved the outdoors. But not just for football and golf! He shared his childhood love of nature and birds (apart from magpies!) with us. I can still picture him retrieving two abandoned hornero (oven-maker) birds' nests (heavy, sun-baked mud nests!) from the top of the gate posts at Pototo's farm in rural Maldonado. One of them sat proudly for years in our big old oak tree! Dad told us the story of his time as a teenager at the farm; how he was the only one who dared to ride on the back of the bull! It promptly took off towards the arroyo (stream) and threw him overboard! There was far more to the Man from Uruguay than el fútbol.

WINNER

Dad taught me to do things properly, to work hard and to play fair. He demonstrated that you have to keep going even when life isn't fair. The long journeys home from Wembley gave him more than enough experience in that!

But for Dad, winning was always possible. No matter who your opponent. His confidence in the underdog was always strong. He knew as a young player the sweetness of beating the 'Giant' - scoring that winning goal in the last ten minutes to make it Sevilla 1 Real Madrid 0, and knocking their rival off the top of the table! He often recounted the story of David and Goliath. He had much in common with the young shepherd boy. He recognised the value of skill over stature.

I remember when he was filming 'Win through Skill'. I remember him playing the Bee Gees' 'You Win Again' over and over again in our living room! Full blast! Before it ever got to the pre-match Ground! 'The Winner Takes it All' by Abba was another favourite, yet this one expressing the bitter reality that we might not always win.

Dad filled our home with songs! So many of them bring tears to my eyes as they are such a powerful reminder of him. Of him still with us. The sound of Sevillanas as we gathered around to watch cine film of our family holidays in Spain, the Uruguayan folklore and Tangos that he played on the piano, and Por Una Cabeza which was played as he walked me down the aisle. Precious memories.

I remember 'Here's to the Man from Uruguay' and 'Danny Bergara's Blue and White Army' sung with gusto both at Edgeley Park and at Wembley. But the version I will never forget was sung at his Farewell at Totley Rise on 9th August 2007. THANK YOU for singing to him and for him as he was lifted up and carried from the Church on his journey to Paradise. It's not the same around here without him but I do have a deep and quiet assurance that the Paradise Jesus spoke of is real. And that Dad is there. And that we will see him again.

Jan Bergara

Dan was a true professional in every sense of the word. Never sent from the dugout in over 25 years working in England as a coach and/or manager, but as he was Latin/Uruguayan it was always assumed that he was volatile. Interestingly when a British manager is sent from the dugout, they never get called volatile!!

Integrity, honesty, generous, fair, loyal, a provider. You could always count on him, he would never let you down. All these qualities were observed by his family, friends and anyone who knew him.

He wore his heart on his sleeve. He didn't know how to lie or be deceitful - rare qualities. One of his favourite phrases was: Lies have short legs, they can't run far!!

This moral code of conduct and sense of justice have been passed on to his children and continues through his grandchildren.

Danny always said he was ahead of his time - born too early, right place, wrong time!

The world was a much richer place for having Dan a part of it. We love him, miss him, but will all be united again one day.........with 'The Man from Uruguay'

Thank You

I would like to thank everyone for their valued contributions to this book and would also like to add a huge heartfelt thank you from Simon, Ellen and myself to Phil for his labour of love in ensuring that Dan's story has been told.